Credits

Author
Munish K. Gupta

Reviewers
Jonas Bonér
David Y. Ross
Domingo Suarez Torres

Acquisition Editor
Usha Iyer

Lead Technical Editor
Unnati Shah

Technical Editors
Mayur Hule
Devdutt Kulkarni
Ankita Shashi

Copy Editor
Insiya Morbiwala

Project Coordinator
Joel Goveya

Proofreader
Julie Jackson

Indexer
Monica Ajmera

Production Coordinator
Nilesh R. Mohite

Cover Work
Nilesh R. Mohite

Akka Essentials

A practical, step-by-step guide to learn and build Akka's actor-based, distributed, concurrent, and scalable Java applications

Munish K. Gupta

[PACKT] open source ✼
PUBLISHING   community experience distilled

BIRMINGHAM - MUMBAI

About the Author

Munish K. Gupta is a Senior Architect working for Wipro Technologies. Based in Bangalore, India, his day-to-day work involves solution architecture for applications with stringent **non-functional requirements** (**NFRs**), Application Performance Engineering, and exploring the readiness of cutting-edge, open source technologies for enterprise adoption.

He advises enterprise customers to help them solve performance and scalability issues, and implement innovative differentiating solutions to achieve business and technology goals. He believes that technology is meant to enable the business, and technology by itself is not a means to an end.

He is very passionate about software programming and craftsmanship. He is always looking for patterns in solving problems, writing code, and making optimum use of tools and frameworks. He blogs about technology trends and Application Performance Engineering at `http://www.techspot.co.in` and about Akka at `http://www.akkaessentials.in`

Akka Essentials

First published: October 2012

Production Reference: 1171012

Published by Packt Publishing Ltd.

Livery Place

35 Livery Street

Birmingham B3 2PB, UK.

ISBN 978-1-84951-828-4

www.packtpub.com

Cover Image by Eleanor Bennett (eleanor.ellieonline@gmail.com)

Acknowledgement

Writing a book is never a single person's job. During the course of this journey, I have relied on many people, both directly and indirectly. I would like to thank the Akka community, from whom I have learned, and continue to learn, every day.

I would like to especially thank Jonas Bonér and David Ross, who reviewed and contributed many helpful suggestions and improvements to my drafts.

I am grateful to my editors, Usha Iyer, Unnati Shah, and Joel Goveya at Packt Publishing for their help in preparing this book. I would like to thank all my colleagues at Wipro Technologies, especially Hari Burle, Sridhar PV, and Aravind Ajad for all their support and encouragement. I have learned so much from each one of you, and for that I am grateful.

Last but not the least, I would like to thank my family. My wife Kompal, who has been a source of constant support throughout this journey. She single-handedly managed the kids and other chores around the house while I was working late nights and on weekends. She was the constant motivator who egged me on to go that extra mile whenever I felt that it was too big a task. I also want to thank my parents and brother Nitin, who provided the moral support throughout this journey. I love you all.

To my children, Dale and Sabal, I am sorry I couldn't be around with you as much as we all wanted, and many times had to get you away from the laptop. I love you very much.

About the Reviewers

Jonas Bonér is a geek, programmer, speaker, musician, writer, and Java champion. He is the CTO and co-founder of Typesafe, and is an active contributor to the open source community. Most notably, he founded the Akka project and the AspectWerkz AOP compiler (now AspectJ). You can know more about him at http://jonasboner.com.

David Y. Ross is a Scala enthusiast and Software Engineer at Klout, the social media startup that empowers its users to discover and be recognized for how they influence the world. As a member of Klout's platform team, David uses Scala and Akka to scale the Klout API to over a billion requests per day. Having previously worked on enterprise Java systems at a large tech company, he is constantly amazed by the productivity and elegance of Scala and Akka.

David attends Bay Area Scala meetups and has given a talk on Klout's use of Akka. He is a fan of Boston's sports teams and esoteric Jazz guitar players.

Domingo Suarez Torres is a Software Developer from Mexico City. He is always looking for tools that can make him a more productive developer. He likes to adopt frameworks that are in their early stages. In Mexico, he has been a pioneer in adopting several languages for the JVM, such as Groovy and Scala, programming languages that are used to build successful businesses. He has founded several user groups to spread the word about new technology.

In the professional field, he has worked for big companies as well as small ones in different sectors, such as financial, health, media, sales, and e-commerce. Currently, he is the CTO for a succesful e-commerce company in Mexico (clickOnero).

He has helped as a technical reviewer for other books, such as *Camel In Action, Claus Ibsen and Jonathan Anstey, Manning Publications* and *Making Java Groovy, Kenneth A. Kousen, Manning Publications.*

www.PacktPub.com

Support files, eBooks, discount offers and more

You might want to visit www.PacktPub.com for support files and downloads related to your book.

Did you know that Packt offers eBook versions of every book published, with PDF and ePub files available? You can upgrade to the eBook version at www.PacktPub.com and as a print book customer, you are entitled to a discount on the eBook copy. Get in touch with us at service@packtpub.com for more details.

At www.PacktPub.com, you can also read a collection of free technical articles, sign up for a range of free newsletters and receive exclusive discounts and offers on Packt books and eBooks.

http://PacktLib.PacktPub.com

Do you need instant solutions to your IT questions? PacktLib is Pack's online digital book library. Here, you can access, read and search across Pack's entire library of books.

Why Subscribe?

- Fully searchable across every book published by Packt
- Copy and paste, print and bookmark content
- On demand and accessible via web browser

Free Access for Packt account holders

If you have an account with Packt at www.PacktPub.com, you can use this to access PacktLib today and view nine entirely free books. Simply use your login credentials for immediate access.

Table of Contents

Preface	**1**
Chapter 1: Introduction to Akka	**7**
Background	**7**
Microprocessor evolution	7
Concurrent systems	8
Container-based applications	10
Actor Model	10
Akka framework	12
Actor systems	13
What is an actor?	13
Fault tolerance	17
Location transparency	18
Transactors	19
Akka use cases	**21**
Summary	**22**
Chapter 2: Starting with Akka	**23**
Application requirements	**23**
Application design	**24**
Start development	**26**
Prerequisites	26
Java	26
Eclipse	27
Maven	27
Scala	27
Akka	28
Java application	30
Creating the Akka Maven project	30
Defining message classes	35
Defining actor classes	36
Defining the execution class	44

Scala application   46
    Defining message classes   47
    Defining actor classes   47
    Defining the execution class   55
Summary   **58**

Chapter 3: Actors   **59**
Actors   **59**
Defining an actor   **61**
Creating actors   **61**
  Actor with default constructor   62
  Actor with non-default constructor   62
  Creating an actor within an actor hierarchy   63
Messaging model   **64**
  Sending messages   65
    Fire and forget messages – tell()   66
    Send and receive messages – ask()   67
  Receiving messages   69
  Replying to messages   70
  Forwarding messages   70
Stopping actors   **71**
Killing actors   **73**
Actor lifecycle monitoring   **73**
HotSwap   **74**
Summary   **76**

Chapter 4: Typed Actors   **77**
What are typed actors?   **78**
Defining an actor   **80**
Creating actors   **82**
  An actor with a default constructor   83
  An actor with a non-default constructor   83
Messaging model   **84**
  Sending messages   84
    Fire and forget messages   85
    Send and receive messages   85
Stopping actors   **86**
Actor lifecycle monitoring   **87**
  Lifecycle callbacks   87
  Receiving messages   88
  Supervisor strategy   90
Creating an actor hierarchy   **91**
Dispatchers and routers   **92**

Using dispatchers 92
application.conf 93
Using routers 93
Summary **94**
Chapter 5: Dispatchers and Routers **95**
Dispatchers **95**
Dispatcher as a pattern 97
Executor in Java 97
Dispatchers in Akka 99
Types of dispatcher 100
Dispatcher 101
Pinned dispatcher 102
Balancing dispatcher 103
Calling thread dispatcher 103
Types of mailboxes 104
Dispatcher usage 105
Routers **109**
Router usage 110
Router usage via application.conf 112
Router usage for distributed actors 113
Dynamically resizing routers 114
Custom router 115
Summary **121**
Chapter 6: Supervision and Monitoring **123**
Let It Crash **123**
Actor hierarchy 124
Supervision **127**
Supervision strategies **130**
One-For-One strategy 133
All-For-One strategy 146
Lifecycle monitoring **154**
Fault tolerance **161**
Summary **163**
Chapter 7: Software Transactional Memory **165**
Transaction management **165**
What is software transactional memory? 166
Coordinated transactions **169**
Money transfer between two accounts 171
Transactor **184**
Money transfer between two accounts – take two 185

Agents	**187**
Creating agents	188
Updating agent values	188
Reading agent values	189
Stopping agents	190
Summary	**190**
Chapter 8: Deployment Ready	**191**
Testing your Akka application	**191**
Writing the first unit test with TestActorRef	192
Access to the underlying actor reference	194
Testing actor behavior	195
Testing exception scenarios	196
Integration testing with TestKit	197
EchoActor testing	202
ForwardingActor testing	203
SequencingActor testing	203
SupervisorActor testing	205
Remote actors testing	207
Managing application configuration using Akka extensions	**208**
Deployment mode	**213**
Microkernel	214
Summary	**216**
Chapter 9: Remote Actors	**217**
Distributed computing	**217**
Actor path	221
Remote actors	**223**
Creating the remote node application	225
Creating the local node application	228
Creating remote actors programmatically	232
Message serialization	**234**
Creating your own serialization technique	235
Remote events	**242**
Summary	**246**
Chapter 10: Management	**247**
Application monitoring	**247**
Typesafe console	**248**
Typesafe console modules	249
Trace	250
Analyze	252
Query	254
Typesafe console	255

Graphical dashboard **257**
 System overview 259
  Node 260
 Dispatchers 262
  Actors 264
  Tags 266
  Errors 268
 Limitations 270
JMX and REST interfaces **270**
 RESTful API 270
 JMX 272
Summary **274**
Chapter 11: Advanced Topics **275**
Durable mailboxes **275**
 Akka support 277
  Dispatcher usage 277
  FileDurableMailboxStorage 279
Actors and web applications **281**
 Installing play 282
 Creating the first HttpActors application 282
 Launching the console 283
Integrating actors with ZeroMQ **289**
 Publisher-subscriber connection 290
  Usage 290
 Request-reply connection 294
  Usage 295
 Router-dealer connection 298
  Usage 299
 Push-pull connection 302
  Usage 303
Summary **306**
Index **307**

Preface

Akka Essentials is meant as a guide for architects, solution providers, consultants, engineers, and anyone planning to design and implement a distributed, concurrent application based on Akka. It will refer to easy-to-explain concept examples, as they are likely to be the best teaching aids. It will explain the logic, code, and configurations needed to build a successful, distributed, concurrent application, as well as the reason behind those decisions.

This book covers the core concepts to design and create a distributed, concurrent application, but it is not meant to be a replacement for the official documentation guide for Akka published at Typesafe.

The driving force of Akka's Actor Model

The existing, Java-based concurrency model does not lend well to the underlying, hardware multiprocessor model. This leads to the Java application not being able to scale up and scale out, to handle the demands of a distributed, scalable, concurrent application.

The Akka framework has taken the "Actor Model" concept to build an event-driven, middleware framework that allows the building of concurrent, scalable, and distributed systems. Akka uses the Actor Model to raise the abstraction level that decouples the business logic from the low-level constructs of threads, locks, and non-blocking I/O.

The Akka framework provides the following features:

- **Concurrency**: The Akka Actor Model abstracts concurrency handling and allows the programmer to focus on the business logic
- **Scalability**: The Akka Actor Model's asynchronous message passing allows applications to scale up on multicore servers

- **Fault tolerance**: Akka borrows the concepts and techniques from Erlang to build the "Let It Crash", fault tolerance model

- **Event-driven architecture**: Akka provides an asynchronous messaging platform for building event-driven architectures

- **Transaction support**: Akka implements transactors that combine the actors and **software transactional memory** (**STM**) into transactional actors

- **Location transparency**: Akka provides a unified programming model for multicore and distributed computing needs

- **Scala/Java APIs**: Akka supports both Java and Scala APIs for building applications

The Akka framework is envisioned as a toolkit and runtime for building highly concurrent, distributed, and fault-tolerant, event-driven applications on the JVM.

What this book covers

Chapter 1, Introduction to Akka, covers the background on the evolution of the microprocessor, the current problems met in the building of concurrent applications, and the Actor Model. We will then jump into what Akka provides, and the high-level features of the Akka framework.

Chapter 2, Starting with Akka, covers the motions of the installation of the development environment and the writing of the first Akka application.

Chapter 3, Actors, covers the overview of the actors. The chapter covers the lifecycle of an actor, how to create actors, how to pass and process messages, and how to stop or kill the actor.

Chapter 4, Typed Actors, covers the overview of the typed actors. It also covers the lifecycle of a typed actor, how to create actors, how to pass and process messages, and how to stop or kill the actor.

Chapter 5, Dispatchers and Routers, covers dispatchers and their workings. The chapter covers the various types of dispatchers and their usage and configuration settings, and the different types of mailboxes and their usage and configuration. This chapter also covers routers, and their different types and usage.

Chapter 6, Supervision and Monitoring, covers fault tolerance, the lifecycle, supervision strategies, and linking strategies when writing large-scale, concurrent programs. The chapter covers the "Let It Crash" paradigm, and how it is managed in the Actor Model using the various supervision strategies.

Chapter 7, Software Transactional Memory, covers the various Akka constructs provided for the transactional concepts (begin/commit/rollback semantics). The chapter walks us through the basics of transaction management and explores the Akka constructs provided for STM—transactors and agents.

Chapter 8, Deployment Ready, covers the three, critical gating criteria that an application needs to pass in order to go into production. This chapter covers the unit and integration testing employed for the Akka application, how to manage environment-specific configuration, and the deployment strategies.

Chapter 9, Remote Actors, covers the requirements of a distributed computing environment and how Akka implements these. It also covers the various methods of creating remote actors, how object serialization happens in Akka, the various serializers provided by Akka, and how you can write your own serializers.

Chapter 10, Management, covers the monitoring capabilities provided by the Typesafe console—the Akka monitoring tool, various graphical dashboards, and real-time statistics. The chapter also covers the key JMX and REST interfaces.

Chapter 11, Advanced Topics, covers topics such as durable mailboxes, the integration of Akka with the play framework, and actor integration with ZeroMQ.

What you need for this book

The book is technical in nature, so the reader needs to have a basic understanding of the following:

- Java/Scala programming language
- Java's thread and concurrency model

Who this book is for

This book is aimed at developers and architects, who are building large distributed, concurrent, and scalable applications using Java/Scala. The book requires the reader to have a knowledge of Java/JEE concepts, but a knowledge of the Actor Model is not necessary.

Conventions

In this book, you will find a number of styles of text that distinguish between different kinds of information. Here are some examples of these styles, and an explanation of their meaning.

Code words in text are shown as follows:"The /lib folder holds the scala-library.jar file."

A block of code is set as follows:

```
package akka.first.app.mapreduce.messages;
import java.util.List;
public final class MapData {
    private final List<WordCount> dataList;
    public List<WordCount> getDataList() {
        return dataList;
    }
    public MapData(List<WordCount> dataList) {
        this.dataList = dataList;
    }
}
```

When we wish to draw your attention to a particular part of a code block, the relevant lines or items are set in bold:

```
package akka.first.app.mapreduce.actors;
import akka.actor.ActorRef;
import akka.actor.UntypedActor;
import akka.first.app.mapreduce.messages.Result;

public class MasterActor extends UntypedActor {
    ActorRef mapActor;
    ActorRef reduceActor;
    ActorRef aggregateActor;
    @Override
    public void onReceive(Object message) throws Exception {

    }
}
```

Any command-line input or output is written as follows:

```
$ cd HttpActors
$ ls
```

New terms and **important words** are shown in bold. Words that you see on the screen, in menus or dialog boxes for example, appear in the text like this:"Open Eclipse and go to **File | New | Project....**"

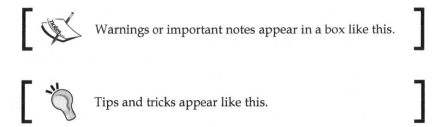

> Warnings or important notes appear in a box like this.

> Tips and tricks appear like this.

Reader feedback

Feedback from our readers is always welcome. Let us know what you think about this book—what you liked or may have disliked. Reader feedback is important for us to develop titles that you really get the most out of.

To send us general feedback, simply send an e-mail to feedback@packtpub.com, and mention the book title via the subject of your message.

If there is a topic that you have expertise in and you are interested in either writing or contributing to a book, see our author guide on www.packtpub.com/authors

Customer support

Now that you are the proud owner of a Packt book, we have a number of things to help you to get the most from your purchase.

Downloading the example code

You can download the example code files for all Packt books you have purchased from your account at http://www.PacktPub.com. If you purchased this book elsewhere, you can visit http://www.PacktPub.com/support and register to have the files e-mailed directly to you.

Errata

Although we have taken every care to ensure the accuracy of our content, mistakes do happen. If you find a mistake in one of our books—maybe a mistake in the text or the code—we would be grateful if you would report this to us. By doing so, you can save other readers from frustration and help us improve subsequent versions of this book. If you find any errata, please report them by visiting http://www.packtpub.com/support, selecting your book, clicking on the **errata submission form** link, and entering the details of your errata. Once your errata are verified, your submission will be accepted and the errata will be uploaded on our website, or added to any list of existing errata, under the Errata section of that title. Any existing errata can be viewed by selecting your title from http://www.packtpub.com/support.

Piracy

Piracy of copyright material on the Internet is an ongoing problem across all media. At Packt, we take the protection of our copyright and licenses very seriously. If you come across any illegal copies of our works, in any form, on the Internet, please provide us with the location address or website name immediately so that we can pursue a remedy.

Please contact us at copyright@packtpub.com with a link to the suspected pirated material.

We appreciate your help in protecting our authors, and our ability to bring you valuable content.

Questions

You can contact us at questions@packtpub.com if you are having a problem with any aspect of the book, and we will do our best to address it.

1
Introduction to Akka

Akka is one of the most popular Actor Model frameworks that provide a complete toolkit and runtime for designing and building highly concurrent, distributed, and fault-tolerant, event-driven applications on the JVM. This chapter will walk you through the motivation and need for building an Akka toolkit.

As Java/Scala developers, we will see the usage of creating applications using the Akka Actor Model, which scales up and scales out seamlessly, and provides levels of concurrency, which is simply difficult to achieve with the standard Java libraries.

Background

Before we delve into what Akka is, let us take a step back to understand how the concept of concurrent programming has evolved in the application development world. The applications have always been tied to the underlying hardware resource capacity. The whole concept of building large, scalable, distributed applications needs to be looked at from the perspective of the underlying hardware resources where the application runs and the language support provided for concurrent programming.

Microprocessor evolution

The advancement of the microprocessor architecture meant the CPU kept becoming faster and faster with doubling of the transistors every 18 months (Moore's law). But soon, the chip design hit the physical limits in terms of how many transistors could be squeezed on to the **printed circuit board** (**PCB**). Subsequently, we moved to multicore processor architecture that has two or more identical processors or processor cores physically close to each other, sharing the underlying bus interface and the cache.

These microprocessors having two or more cores effectively increased the processor's performance by the same factor as the number of cores, limited only by the amount of serial code (Amdahl's law).

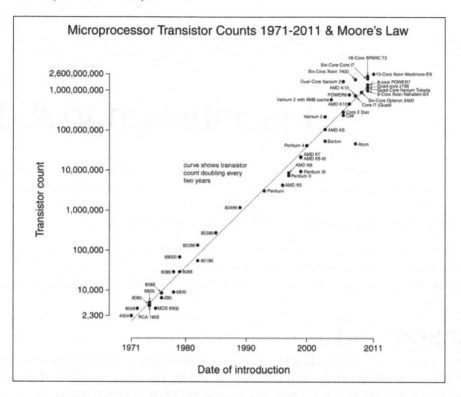

The preceding diagram from wiki, http://en.wikipedia.org/wiki/Transistor_count shows how the transistor count was doubled initially over the period of 18 months (following the Moore's Law) and how the multiprocessor architecture for consumer machines has evolved over the last 6-7 years.

> Clock speeds are not increasing; processors are getting more parallel and not faster.

Concurrent systems

When writing large concurrent systems, the traditional model of shared state concurrency makes use of changing shared memory locations. The system uses multithreaded programming coupled with synchronization monitors to guard against potential deadlocks. The entire multithreading programming model is based on how to manage and control the concurrent access to the shared, mutable state.

Manipulating shared, mutable state via threads makes it hard at times to debug problems. Usage of locks may guarantee the correct behavior, but it is likely to lead to the effect of threads running into a deadlock problem, with each acquiring locks in a different order and waiting for each other, as shown in the following diagram:

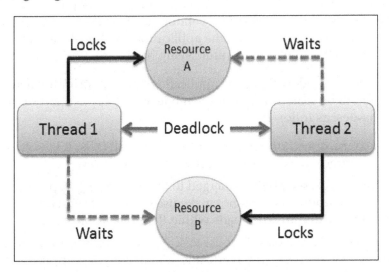

Working with threads requires a much higher level of programming skills and it is very difficult to predict the behavior of the threads in a runtime environment.

Java provides shared memory threads with locks as the primary form of concurrency abstractions. However, shared memory threads are quite heavyweight and incur severe performance penalties from context-switching overheads.

A newer Java API around fork/join, based on work-stealing algorithms, makes the task easier, but it still takes a fair bit of expertise and tuning to write the application.

> Writing multithreaded applications that can take advantage of the underlying hardware is very error-prone and not easy to build.
>
> Scaling up Java programs is difficult; scaling out Java programs is even more difficult.

Container-based applications

Java Platform, Enterprise Edition (JEE) was introduced as a platform to develop and run distributed multitier Java applications. The entire multitier architecture is based on the concept of breaking down the application into specialized layers that process the smaller pieces of logic. These multitier applications are deployed in containers (called application servers) provided by vendors, such as IBM or Oracle, which host and provide the infrastructure to run the application. The application server is tuned to run the application and utilize the underlying hardware.

The container-based model allows the applications to be distributed across nodes and allows them to be scaled. The runtime model of the application servers has its own share of issues, as follows:

- In case of runtime failures, the entire request call fails. It is very difficult to retry any method execution or recovery from failures.

- The application scalability is tagged to the underlying application container settings. An application cannot make use of different threading models to account for different workloads within the same application.

- Using the container-based model to scale out the applications requires a large set of resources, and overheads of managing the application across the application server nodes are very high.

 Container-based applications are bounded by the rules of the container's ability to scale up and scale out, resulting in suboptimal performance.

The JEE programming model of writing distributed applications is not the best fit for a scale-out application model.

Given that the processors are becoming more parallel, the applications are getting more distributed, and traditional JVM programming techniques are not helpful. So, there is a need for a different paradigm to solve the problem.

Actor Model

In 1973, Carl Hewitt, Peter Bishop, and Richard Steiger wrote a paper—*A Universal Modular ACTOR Formalism for Artificial Intelligence*, which introduced the concept of Actors. Subsequently, the Actor Model was implemented in the Erlang language by Joe Armstrong and Ericsson implemented the AXD 301 telecom switch that went onto achieve reliability of 99.9999999 percent (nine 9's).

The Actor Model takes a different approach to solving the problem of concurrency, by avoiding the issues caused by threads and locks. In the Actor Model, all objects are modeled as independent, computational entities that only respond to the messages received. There is no shared state between actors, as follows:

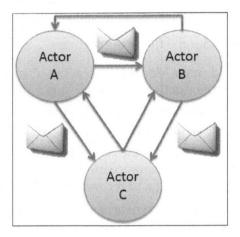

Actors change their state only when they receive a stimulus in the form of a message. So unlike the object-oriented world where the objects are executed sequentially, the actors execute concurrently.

The Actor Model is based on the following principles:

- The immutable messages are used to communicate between actors. Actors do not share state, and if any information is shared, it is done via message only. Actors control the access to the state and nobody else can access the state. This means there is no shared, mutable state.

- Each actor has a queue attached where the incoming messages are enqueued. Messages are picked from the queue and processed by the actor, one at a time. An actor can respond to the received message by sending immutable messages to other actors, creating a new set of actors, updating their own state, or designating the computational logic to be used when the next message arrives (behavior change).

- Messages are passed between actors asynchronously. It means that the sender does not wait for the message to be received and can go back to its execution immediately. Any actor can send a message to another actor with no guarantee on the sequence of the message arrival and execution.

- Communication between the sender and receiver is decoupled and asynchronous, allowing them to execute in different threads. By having invocation and execution in separate threads coupled with no shared state, allows actors to provide a concurrent and scalable model.

Akka framework

The Akka framework has taken the Actor Model concept to build an event-driven, middleware framework that allows building concurrent, scalable, distributed systems. Akka uses the Actor Model to raise the abstraction level that decouples the business logic from low-level constructs of threads, locks, and non-blocking I/O.

The Akka framework provides the following features:

- **Concurrency**: Akka Actor Model abstracts the concurrency handling and allows the programmer to focus on the business logic.

- **Scalability**: Akka Actor Model's asynchronous message passing allows applications to scale up on multicore servers.

- **Fault tolerance**: Akka borrows the concepts and techniques from Erlang to build a "Let It Crash" fault-tolerance model using supervisor hierarchies to allow applications to fail fast and recover from the failure as soon as possible.

- **Event-driven architecture**: Asynchronous messaging makes Akka a perfect platform for building event-driven architectures.

- **Transaction support**: Akka implements transactors that combine actors and **software transactional memory** (**STM**) into transactional actors. This allows composition of atomic message flows with automatic retry and rollback.

- **Location transparency**: Akka treats remote and local process actors the same, providing a unified programming model for multicore and distributed computing needs.

- **Scala/Java APIs**: Akka supports both Java and Scala APIs for building applications.

The Akka framework is envisaged as a toolkit and runtime for building highly concurrent, distributed, and fault-tolerant, event-driven applications on the JVM.

 Akka is open source and available under the Apache License, Version 2 at `http://akka.io`.

Akka was originally created by Jonas Bonér and is currently available as part of the open source Typesafe Stack.

Next, we will see all the key constructs provided by Akka that are used to build a concurrent, fault-tolerant, and scalable application.

Actor systems

Actor is an independent, concurrent computational entity that responds to messages. Before we jump into actor, we need to understand the role played by the actor in the overall scheme of things. Actor is the smallest unit in the grand scheme of things. Concurrent programs are split into separate entities that work on distinct subtasks. Each actor performs his quota of tasks (subtasks) and when all the actors have finished their individual subtasks, the bigger task gets completed.

Let's take an example of an IT project that needs to deliver a defined functionality to the business. The project is staffed with people who bring different skill sets to the table, mapped for the different phases of the project as follows:

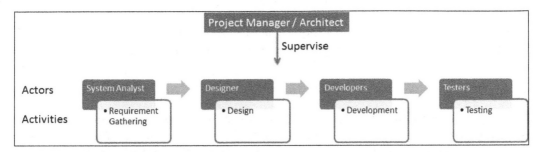

The whole task of building something is divided into subtasks/activities that are handled by specialized actors adept in that subtask. The overall supervision is provided by another actor—project manager or architect.

In the preceding example, the project needs to exist and it should provide the structure for the various actors (project manager, architect, developer, and so on) to start playing their roles. In the absence of the project, the actor roles have no meaning and existence. In Akka world, the project is equivalent to the actor system.

 The **actor system** is the container that manages the actor behavior, lifecycle, hierarchy, and configuration among other things. The actor system provides the structure to manage the application.

What is an actor?

Actor is modeled as the object that encapsulates state and behavior. All the messages intended for the actors are parked in a queue and actors process the messages from that queue.

Actors can change their state and behavior based on the message passed. This allows them to respond to changes in the messages coming in. An actor has the constituents that are listed in the following sections.

State

The actor objects hold instance variables that have certain state values or can be pure computational entities (stateless). These state values held by the actor instance variable define the state of the actor. The state can be characterized by counters, listeners, or references to resources or state machine. The actor state is changed only as a response to a message. The whole premise of the actor is to prevent the actor state getting corrupted or locked via concurrent access to the state variables.

Akka implements actors as a reactive, event-driven, lightweight thread that shields and protects the actor's state. Actors provide the concurrent access to the state allowing us to write programs without worrying about concurrency and locking issues.

When the actors fail and are restarted, the actors' state is reinitialized to make sure that the actors behave in a consistent manner with a consistent state.

Behavior

Behavior is nothing but the computation logic that needs to be executed in response to the message received. The actor behavior might include changing the actor state. The actor behavior itself can undergo a change as a reaction to the message. It means the actor can swap the existing behavior with a new behavior when a certain message comes in. The actor defaults to the original behavior in case of a restart, when encountering a failure:

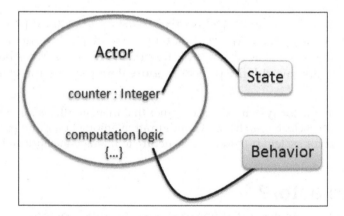

Mailbox

An actor responds to messages. The connection wire between the sender sending a message and the receiver actor receiving the message is called the **mailbox**. Every actor is attached to exactly one mailbox. When the message is sent to the actor, the message gets enqueued in its mailbox, from where the message is dequeued for processing by the receiving actor. The order of arrival of the messages in the queue is determined in runtime based on the time order of the send operation. Messages from one sender actor to another definite receiver actor will be enqueued in the same order as they are sent:

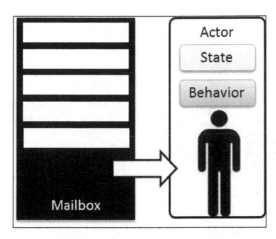

Akka provides multiple mailbox implementations. The mailboxes can be bounded or unbounded. A bounded mailbox limits the number of messages that can be queued in the mailbox, meaning it has a defined or fixed capacity for holding the messages.

At times, applications may want to prioritize a certain message over the other. To handle such cases, Akka provides a priority mailbox where the messages are enqueued based on the assigned priority. Akka does not allow scanning of the mailbox. Messages are processed in the same order as they are enqueued in the mailbox.

Akka makes use of dispatchers to pass the messages from the queue to the actors for processing. Akka supports different types of dispatchers. We will cover more about dispatchers and mailboxes in *Chapter 5, Dispatchers and Routers*.

Actor lifecycle

Every actor that is defined and created has an associated lifecycle. Akka provides hooks such as preStart that allow the actor's state and behavior to be initialized. When the actor is stopped, Akka disables the message queuing for the actor before PostStop is invoked. In the postStop hook, any persistence of the state or clean up of any hold-up resources can be done:

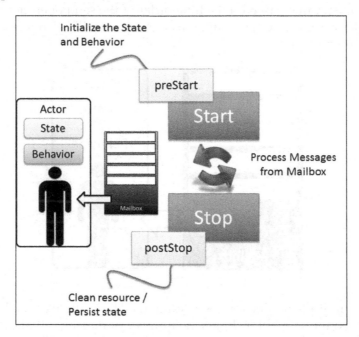

Further, Akka supports two types of actors—untyped actors and typed actors. We will cover untyped and typed actors in *Chapter 3*, *Actors*, and *Chapter 4*, *Typed Actors*, respectively.

Fault tolerance

Akka follows the premise of the actor hierarchy where we have specialized actors that are adept in handling or performing an activity. To manage these specialized actors, we have supervisor actors that coordinate and manage their lifecycle. As the complexity of the problem grows, the hierarchy also expands to manage the complexity. This allows the system to be as simple or as complex as required based on the tasks that need to be performed:

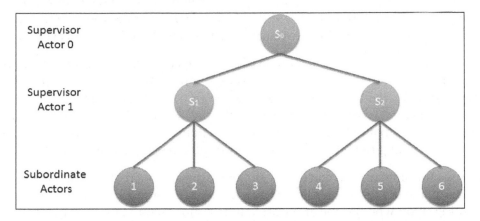

The whole idea is to break down the task into smaller tasks to the point where the task is granular and structured enough to be performed by one actor. Each actor knows which kind of message it will process and how he reacts in terms of failure. So, if the actor does not know how to handle a particular message or an abnormal runtime behavior, the actor asks its supervisor for help. The recursive actor hierarchy allows the problem to be propagated upwards to the point where it can be handled. Remember, every actor in Akka has one and only one supervisor.

This actor hierarchy forms the basis of the Akka's "Let It Crash" fault-tolerance model. Akka's fault-tolerance model is built using the actor hierarchy and supervisor model. We will cover more details about supervision in *Chapter 6, Supervision and Monitoring*.

Location transparency

For a distributed application, all actor interactions need to be asynchronous and location transparent. Meaning, location of the actor (local or remote) has no impact on the application. Whether we are accessing an actor, or invoking or passing the message, everything remains the same.

To achieve this location transparency, the actors need to be identifiable and reachable. Under the hood, Akka uses configuration to indicate whether the actor is running locally or on a remote machine. Akka uses the actor hierarchy and combines it with the actor system address to make each actor identifiable and reachable.

Akka uses the same philosophy of the **World Wide Web (WWW)** to identify and locate resources on the Web. WWW makes use of the **uniform resource locator (URL)** to identify and locate resources on the Web. The URL consists of — `scheme://domain:port/path`, where `scheme` defines the protocol (HTTP or FTP), `domain` defines the server name or the IP address, `port` defines the port where the process listens for incoming requests, and `path` specifies the resource to be fetched.

Akka uses the similar URL convention to locate the actors. In case of an Akka application, the default values are `akka://hostname/` or `akka://hostname:2552/` depending upon whether the application uses remote actors or not, to identify the application. To identify the resource within the application, the actor hierarchy is used to identify the location of the actor:

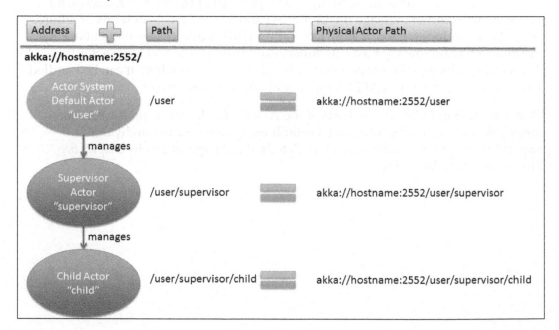

The actor hierarchy allows the unique path to be created to reach any actor within the actor system. This unique path coupled with the address creates a unique address that identifies and locates an actor.

Within the application, each actor is accessed using an `ActorRef` class, which is based on the underlying actor path. `ActorRef` allows us to transparently access the actors without knowing their locations. Meaning, the location of the actor is transparent for the application. The location transparency allows you to build applications without worrying how the actors communicate underneath.

 Akka treats remote and local process actors the same—all can be accessed by an address URL.

Transactors

To provide transaction capabilities to actors, Akka transactors combine actors with STM to form transactional actors. This allows actors to compose atomic message flows with automatic retry and rollback.

Working with threads and locks is hard and there is no guarantee that the application will not run into locking issues. To abstract the threading and locking hardships, STM, which is a concurrency control mechanism for managing access to shared memory in a concurrent environment, has gained a lot of acceptance.

STM is modeled on similar lines of database transaction handling. In the case of STM, the Java heap is the transactional data set with begin/commit and rollback constructs. As the objects hold the state in memory, the transaction only implements the characteristics—atomicity, consistency, and isolation.

For actors to implement a shared state model and provide a consistent, stable view of the state across the calling components, Akka transactors provide the way. Akka transactors combine the Actor Model and STM to provide the best of both worlds allowing you to write transactional, asynchronous, event-based message flow applications and gives you composed atomic arbitrary, deep message flows. We will cover transactors in more details in the *Chapter 7, Software Transactional Memory*.

So far, we have seen the key constructs that form the basis of Akka:

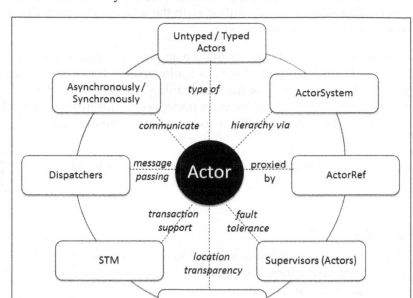

As we move ahead and delve deep into the constructs provided by the Akka framework, we need to make sure that we keep in mind the following concepts:

- An **actor** is a computation unit with state, behavior, and its own mailbox
- There are two types of actors—untyped and typed
- Communication between actors can be asynchronous or synchronous
- Message passing to the actors happens using dispatchers
- Actors are organized in a hierarchy via the actor system
- Actors are proxied via `ActorRef`
- Supervisor actors are used to build the fault-tolerance mechanism
- Actor path follows the URL scheme, which enables location transparency
- STM is used to provide transactional support to multiple actor state updates

We will explore each of these concepts in detail in the coming chapters.

Akka use cases

Now that we have seen what Akka is and the key features of Akka, let's delve into the use cases where Akka fits in best. Any business use case that requires the application to scale up and scale out, be fault tolerant, or provide **High Availability (HA)**, requires massive concurrency/parallelism, which is a prime target for use of the Akka Actor Model. The following are the use cases for Akka:

- **Transaction processing**: This includes processing large data streams, where the incoming data is either time series or transactional data. The stream pumps in large amount of data that needs to be processed in parallel and concurrently. The output of the data processing might be used in real time or might be fed into analytical systems. Finance, banking, securities, trading, telecom, social media, analytics, and online gaming are some of the domain enterprises that deal with large data coming in from multiple sources, which needs to be processed, analyzed, and reported.

- **Service providers**: Another area is where the application provides services to various other clients via variety of service means such as SOAP, REST, Cometd, or WebSockets. The application generally caters to a massive amount of stateless requests that need to be processed fast and concurrently.

- **Batch processing**: Batch processing used across enterprise domains is another area where Akka shines very well. Dealing with large data, applying paradigms such as divide and conquer, map-reduce, master-worker, and grid computing allows massive data to be processed. The data might be coming in via real-time feeds, or it might be unstructured data (coming via logfiles) or data read from existing data stores.

- **Data mining/analytics/Business Intelligence**: Most enterprises generate large amounts of data—structured as well as unstructured. Applications that mine this data from existing transactional stores or data warehouses can use Akka to process and analyze these massive sets of data.

- **Service gateways/hubs**: Service gateways or hubs connect multiple systems or applications together, and provide mediation and transformation services. An Akka-based application can provide those scale-up and scale-out options along with high availability for applications in this space.

- **Apps requiring concurrency/parallelism**: Any application that needs to process data in parallel or provide/support concurrency can make use of Akka. Akka provides a faster time to market for such applications, as writing and testing such applications is far easier and less error-prone compared to traditional thread-based concurrent applications. Akka JARs can be easily dropped into existing Java or Scala applications and the applications can start making use of the Actor Model.

At times, Akka needs to be used in conjunction with other frameworks or libraries to build the complete application. Some of the common frameworks that work very well with Akka are Play framework, ZeroMQ, Apache Camel, and Spring framework, among others. We will explore the usage of Play framework and ZeroMQ with Akka.

Summary

This completes the introduction to Akka, where we saw the evolution of the microprocessors, the problems with writing/using the Java concurrency models for distributed applications, and how Akka's Actor Model provides an answer to the two problems. We also learned the key constructs that define the Akka framework and sample use cases where Akka is a prime candidate for use.

In the next chapter, we will get started with Akka, we will go through the motions of installing the development environment and write our first Akka application.

2
Starting with Akka

In this chapter we will go through the motions of installing and configuring our development environment and writing our first Akka application.

We will use Eclipse as our medium of **Integrated Development Environment (IDE)** and go through the motions of installing, configuring, and doing development with Akka.

We assume that you are well aware of Java/Scala and starting your Akka actor's journey.

Downloading the example code

You can download the example code files for all Packt books you have purchased from your account at http://www. PacktPub.com. If you purchased this book elsewhere, you can visit http://www.PacktPub.com/support and register to have the files e-mailed directly to you.

Application requirements

For our first Akka application, we are going to implement the Word Count using the `MapReduce` method. The premise of the application is to accept complete sentences as a string and count the number of words across the input sentences.

We will take certain English sentences and run them through our Word Count Map Reduce application to count the number of occurrences of each word. The overall application will be broken into multiple tasks, such as performing specialized computations and computing the word count. The following diagram explains the different computational duties that will be assigned for each of the tasks:

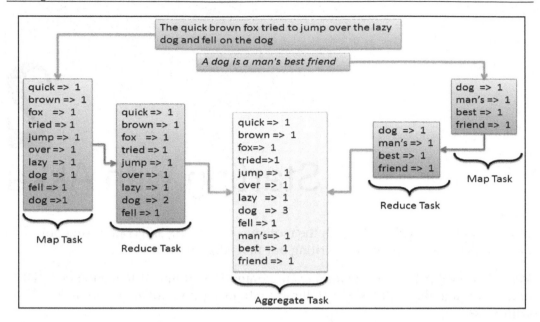

Each sentence goes through the notions of the following:

- **Map task**: It is defined as mapping the words within the sentence. We count the actual words in the sentence and discard certain STOP words such as "a", "is", "the", "to", and so on. For the selected words, we assign the numerical count value of 1. Subsequently, the list is passed on to the Reduce task.

- **Reduce task**: It is defined as reducing the list of words to individual occurrences for each sentence. Here, we check the occurrences of the same word within the first list and if certain words are found, we increase the count. The reduced list is further passed to the Aggregate task.

- **Aggregate task**: It is defined as aggregating the reduce lists across sentences into one common list.

Application design

We have the basic computational units identified in the beginning for each of the tasks that will be performed on the sentence in order to count the words. We model our actors around the same computational task model and create the following three actors for each task:

- Map actor
- Reduce actor
- Aggregate actor

To create and manage the lifecycle of these actors, we create another actor called Master actor. The communication between actors will happen via immutable messages as follows:

1. The Master actor sends the sentence as a string to the Map actor.

2. The Map actor maps the words in the sentence and returns the `MapData` message to the The Master actor. Master actor sends the `MapData` message to the Reduce actor.

3. The Reduce actor acts on the `MapData` message and reduces the words. The reduced word list is sent to the Aggregate actor as `ReduceData` via the Master actor.

4. The Aggregate actor receives `ReduceData` and updates its internal state, which has the complete list of the data.

5. The Master actor can send a `Result` message to the Aggregate actor and it will return the aggregated list as a response to that message.

All the actors are created and running within an actor system, as shown in the following diagram:

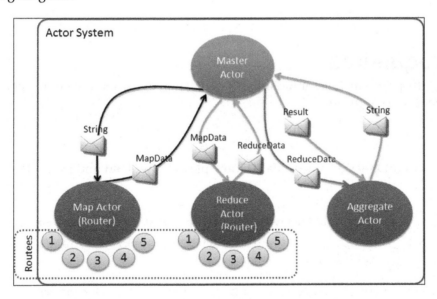

As part of the application development, we need to perform the following activities:

- Define structure for the messages
- Define four actors and write the respective computational logic in each of them
- Write an actor system that will create the actors and run against a set of data to perform the calculations

Start development

Let's get started for the development of the solution. To start working on the solution, we need to get the development environment set up. Let's understand what we need for the development environment and prerequisites.

The following are the tooling requirements for development of the application in Java or Scala. If you already have some of these tools installed, you can skip those particular sections and just deploy the rest of the tooling:

Tooling/framework	Java	Scala
Java	Java SDK 1.6 minimum	Java SDK 1.6 minimum
Akka	2.0.1 and above	2.0.1 and above
Maven plugin for Eclipse	3.0.2	3.0.2
Scala IDE plugin for Eclipse	NA	2.0.2
Eclipse	3.6 and above	3.6 and above
Scala Simple Build Tool (SBT) (an alternative for Scala IDE plugin for Eclipse)	NA	0.10 and above

Prerequisites

Let's get the prerequisites for having the application development environment installed and configured.

Java

Based on your OS—Windows/Mac/Linux, please download and install Java 6 or Java 7.

 Check out the Java installation options at the following website:
`http://www.oracle.com/technetwork/java/javase/downloads/index.html`

After installation of Java, make sure you set up the %JAVA_HOME% environment variable to point to the Java installation. Also add the JAVA_HOME variable to the PATH environment variable.

Eclipse

For the development environment, we will download and install Eclipse. For Akka development, we will download Eclipse 4.2 (Juno) version. If you have earlier versions such as Indigo or Helios, they will work fine as well.

 Eclipse 4.2 (Juno) can be downloaded from the following website: `http://www.eclipse.org/downloads/`

Maven

Maven is a well-known application build automation tool. Maven uses an XML file (`pom.xml`) to manage the application dependencies on external modules and libraries. Maven supports both Java and Scala.

We will install Maven plugin for use within our Eclipse IDE. We will use the Eclipse update site URL to add the Maven plugin to the Eclipse IDE. Refer to the following URL for the Maven Eclipse update site:

`http://www.eclipse.org/m2e/download/`

If you can access source code repositories from Maven, then you need not install Akka or Scala separately. Once you specify the dependent modules and repository source, Maven can download and make the right JARs available.

Scala

If you intend to build the Akka application using Scala, there are two options as follows:

- Use the Scala IDE plugin for Eclipse
- Download and install SBT

To install the Scala IDE plugin for use within our Eclipse, we will use the Eclipse update site URL to add the Scala IDE plugin to the Eclipse IDE. Refer to the following URL for the Scala Eclipse update site:

`http://typesafe.com/stack/scala_ide_download`

When you install the plugin, the required Scala language libraries will be downloaded and installed, so you do not need to do any separate Scala installation.

SBT or **Simple Build Tool** is a build system written in Scala. You can install SBT and refer to https://github.com/harrah/xsbt/wiki or https://github.com/harrah/xsbt/wiki/Getting-Started-Setup for details about creating a Scala project.

Akka

If we are building projects using Maven, then we specify the Akka repository URL and the required module name; Maven will automatically download and add the dependency to the project.

In case you do not want to use Maven, Typesafe provides a simple way to install the SBT along with giter8, which provides starter templates for Scala/Akka projects. Check out http://typesafe.com/resources/typesafe-stack/downloading-installing.html.

You can also download the current, stable release version of Akka from http://akka.io/downloads/. Once you have downloaded the Akka distribution, unzip it in the folder you would like to have Akka installed in. I am choosing to install Akka in D:\tools, simply by unzipping it to this directory.

Once unzipped, the Akka folder structure looks as shown the following screenshot:

```
D:\Tools>cd akka-2.0.3

D:\Tools\akka-2.0.3>dir
 Volume in drive D is Local Disk
 Volume Serial Number is 221D-00DE

 Directory of D:\Tools\akka-2.0.3

09/20/2012  08:15 AM    <DIR>          .
09/20/2012  08:15 AM    <DIR>          ..
09/20/2012  08:14 AM    <DIR>          bin
09/20/2012  08:14 AM    <DIR>          config
09/20/2012  08:14 AM    <DIR>          deploy
09/20/2012  08:14 AM    <DIR>          doc
09/20/2012  08:15 AM    <DIR>          lib
08/15/2012  05:22 PM               906 README
09/20/2012  08:15 AM    <DIR>          src
               1 File(s)            906 bytes
               8 Dir(s)  56,106,917,888 bytes free
```

The directory structure of Akka is divided into the following folders, and in each of the folders the following files are kept:

Folder	Usage
bin	Holds the scripts to start/stop the Akka microkernel
config	Placeholder for the Akka application configuration files
deploy	Holds the Akka application JAR files that will be run within microkernel mode
doc	Holds the documentation about Akka usage, APIs, and doc JARs
lib	Holds the Scala JAR files
lib/akka	Holds the Akka JAR files
src	Holds the source code for the Akka JAR files

The /lib folder holds the scala-library.jar file, which is the core Scala JAR for running the Scala code, and /lib/akka holds the Akka JARs. All the core Akka JARs along with the required external dependency JARs are available here.

Akka has a modular approach and each of the Akka functional modules have been packaged as a separate JAR. Based on the functional modules being used, module-specific JARs need to be added to the project.

The Akka modules are as follows:

Modules	Functionality
akka-actor	Standard actors, untyped actors
akka-remote	Remote actors
akka-slf4j	**Simple Logging Facade for Java (SLF4J)** event-handler listener for logging with SLF4J
akka-testkit	Testing toolkit for actors
akka-kernel	Microkernel for running a bare-bones mini application server
akka-<storage-system>-mailbox	File-based Akka durable mailboxes
akka-transactor	**software transactional memory (STM)** support
akka-agent	STM agent support
akka-dataflow	Oz-style dataflow concurrency support
akka-camel	Apache Camel support
akka-osgi	OSGI deployment support
Akka-zeromq	ZeroMQ support

Java application

Once we have finished with the basic installation prerequisites, let's go ahead and create the project and start writing code for our first Akka application.

Creating the Akka Maven project

To create the Akka Maven project, perform the following steps:

1. Open Eclipse and go to **File | New | Project...**. In the **Select a wizard** dialog box, type in maven under the **Wizards** section to get the focus on **Maven Project**, as shown in the following screenshot:

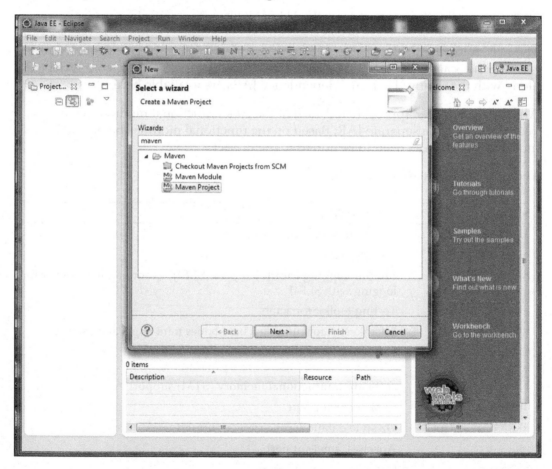

2. Select the **Maven Project** option and click on **Next**. The **New Maven Project** dialog box appears, which asks for project name and workspace, as shown in the following screenshot:

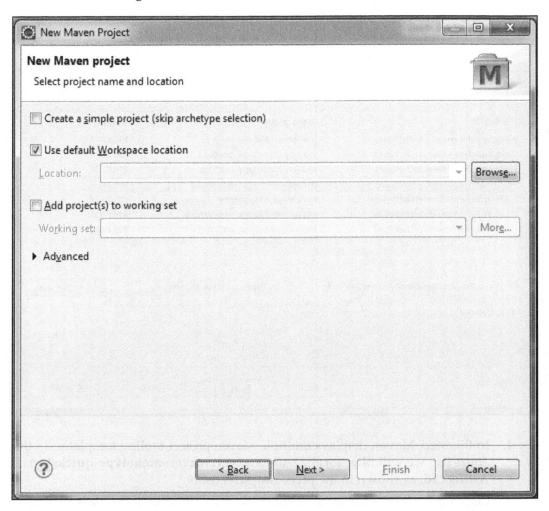

3. Click the on the **Next** button and move on to the next step:

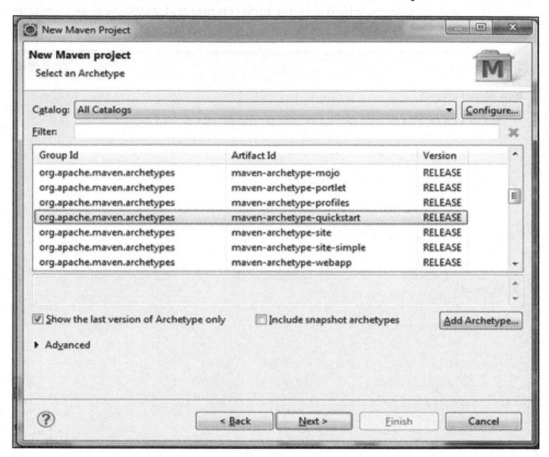

4. In this step, Maven displays multiple Maven project tooling templates. In this entire list, we will filter for the template with **maven-archetype-quickstart** as **Artifact Id**, as shown in the preceding screenshot.

Once we have selected the template type, we will click on the **Next** button.

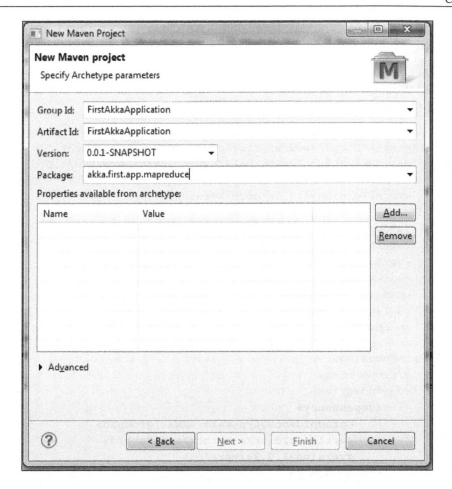

5. Here, we will provide **FirstAkkaApplication** as **Group Id** and **Artifact Id**
    and **akka.first.app.mapreduce** as **Package**. Click on the **Finish** button and
    the project will be created in the workspace. The project layout will look like
    the following screenshot:

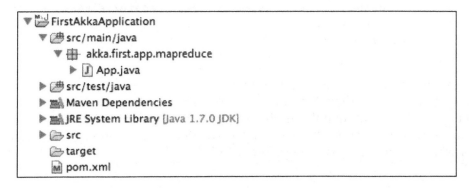

There is already one Java source file—**App.java**. Just go ahead and delete that file.

6. Next, we will open the pom.xml file and make the necessary changes. We will add the module dependency and the repository from where the dependency can be downloaded as follows:

```xml
<project xmlns="http://maven.apache.org/POM/4.0.0"
xmlns:xsi="http://www.w3.org/2001/XMLSchema-instance"
    xsi:schemaLocation="http://maven.apache.org/POM/4.0.0 http://
maven.apache.org/xsd/maven-4.0.0.xsd">
    <modelVersion>4.0.0</modelVersion>

    <groupId>FirstAkkaApplication</groupId>
    <artifactId>FirstAkkaApplication</artifactId>
    <version>0.0.1-SNAPSHOT</version>
    <packaging>jar</packaging>
    <name>FirstAkkaApplication</name>
    <url>http://maven.apache.org</url>
    <properties>
        <project.build.sourceEncoding>UTF-8</project.build.
sourceEncoding>
    </properties>
    <dependencies>
        <dependency>
            <groupId>com.typesafe.akka</groupId>
            <artifactId>akka-actor</artifactId>
            <version>2.0.3</version>
        </dependency>
    </dependencies>
    <repositories>
        <repository>
            <id>typesafe</id>
            <name>Typesafe Repository</name>
            <url>http://repo.typesafe.com/typesafe/releases/</url>
        </repository>
    </repositories>
</project>
```

We added the repository name and location to http://repo.typesafe.com/typesafe/releases/ and added the akka-actor dependency module with version number 2.0.3, to specify that the application uses akka-actor JAR and the associated version being used is 2.0.3. The actor JAR has no dependency on any other module and is sufficient for demonstrating our example.

In case you are not using Maven, you can also create a simple Java project in Eclipse and add the following JAR dependencies:

Dependent JARs	Location
scala-library.jar	\<akka unzip path\>akka-2.0.3\lib\
akka-actor-2.0.3.jar	\<akka unzip path\>akka-2.0.3\lib\akka

Defining message classes

Once the bare project skeleton is set up, we will start with writing message classes. So for the messages, we define the message classes in the package—akka.first. app.mapreduce.messages.

MapData.java

The following code snippet shows a MapData message:

```java
package akka.first.app.mapreduce.messages;
import java.util.List;
public final class MapData {
    private final List<WordCount> dataList;
    public List<WordCount> getDataList() {
        return dataList;
    }
    public MapData(List<WordCount> dataList) {
        this.dataList = dataList;
    }
}
```

MapData is the message that is passed from the Map actor to the Reduce actor. The message consists of a list of the WordCount objects. The WordCount object holds the word along with the associated number of instances occurring within the sentence.

WordCount.java

The WordCount class is defined as follows:

```java
package akka.first.app.mapreduce.messages;

public final class  WordCount {
    private final String word;
    private final Integer count;
    public WordCount(String inWord, Integer inCount) {
        word = inWord;
        count = inCount;
    }
```

```
    public String getWord() {
        return word;
    }
    public Integer getCount() {
        return count;
    }
}
```

ReduceData is the message passed between the Reduce actor and the Aggregate actor. The Reduce actor will reduce the message passed in MapData and pass the results as ReduceData to the Aggregate actor.

ReduceData.java

The ReduceData class can be defined as follows:

```
package akka.first.app.mapreduce.messages;
import java.util.HashMap;
public final class ReduceData {
    private final HashMap<String, Integer> reduceDataList;
    public HashMap<String, Integer> getReduceDataList() {
        return reduceDataList;
    }
    public ReduceData(HashMap<String, Integer> reduceDataList) {
        this.reduceDataList = reduceDataList;
    }
}
```

Result is the message passed by the Master actor to the Aggregate actor whenever the aggregated results need to be obtained. In this case, the class has no instance variable.

Result.java

The Result class can be defined as follows:

```
package akka.first.app.mapreduce.messages;
public final class Result {
}
```

Defining actor classes

Next, we will start with the definition of the actor classes. The actors are created in the akka.first.app.mapreduce.actors package.

MapActor.java

Let's start with the MapActor class whose responsibility was to take in the English sentence as a String object, identify the words in the sentence, and not count the STOP words. Once finished, MapActor will send the mapped data list to the Master actor, who will send it to Reduce actor:

```
package akka.first.app.mapreduce.actors;
public class MapActor extends UntypedActor {
    @Override
    public void onReceive(Object message) throws Exception {
        if (message instanceof String) {
            String work = (String) message;
            // map the words in the sentence and send the result
            to MasterActor
            getSender().tell(evaluateExpression(work));
        } else
            unhandled(message);
    }
    private MapData evaluateExpression(String line) {
        //logic to map the words in the sentences
    }
}
```

We create the MapActor class, which extends UntypedActor. The UntypedActor class requires you to implement the onReceive() method call, where the messages passed on to the actor are received. The onReceive() method is the message handler for the actor:

- In the onReceive() method call, messages are received as Java objects.

- For MapActor , we are interested in the String messages. We check for the String messages, and if found we cast the object to the string and pass the message to another private method — evaluateExpression(). If another message type is passed, we invoke the unhandled() method. The unhandled() method is provided by the UntypedActor class.

- evaluateExpression() takes in the string and performs the logic for the string being mapped. The data is enclosed in the MapData object and passed back.

- Once the sentence has been mapped into the MapData object, we need to pass MapData as a message to the Master actor.

Next, to evaluate the sentence and not count the STOP words, we will need the list of STOP words. So we will define the STOP words' list, as something like the following code snippet:

```
String[] STOP_WORDS = { "a", "am", "an", "and", "are", "as", "at",
"be","do", "go", "if", "in", "is", "it", "of", "on", "the", "to" };
List<String> STOP_WORDS_LIST = Arrays.asList(STOP_WORDS);
```

Further, in order to pass the message to the Master actor, we will need reference to the `MasterActor` object. In this case, we get the reference for the Master actor via the `getSender()` construct.

Next, we will define the logic in the `evaluateExpression()` method to complete the logic as follows:

```
private MapData evaluateExpression(String line) {
    List<WordCount> dataList = new ArrayList<WordCount>();
    StringTokenizer parser = new StringTokenizer(line);
    while (parser.hasMoreTokens()) {
        String word = parser.nextToken().toLowerCase();
        if (!STOP_WORDS_LIST.contains(word)) {
            dataList.add(new WordCount(word,Integer.valueOf(1)));
        }
    }
    return new MapData(dataList);
}
```

In `evaluateExpression ()`, we use `StringTokenizer` to break down the string into individual words. Subsequently, we loop through the list and cross-check whether the word is a STOP word or not. If not a STOP word, we add the word along with the default instance count − 1 into a map, which is added to the `MapData` message and returned back.

The complete source code for Map actor looks like the following code snippet:

```
package akka.first.app.mapreduce.actors;
import java.util.*;
import java.util.StringTokenizer;
import akka.actor.UntypedActor;
import akka.first.app.mapreduce.messages.MapData;
import akka.first.app.mapreduce.messages.WordCount;

public class MapActor extends UntypedActor {
    String[] STOP_WORDS = { "a", "am", "an", "and", "are", "as", "at",
    "be",
            "do", "go", "if", "in", "is", "it", "of", "on", "the",
            "to" };
```

```
        private List<String> STOP_WORDS_LIST =
        Arrays.asList(STOP_WORDS);
        @Override
        public void onReceive(Object message) throws Exception {
            if (message instanceof String) {
                String work = (String) message;
                // map the words in the sentence and send the result
                to MasterActor
                getSender().tell(evaluateExpression(work));
            } else
                unhandled(message);
        }
        private MapData evaluateExpression(String line) {
            List<WordCount> dataList = new ArrayList<WordCount>();
            StringTokenizer parser = new StringTokenizer(line);
            while (parser.hasMoreTokens()) {
                String word = parser.nextToken().toLowerCase();
                if (!STOP_WORDS_LIST.contains(word)) {
                    dataList.add
                    (newWordCount(word,Integer.valueOf(1)));
                }
            }
            return new MapData(dataList);
        }
    }
```

ReduceActor.java

Map actor will send the `MapData` message to the Master actor, who passes it to the Reduce actor. The Reduce actor will go through the list of words and reduce for duplicate words, and accordingly increase the number of instances counted for such words. The reduced list is then sent back to the Master actor:

```
package akka.first.app.mapreduce.actors;
import java.util.*;
import akka.actor.UntypedActor;
import akka.first.app.mapreduce.messages.MapData;
import akka.first.app.mapreduce.messages.ReduceData;
import akka.first.app.mapreduce.messages.WordCount;

public class ReduceActor extends UntypedActor {
    @Override
    public void onReceive(Object message) throws Exception {
        if (message instanceof MapData) {
            MapData mapData = (MapData) message;
            // reduce the incoming data and forward the result to
            Master actor
```

```
            getSender().tell(reduce(mapData.getDataList()));
        } else
            unhandled(message);
    }
    private ReduceData reduce(List<WordCount> dataList) {
HashMap<String, Integer> reducedMap = new HashMap<String,
Integer>();
        for (WordCount wordCount : dataList) {
            if (reducedMap.containsKey(wordCount.getWord())) {
                Integer value = (Integer)
                reducedMap.get(wordCount.getWord());
                value++;
                reducedMap.put(wordCount.getWord(), value);
            } else {
                reducedMap.put(wordCount.getWord(),
                Integer.valueOf(1));
            }
        }
        return new ReduceData(reducedMap);
    }
}
```

The ReduceActor class is very similar to MapActor. We extend the ReduceActor class with UntypedActor and implement the onReceive() method. We capture the messages that belong to the MapData type and ignore the rest. When the MapData message is received, we extract the data list from the message and pass the same to the reduce() method, which reduces this list and returns back the ReduceData message, which is then passed on to the Master actor.

AggregateActor.java

Aggregate actor receives the reduced data list from the Master actor and aggregates it into one big list. Aggregate actor will maintain a state variable that will hold the list of words and get updated on receipt of the reduced data list message:

```
package akka.first.app.mapreduce.actors;
import java.util.*;
import akka.actor.UntypedActor;
import akka.first.app.mapreduce.messages.*;

public class AggregateActor extends UntypedActor {
    private Map<String, Integer> finalReducedMap =
    new HashMap<String, Integer>();
    @Override
    public void onReceive(Object message) throws Exception {
        if (message instanceof ReduceData) {
            ReduceData reduceData = (ReduceData) message;
```

```
                    aggregateInMemoryReduce(reduceData.
                    getReduceDataList());
            } else if (message instanceof Result) {
                getSender().tell(finalReducedMap.toString());
            } else
                unhandled(message);
    }
    private void aggregateInMemoryReduce(Map<String,
    Integer> reducedList) {
        Integer count = null;
        for (String key : reducedList.keySet()) {
            if (finalReducedMap.containsKey(key)) {
                count = reducedList.get(key) +
                finalReducedMap.get(key);
                finalReducedMap.put(key, count);
            } else {
                finalReducedMap.put(key, reducedList.get(key));
            }
        }
    }
}
```

We define the `AggregateActor` class and extend `UntypedActor`. In this actor, we also define a state variable that holds the final reduced map across multiple sentences, as follows:

```
private Map<String, Integer> finalReducedMap = new
HashMap<String, Integer>();
```

In the `onReceive()` method, we intercept two kinds of messages as follows:

- `ReduceData` messages are received from the Master actor. These messages are then sent to the private method — `aggregateInMemoryReduce()`, where we add the data to the existing data set stored in the `finalReducedMap` variable.

- A `Result` message is sent from the Master actor, and as a response to this message, we send back the results of the `finalReducedMap` variable.

MasterActor.java

Master actor is a Supervisor actor and responsible for the instantiation of the child actors. Master actor is the gateway for all messages that are passed on to the other actors, namely the Map actor and Aggregate actor.

Let's go ahead and create the `MasterActor` class as follows:

```
package akka.first.app.mapreduce.actors;
import akka.actor.ActorRef;
import akka.actor.UntypedActor;
import akka.first.app.mapreduce.messages.Result;

public class MasterActor extends UntypedActor {
    ActorRef mapActor;
    ActorRef reduceActor;
    ActorRef aggregateActor;
    @Override
    public void onReceive(Object message) throws Exception {


    }
}
```

The `MasterActor` class extends `UntypedActor` and implements the `onReceive()` message handler method for the Master actor. The `onReceive()` method listens to the following kinds of messages:

- `String` messages that need to be passed to the Map actor
- `MapData` objects received from the Map actor that are passed to the Reduce actor
- `ReduceData` objects received from the Reduce actor that are passed to the Aggregate actor
- `Result` messages that need to be forwarded to the Aggregate actor for getting the result

The key here is the creation of the child actors—Map actor, Reduce actor, and Aggregate actor. We have defined state variables for the Master actor and the next step will be instantiating these actors as follows:

```
ActorRef mapActor = getContext().actorOf(
    new Props(MapActor.class).withRouter(new
    RoundRobinRouter(5)), "map");
```

Here we instantiate the Map actor, using the `getContext().actorOf()` method. The method takes in `Props` with the class name of the actor that needs to be created. In this case, we want to create the Map actor as a router actor. So, on the `Prop` we invoke the `withRouter()` method passing the `RoundRobinRouter` type and number of instances. The router allows us to create a pool of similar actors (called **routes**), enabling us to spread the load across multiple actors.

Next, we will create the Reduce actor as follows:

```
ActorRef reduceActor = getContext().actorOf(
    new Props(ReduceActor.class).withRouter(new
RoundRobinRouter(5)),"reduce");
```

We use the same method for creating the Aggregate actor, but without the router. We skip the router, because the Aggregate actor has states, and having multiple instances of the same actor defeats the purpose:

```
ActorRef aggregateActor = getContext().actorOf(
    new Props(AggregateActor.class), "aggregate");
```

The complete code for the Master actor is as follows:

```
package akka.first.app.mapreduce.actors;
import akka.actor.ActorRef;
import akka.actor.Props;
import akka.actor.UntypedActor;
import akka.first.app.mapreduce.messages.*;
import akka.routing.RoundRobinRouter;

public class MasterActor extends UntypedActor {
    ActorRef mapActor = getContext().actorOf(
        new Props(MapActor.class).withRouter(new
        RoundRobinRouter(5),     "map");
    ActorRef reduceActor = getContext().actorOf(
        new Props(ReduceActor.class).withRouter(new
        RoundRobinRouter(5)),"reduce");
    ActorRef aggregateActor = getContext().actorOf(
            new Props(AggregateActor.class), "aggregate");
    @Override
    public void onReceive(Object message) throws Exception {
        if (message instanceof String) {
            mapActor.tell(message,getSelf());
        } else if (message instanceof MapData) {
            reduceActor.tell(message,getSelf());
        } else if (message instanceof ReduceData) {
            aggregateActor.tell(message);
        } else if (message instanceof Result) {
            aggregateActor.forward(message, getContext());
        } else
            unhandled(message);
    }
}
```

This completes the definition of the actors. Next, we create the runtime class that will instantiate and invoke these actors.

Defining the execution class

This class will bring together all the pieces and provide us the executable to run and test our program. We create the Java class—MapReduceApplication.java in the akka.first.app.mapreduce package.

MapReduceApplication.java

The MapReduceApplication.java class can be defined as follows:

```
package akka.first.app.mapreduce;
import akka.actor.ActorRef;
import akka.actor.ActorSystem;
import akka.actor.Props;
import akka.dispatch.Await;
import akka.dispatch.Future;
import akka.first.app.mapreduce.actors.MasterActor;
import akka.first.app.mapreduce.messages.Result;
import akka.pattern.Patterns;
import akka.util.Duration;
import akka.util.Timeout;

public class MapReduceApplication {
    public static void main(String[] args) throws Exception {
        Timeout timeout = new Timeout(Duration.parse("5 seconds"));
        ActorSystem _system = ActorSystem.create("MapReduceApp");
        ActorRef master = _system.actorOf(new
        Props(MasterActor.class),
                "master");
        master.tell("The quick brown fox tried to jump over the
        lazy dog and fell on the dog");
        master.tell("Dog is man's best friend");
        master.tell("Dog and Fox belong to the same family");
        Thread.sleep(5000);
        Future<Object> future = Patterns.ask(master, new
        Result(), timeout);
        String result = (String) Await.result(future,
        timeout.duration());
        System.out.println(result);
        _system.shutdown();
    }
}
```

`MapReduceApplication` can be seen as a series of steps, as follows:

1. First we go ahead and create `ActorSystem`—a container in which the actors are instantiated. Using `ActorSystem`, we create the Master actor as follows:

    ```
    ActorSystem _system = ActorSystem.create("MapReduceApp");
    ActorRef master = _system.actorOf(new
    Props(MasterActor.class),"master");
    ```

2. Using the `MasterActor` reference, we pass sentence string messages to the actor as follows:

    ```
    master.tell("The quick brown fox tried to jump over the lazy dog
    and fell on the dog");
    master.tell("Dog is man's best friend");
    master.tell("Dog and Fox belong to the same family");
    ```

3. Next, we send the `Result` message to the Master actor to see the results as follows:

    ```
    Future<Object> future = Patterns.ask(master, new Result(),
    timeout);
    String result = (String) Await.result(future,
    timeout.duration());
    System.out.println(result);
    ```

4. Lastly, we shut down the actor system as follows:

    ```
    _system.shutdown();
    ```

We have `Thread.sleep()` because there is no guarantee in which order the messages are processed. The first `Thread.sleep()` method ensures that all the string sentence messages are processed completely before we send the `Result` message.

With this, we completed the application part. Let's compile and execute the application to see the results. From within the Eclipse you can use the `Run` command to run `MapReduceApplication`. When you run the application, you should see the following in the console window:

```
{fell=1, fox=2, belong=1, quick=1, tried=1, man's=1, same=1, jump=1,
over=1, family=1, best=1, brown=1, lazy=1, dog=4, friend=1}
```

Congratulations, you just wrote your first Word Count Map Reduce program for Java using the Akka Actor Model.

Scala application

For the Scala developers, we will use SBT to create and build the Scala project. Once you have followed the instructions to install the SBT, we will go ahead to create our first Akka application. Perform the following steps to do so:

1. We will create the `firstAkkaApplication` project directory in a working folder. In this case we are using the folder – `/home/ubuntu` to create the `firstAkkaApplication` folder.

2. Once the project folder is created, create a `build.sbt` file and add the contents to it, as shown in the following screenshot:

```
build.sbt
 1   name := "firstAkkaApplication"
 2
 3   version := "1.0"
 4
 5   scalaVersion := "2.9.1"
 6
 7   resolvers += "Typesafe Repository" at "http://repo.typesafe.com/typesafe/releases/"
 8
 9   libraryDependencies += "com.typesafe.akka" % "akka-actor" % "2.0.3"
10
```

Key parameter values are the name of the project, version of the project, Scala version being used, URL for Typesafe repository, and library dependencies for Akka. In this case we are only using the `akka-actor` library.

3. Next, we create the folder – `src/main/scala` in the `firstAkkaApplication` project and within the same, we will create our package structure – `akka.first.app.mapreduce`:

```
firstAkkaApplication
    + src
       + main
          + scala
              + akka                          package structure
                 + first
                    + app
                       + mapreduce
    build.sbt
```

4. Once we have finished this, we can go ahead and write our Scala code in the defined package structure.

In case you are not using the SBT, you can also create a simple Scala project in Eclipse and add the following JAR dependencies:

Dependent JARs	Location
`scala-library.jar`	`<akka unzip path>akka-2.0.3\lib\`
`akka-actor-2.0.3.jar`	`<akka unzip path>akka-2.0.3\lib\akka`

Defining message classes

Once the bare project skeleton is set up, we will start with writing message classes. We will define the classes in `MapReduceApplication.scala`, which is created in the `akka.first.app.mapreduce` package as follows:

```
sealed trait MapReduceMessage
case class WordCount(word: String, count: Int) extends
MapReduceMessage
case class MapData(dataList: ArrayBuffer[WordCount]) extends
MapReduceMessage
case class ReduceData(reduceDataMap: Map[String, Int]) extends
MapReduceMessage
case class Result extends MapReduceMessage
```

A `WordCount` object holds the word along with the associated number of instances occurring within the sentence. `MapData` is the message that is passed from the Map actor to the Reduce actor. The message consists of a list of `WordCount` objects.

`ReduceData` is the message passed between the Reduce actor and the Aggregate actor. The Reduce actor will reduce the message passed in `MapData` and pass the results as `ReduceData` to the Aggregate actor.

`Result` is the message passed by the Master actor to the Aggregate actor whenever the aggregated results need to be obtained. In this case, the class has no instance variable.

We have also defined a sealed marker trait—`MapReduceMessage`, which is extended by all the case classes.

Defining actor classes

Next, we will start with the definition of the actor classes. The actors are created in the `akka.first.app.mapreduce.actors` package.

MapActor.scala

Let's start with the MapActor class, whose responsibility is to take in the English sentence as a String object, identify the words in the sentence, and not count the STOP words. Once finished, the Map actor will return the mapped data list back to the Master actor:

```scala
class MapActor extends Actor {
    def receive: Receive = {
        case message: String =>
            reduceActor ! evaluateExpression(message)
    }
    def evaluateExpression(line: String): MapData = MapData {
            //logic to map the words in the sentences
        }
}
```

We create the MapActor class, which extends Actor. Actor, requiring you to implement the receive() method call, where the messages passed on to the actor are received. The receive() method is the message handler for the actor. The following steps are needed to be performed:

1. We implement the receive() method calls, which intercepts and filters the incoming messages based on the instance type.

2. For the MapActor class, we are interested in the String messages. We check for the String messages, and if found we cast the object to the string and pass the message to another private method—evaluateExpression().

3. evaluateExpression() takes in the string and performs the logic for the string being mapped. The data is enclosed in the MapData object and is passed back.

4. Once the sentence has been mapped into the MapData object, we need to pass the MapData as a message to the Master actor. We use the implicit sender actor to pass the result back.

Next, to evaluate the sentence and not count the STOP words, we will need the list of STOP words. So we will define the STOP words' list, as something like the following line of code:

```scala
val STOP_WORDS_LIST = List("a", "am", "an", "and", "are", "as", "at",
"be","do", "go", "if", "in", "is", "it", "of", "on", "the", "to")
```

Next, we will define the logic in the `evaluateExpression()` method to complete the logic as follows:

```
def evaluateExpression(line: String): MapData = MapData {
  line.split("""\s+""").foldLeft(ArrayBuffer.empty[WordCount]) {
    (index, word) =>
      if (!STOP_WORDS_LIST.contains(word.toLowerCase))
        index += WordCount(word.toLowerCase, 1)
      else
        index
  }
}
```

In the `evaluateExpression()` method, we use the `split()` method to break down the string into individual words and return the same result as `Array[String]`. On the array, we invoke the `foldLeft()` method with an empty map as the return type. `foldLeft()` applies a binary operator to a start value and all elements of the array, going left to right. Subsequently, we loop through the list and cross-check whether the word is a STOP word or not. If not a STOP word, we add the word along with the default instance count — 1 into a map, which is added to the `MapData` message and returned back.

The complete source code for the `MapActor` class looks like the following code snippet:

```
package akka.first.app.mapreduce.actors

import akka.actor.Actor
import akka.actor.ActorRef
import akka.first.app.mapreduce.MapData
import akka.first.app.mapreduce.WordCount
import scala.collection.mutable.ArrayBuffer

class MapActor extends Actor {
  val STOP_WORDS_LIST = List("a", "am", "an", "and", "are", "as",
    "at", "be", "do", "go", "if", "in", "is", "it", "of", "on", "the",
    "to")
  val defaultCount: Int = 1
  def receive: Receive = {
    case message: String =>
      sender ! evaluateExpression(message)
  }
  def evaluateExpression(line: String): MapData = MapData {
    line.split("""\s+""").foldLeft(ArrayBuffer.empty[WordCount]) {
      (index, word) =>
```

```
          if(!STOP_WORDS_LIST.contains(word.toLowerCase))
            index += WordCount(word.toLowerCase, 1)
        else
          index
   }
  }
}
```

ReduceActor.scala

Master actor will send the `MapData` message to the Reduce actor. The Reduce actor will go through the list of words and reduce it by looking for duplicate words, and accordingly, increase the count for the number of instances of such words. The reduced list is then sent to the Aggregate actor:

```
class ReduceActor extends Actor {

  def receive: Receive = {
    case MapData(dataList) =>
      sender ! reduce(dataList)
  }
def reduce(words: IndexedSeq[WordCount]): ReduceData = ReduceData {
      //Reduces the list for duplicate words in
      the mapped data list
    }
}
```

The `ReduceActor` class is very similar to the `MapActor` class. We extend the `ReduceActor` class with `Actor` and implement the `receive()` message handler method as follows:

```
def receive: Receive = {
  case MapData(dataList) =>
    sender ! reduce(dataList)
}
```

We filter the messages that belong to the `MapData` type and ignore the rest. When the `MapData` message is received, we extract the data list from the message and pass the same to the `reduce()` method. The `reduce()` method reduces this list and returns back the `MasterData` message, which is then passed on to the Aggregate actor.

The complete code for the `ReduceActor` class looks like the following code snippet:

```scala
package akka.first.app.mapreduce.actors
import scala.collection.immutable.Map

import akka.actor.Actor
import akka.first.app.mapreduce.MapData
import akka.first.app.mapreduce.ReduceData
import akka.first.app.mapreduce.WordCount

class ReduceActor extends Actor {
  def receive: Receive = {
    case MapData(dataList) =>
      sender ! reduce(dataList)
  }
  def reduce(words: IndexedSeq[WordCount]): ReduceData = ReduceData {
    words.foldLeft(Map.empty[String, Int]) {  (index, words) =>
      if (index contains words.word)
        index + (words.word -> (index.get(words.word).get + 1))
      else
        index + (words.word -> 1)
    }
  }
}
```

AggregateActor.scala

Aggregate actor receives the reduced data list from the Master actor and aggregates it into one big list. The Aggregate actor will maintain a state variable that will hold the list of words and get updated on the receipt of the reduced data list message. In addition, the Aggregate actor will also receive the `Result` message and reply with the result of the state variable as a response to the message:

```scala
class AggregateActor extends Actor {
  val finalReducedMap = new HashMap[String, Int]
  def receive: Receive = {
    case ReduceData(reduceDataMap) =>
      aggregateInMemoryReduce(reduceDataMap)
    case Result =>
      sender ! finalReducedMap.toString()
  }
  def aggregateInMemoryReduce(reducedList: Map[String, Int]):
  Unit = {
    //add the received Map to the state variable finalReduceMap
  }
}
```

We define the `AggregateActor` class and extend `Actor`. In this `Actor`, we also define a state variable that holds the final reduced map across multiple sentences:

```
val finalReducedMap = new HashMap[String, Int]
```

In the `receive()` method, we intercept two kinds of messages as follows:

- `ReduceData` messages are received from the Master actor. These messages are then sent to the private method—`aggregateInMemoryReduce()`, where we add the data to the existing data set stored in the `finalReducedMap` variable.

- A `Result` message is sent from the Master actor, and as a response to this message, we return the results of the `finalReducedMap` variable as string.

The complete code for the `AggregateActor` class looks like the following code snippet:

```
package akka.first.app.mapreduce.actors

import scala.collection.immutable.Map
import scala.collection.mutable.HashMap

import akka.actor.Actor
import akka.first.app.mapreduce.ReduceData
import akka.first.app.mapreduce.Result

class AggregateActor extends Actor {
  val finalReducedMap = new HashMap[String, Int]
  def receive: Receive = {
    case ReduceData(reduceDataMap) =>
      aggregateInMemoryReduce(reduceDataMap)
    case Result =>
      sender ! finalReducedMap.toString()
  }
  def aggregateInMemoryReduce(reducedList: Map[String, Int]): Unit = {
    for ((key,value) <- reducedList) {
      if (finalReducedMap contains key)
        finalReducedMap(key) = (value + finalReducedMap.get(key).get)
      else
        finalReducedMap += (key -> value)
    }
  }
}
```

MasterActor.scala

Master actor is a Supervisor actor and responsible for the instantiation of the child actors. Master actor is the gateway for all messages that are passed on to the other actors, namely the Map actor and Aggregate actor.

Let's go ahead and create the `MasterActor` class as follows:

```
class MasterActor extends Actor {

    val mapActor
    val reduceActor
    val aggregateActor

    def receive: Receive = {
        case line: String =>  mapActor ! line
            case mapData: MapData =>  reduceActor ! mapData
            case reduceData: ReduceData =>
            aggregateActor ! reduceData
            case Result =>  aggregateActor forward Result
    }
}
```

The `MasterActor` class extends `Actor` and implements the `receive()` message handler for the Master actor. The `receive()` method listens to the following kinds of messages:

- `String` messages that need to be passed to the Map actor
- `MapData` objects received from the Map actor that are passed to the Reduce actor
- `ReduceData` objects received from the Reduce actor that are passed to the Aggregate actor
- `Result` messages that need to be forwarded to the Aggregate actor for getting the result

The key here is the creation of the child actors — Map actor, Reduce actor, and Aggregate actor, as follows:

```
    val mapActor
    val reduceActor
    val aggregateActor
```

We have defined state variables for the Master actor and the next step will be instantiating these actors as follows:

```
val mapActor = context.actorOf(Props[MapActor].withRouter(
    RoundRobinRouter(nrOfInstances = 5)), name = "map")
```

Here we instantiate the Map actor, using the `context.actorOf()` method. This method takes in `Props` with the class name of the actor that needs to be created. In this case, we want to create the Map actor as a router actor. So, on the `Prop` we invoke the `withRouter()` method, passing the `RoundRobinRouter` type and number of instances. The router allows us to create a pool of similar actors (called routes), enabling us to spread the load across multiple actors.

Next, we will create the Reduce actor as follows:

```
val reduceActor:ActorRef = context.actorOf(Props(new ReduceActor
(aggregateActor)),name="reduce")
```

We use the same method for creating the Aggregate actor, but without a router. We skip the router because the Aggregate actor has state, and having multiple instances of the same actor defeats the purpose:

```
val aggregateActor = context.actorOf(Props[AggregateActor],
name = "aggregate")
```

The complete code for the `MasterActor` class looks like the following code snippet:

```
package akka.first.app.mapreduce.actors

import akka.actor.Actor
import akka.actor.ActorRef
import akka.actor.Props
import akka.first.app.mapreduce._
import akka.routing.RoundRobinRouter

class MasterActor extends Actor {
  val mapActor = context.actorOf(Props[MapActor].withRouter(
    RoundRobinRouter(nrOfInstances = 5)), name = "map")
  val reduceActor = context.actorOf(Props[ReduceActor].withRouter(
    RoundRobinRouter(nrOfInstances = 5)), name = "reduce")
  val aggregateActor = context.actorOf(Props[AggregateActor],
  name = "aggregate")

  def receive: Receive = {
    case line: String =>
      mapActor ! line
    case mapData: MapData =>
      reduceActor ! mapData
    case reduceData: ReduceData =>
      aggregateActor ! reduceData
    case Result =>
      aggregateActor forward Result
  }
}
```

This completes the definition of the actors. Next we create the runtime class that will instantiate and invoke these actors.

Defining the execution class

This class will bring together all the pieces and provide us the executable to run and test our program. We create the Scala class—MapReduceApplication.scala in the akka.first.app.mapreduce package.

MapReduceApplication.scala

The MapReduceApplication.scala class can be defined as follows:

```scala
package akka.first.app.mapreduce

import scala.collection.immutable.Map
import scala.collection.mutable.ArrayBuffer

import akka.actor.actorRef2Scala
import akka.actor.ActorSystem
import akka.actor.Props
import akka.dispatch.Await
import akka.first.app.mapreduce.actors.MasterActor
import akka.util.duration.intToDurationInt
import akka.util.Timeout

sealed trait MapReduceMessage
case class WordCount(word: String, count: Int) extends
MapReduceMessage
case class MapData(dataList: ArrayBuffer[WordCount]) extends
MapReduceMessage
case class ReduceData(reduceDataMap: Map[String, Int]) extends
MapReduceMessage
case class Result extends MapReduceMessage

object MapReduceApplication extends App {
  val _system = ActorSystem("MapReduceApp")
  val master = _system.actorOf(Props[MasterActor], name = "master")
  implicit val timeout = Timeout(5 seconds)

  master ! "The quick brown fox tried to jump over the lazy dog and
fell on the dog"
  master ! "Dog is man's best friend"
  master ! "Dog and Fox belong to the same family"
```

```
Thread.sleep(500)

val future = (master ? Result).mapTo[String]
val result = Await.result(future, timeout.duration)
println(result)
_system.shutdown
}
```

MapReduceApplication can be seen as a series of steps, as follows:

1. First we go ahead and create ActorSystem—a container in which the actors are instantiated. Using ActorSystem, we create the Master actor as follows:

   ```
   val _system = ActorSystem("MapReduceApp")
   val master = _system.actorOf(Props[MasterActor],
   name = "master")
   ```

2. Using the MasterActor reference, we pass sentence string messages to the actor:

   ```
   master ! "The quick brown fox tried to jump over the lazy dog
   and fell on the dog"
   master ! "Dog is man's best friend"
   master ! "Dog and Fox belong to the same family"
   ```

3. Next, we send the Result message to the Master actor to see the results as follows:

   ```
   val future = (master ? new Result).mapTo[String]
   val result = Await.result(future, timeout.duration)
   println(result)
   ```

4. Lastly, we shut down the actor system as follows:

   ```
   _system.shutdown
   ```

We have Thread.sleep() because there is no guarantee in which order the messages are processed. The first Thread.sleep() method ensures that all the string sentence messages are processed completely before we send the Result message. The second Thread.sleep() method ensures that the shutdown message is not processed before the Result message.

With this, we have completed the application part. Let's compile and execute the application to see the results.

For compiling the application, we go to the command prompt in the project folder and run the sbt command. Once we get the sbt prompt, we can type the compile command. Once the Scala application compiles, we can call the run command to run MapReduceApplication.scala as a Scala application, as shown in the following screenshot:

```
ubuntu@domU-12-31-39-0A-29-6A:~/firstAkkaApplication$ sbt
Starting sbt: invoke with -help for other options
[info] Set current project to FirstAkkaApplication (in build file:/home/ubuntu/firstAkkaApplication/)
> compile
[info] Updating {file:/home/ubuntu/firstAkkaApplication/}default-495dde...
[info] Resolving org.scala-lang#scala-library;2.9.1 ...
[info] Resolving com.typesafe.akka#akka-actor;2.0.3 ...
[info] Resolving com.typesafe#config;0.3.1 ...
[info] Done updating.
[info] Compiling 5 Scala sources to /home/ubuntu/firstAkkaApplication/target/scala-2.9.1/classes...
[warn] there were 1 deprecation warnings; re-run with -deprecation for details
[warn] one warning found
[success] Total time: 37 s, completed Sep 20, 2012 11:49:06 AM
> run
[info] Running akka.first.app.mapreduce.MapReduceApplication
Map(best -> 1, brown -> 1, jump -> 1, fell -> 1, fox -> 2, belong -> 1, over -> 1, quick -> 1, family -> 1, dog
 -> 4, man's -> 1, same -> 1, lazy -> 1, tried -> 1, friend -> 1)
[success] Total time: 4 s, completed Sep 20, 2012 11:49:14 AM
>
```

When we run the application, we will see the following in the console window:

```
Map(best -> 1, brown -> 1, jump -> 1, fell -> 1, fox -> 2, belong -> 1,
over -> 1, quick -> 1, family -> 1, dog -> 4, man's -> 1, same -> 1, lazy
-> 1, tried -> 1, friend -> 1)
```

Congratulations, you just wrote your first Word Count Map Reduce program for Scala using the Akka Actor Model. You can enhance this program to read large text files and pump in the data, and see how the application performs and scales up.

Summary

In this chapter, we saw and learned the following:

- How to set up the development environment for Java/Scala
- How to write and create actors—state and behavior
- How to pass the messages across actors
- How to create and execute `ActorSystem` and run the actors within `ActorSystem`
- How to model and create a Word Count Map Reduce application using the Akka actors

This provided a summary of the Actor Model and some of the runtime constructs. In the coming chapter, we will discuss actors further, and see the features and functionality provided by them.

3

Actors

In this chapter, we will see more on the actors. We will cover the following:

- How to create actors
- How to send/receive messages
- How to reply to messages
- How to forward messages
- How to stop actors

This will provide an understanding of the core building blocks. Actors provide the higher level of abstraction that allows us to build highly scalable and concurrent applications. Actors are the entities that define the Actor Model.

Downloading the example code

You can download the example code files for all Packt books you have purchased from your account at http://www.PacktPub.com. If you purchased this book elsewhere, you can visit http://www.PacktPub.com/support and register to have the files e-mailed directly to you.

Actors

Actors are the constructs that provide the basis for the Akka application. Actors provide the abstraction for transparent distribution and the basis for a truly scalable and fault-tolerant application. Actors provide the following:

- Simple and high-level abstracted toolkit for concurrency and parallelism
- Asynchronous, non-blocking, event-driven programming model (using messages)
- Lightweight event-driven processes

Actors are objects that encapsulate state and behavior. An actor can change another actor's state only by sending it a message. From the Actor Model perspective, the actors are the computational units that react to the messages sent to them, and can reply or send messages to other actors. Actors communicate with other actors using the address of the target actor's mailbox. Communication between actors is completely asynchronous and non-blocking; actors only react to the messages being sent to them.

An actor's lifecycle has multiple stages. When the actor is created, it moves into the start stage where it picks up the messages from its mailbox and starts processing them. The messages are processed one at a time in the order they are received. When the actor gets a signal to shut down, it stops processing the messages and terminates itself.

An actor's lifecycle broadly consists of three phases as follows:

- Actor is initialized and started
- Actor receives and processes messages by executing a specific behavior
- Actor stops itself when it receives a termination message

Additionally, an Akka actor has additional, optional hooks that can be used to manage the state where it experiences a lifecycle change. The additional hooks are as follows:

- `preStart()` and `postStop()` can be implemented to initialize/clean any resources used by the actor to process the messages
- `preRestart()` and `postRestart()` allow the actor to manage the state in case an exception has been raised and Supervisor actor restarts the actor

Next, we will cover how to create actors, how they handle messages, and how to stop actors. So, we will cover the three important phases of an actor's lifecycle, as shown in the following diagram:

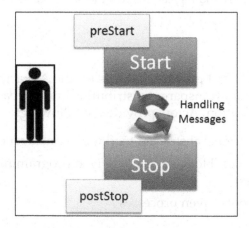

Defining an actor

To define an actor, the class needs to extend the actor and implement the required abstract method for handling messages.

Java:

```
public class MyActor extends UntypedActor {
  public void onReceive(Object message) throws Exception {
  }
}
```

Scala:

```
class MyActor extends Actor {
  def receive = {
  }
}
```

An `Actor` class can also have non-default constructors. So any data that needs to be passed at the time of the object creation can be passed to the `Actor` object. In Scala, the `receive` block is actually a partial function, which allows the usage of pattern matching syntax.

Creating actors

Once an actor is defined, the `Actor` instance needs to be created and started. All actors are created in the context of an actor system or another actor. As part of the actor creation itself, the actor gets started. Before it starts accepting and processing messages, the actor can implement a method called `preStart`, which can handle any initialization required by the actor:

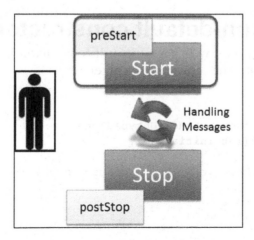

To create an actor, Akka provides a construct called `Props`. `Props` is a configuration class, which takes in the actor along with the various configurations that need to be applied to it.

Actor with default constructor

Let's first take an example of creating an `Actor` object having a default constructor.

Java:

```
ActorSystem _system = ActorSystem.create("MyActorSystem");
ActorRef myActor = _system.actorOf(new Props(MyActor.class),
"myActor");
```

Scala:

```
val system = ActorSystem("MyActorSystem")
val myActor = system.actorOf(Props[MyActor], name = "myActor")
```

To create an Actor, we created the `ActorSystem` class and invoked the `actorOf()` method on the same. The `actorOf()` method accepted two arguments—first was the `Props` object and second was the actor's name passed as a `String` object. The `Props` object accepted the `Actor` class object, which needed to instantiated and started. The actor is started after the object has been instantiated. In the preceding example, we have created an actor using a default constructor.

The instantiated actor is held using `ActorRef`. `ActorRef` provides an immutable and serial able handle to the underlying actor. In essence, `ActorRef` encapsulates the actor and only supports the passing of messages to the actor. Each actor can access internally its local instance reference through the `self` field. The `ActorRef` classes can be shared among other actors by passing them as messages.

Actor with non-default constructor

Next, we will create an actor with a non-default constructor. Let's say we have an actor class that looks like the code snippets given next.

Java:

```
public class MyActor extends UntypedActor {
  public MyActor(int initialise){
  }
  public void onReceive(Object message) throws Exception {
  }
}
```

Scala:

```scala
class MyActor(initialise:Int) extends Actor {
  def receive = {
  }
}
```

Now, to create an actor with the non-default constructor, the syntax is given next.

Java:

```java
ActorSystem _system = ActorSystem.create("MyActorSystem");
ActorRef myActor = _system.actorOf(
new Props(new UntypedActorFactory() {
  public UntypedActor create() {
    return new MyActor(10);
  }
}),
"myActor");
```

Scala:

```scala
val system = ActorSystem("MyActorSystem")
val myActor = system.actorOf(Props(new MyActor(10)), name = "myActor")
```

In case of Java, we used the `UntypedActorFactory` function to create an instance of the actor with the non-default constructor and pass it on to the `Props` object.

In case of Scala, we created `new MyActor(10)` using the Scala call-by-name block. The call-by-name block passes a code within the block to the callee. Each time the callee accesses the parameter, the code block is executed and the value is calculated.

In all of the preceding cases, we created the actor as a top-level `Actor` object managed directly by `ActorSystem`.

Creating an actor within an actor hierarchy

Now, Akka follows the premise of an actor hierarchy where we have specialized actors that are adept in handling or performing an activity, and, we have Supervisor actors that coordinate and manage the lifecycle of the specialized actors. We will cover Supervisor actors in more detail in *Chapter 6, Supervision and Monitoring*. In case we want to create actors that are part of the actor hierarchy, then we use the following syntax to create actors.

Java:

```
public class SupervisorActor extends UntypedActor {
   ActorRef myWorkerActor = getContext().actorOf(new
Props(MyWorkerActor.class), "myWorkerActor");
}
```

Scala:

```
class SupervisorActor extends Actor {
val myWorkerActor = context.actorOf(Props[MyWorkerActor],
"myWorkerActor")
}
```

In this case, within the Actor object, we created the child using the parent context.

As part of starting the actor, the preStart() method is invoked before the actor can start processing the messages. Any initializations required for functioning of the actor can be handled here. For example, if the actor needs to get data from a database, then the connection object can be initialized and opened here.

Java:

```
@Override
public void preStart() {
 //Initialise the resources to be used by actor e.g. db
 //connection opening
 }
```

Scala:

```
override def preStart() = {
//Initialise the resources to be used by actor e.g. db
//connection opening
}
```

Messaging model

The basic premise of an Actor Model is communication via messages. Actor state responds or reacts based on the message that is passed on to the actor. All messages passed should be immutable. In case you pass mutable messages to the actors, the application might behave in weird ways because of the shared mutable message.

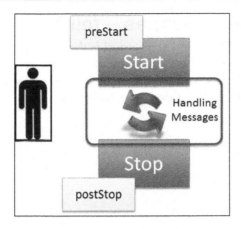

Sending messages

Once the actor reference is available, messages can be passed to an actor in two modes, as follows:

- **Fire and forget**: This is a one-way message model, where the producer of the message expects no reply from the consumer. The message is sent asynchronously and the method returns immediately. Akka actors make use of the `tell()` method to indicate the fire and forget mode of messaging.

- **Send and receive**: In this mode, the producer of the message expects a reply from the consumer and will wait for that reply. In this mode also, the message is sent asynchronously and `future` is returned, which represents a potential reply. In the case of send and receive message mode, actors use the `ask()` method for sending a message and wait on `future` for the reply.

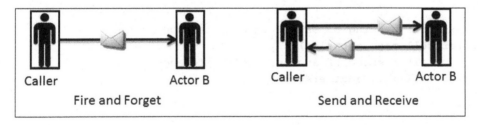

 `future` is a data structure used to retrieve the result of some concurrent operation.

Remember, in the preceding diagram the caller may or may not be an actor.

Fire and forget messages – tell()

Sending a message using the `tell()` method is the easiest way. Get hold of the actor reference and invoke the `tell()` method by passing the message object. The `tell()` method returns immediately and provides the best concurrency and scalability performance, as there is no dependency or waiting on other threads.

Java:

```
actor.tell(msg);
```

Scala:

```
actor ! msg
//or
actor.tell(msg)
//or
actor tell msg
```

In Scala, the `tell()` method can be invoked using the `!` notation.

The `tell()` method accepts two arguments. First is the message object and second is the sender actor's reference. The target actor can then use the passed-by-actor reference to reply back. By default, the caller's actor reference is passed implicitly if nothing is specified. But if the caller is not an actor or if the actor that invoked no longer exists, then the reply is sent to the dead letter actor. In Akka, `DeadLetterActorRef` is the default implementation of the dead letters' service, where all messages are rerouted whose callers are shut down or nonexistent.

You can also pass the reference of another actor who might be interested in the reply.

Java:

```
//explicit passing of sender actor reference
actor.tell(msg, getSelf());
//explicit passing of another actor reference
actor.tell(msg, anotherActorRef);
```

Scala:

```
//implicit passing of sender actor reference
actor ! msg
//explicit passing of another actor reference
actor.tell(msg, anotherActorRef)
```

Send and receive messages – ask()

The mode of sending a message and receiving a reply is a two-step process. In order to avoid blocking calls, the `future` constructs are used along with actors. The `future` construct is used to retrieve the result of a concurrent operation. The operation is invoked by the actor and the result can be accessed synchronously or asynchronously. As both actors and `future` constructs are involved in sending and receiving messages, the `ask()` method is implemented as a use pattern, where the actor along with the message and time to wait for a reply is passed. `Pattern.ask()` returns a `Future` object on which we await the results.

Java:

```java
//Key Imports
import static akka.pattern.Patterns.ask;
import static akka.pattern.Patterns.pipe;
import java.util.concurrent.TimeUnit;
import akka.dispatch.Future;
import akka.dispatch.Futures;
import akka.dispatch.Mapper;
import akka.util.Duration;
import akka.util.Timeout;


public class ProcessOrderActor extends UntypedActor {
    final Timeout t = new Timeout(Duration.create(5,
                    TimeUnit.SECONDS));
    ActorRef orderActor = getContext().actorOf(
                new Props(OrderActor.class));
    ActorRef addressActor = getContext().actorOf(
                new Props(AddressActor.class));
    ActorRef orderAggregateActor = getContext().actorOf(
                new Props(OrderAggregateActor.class));


    @Override
    public void onReceive(Object message) throws Exception {
        if (message instanceof Integer) {
            Integer userId = (Integer) message;
            final ArrayList<Future<Object>> futures =
                        new ArrayList<Future<Object>>();
            //make concurrent calls to actors
            futures.add(ask(orderActor, userId, t));
            futures.add(ask(addressActor, userId, t));

            //set the sequence in which the reply are expected
            final Future<Iterable<Object>> aggregate =
                        Futures.sequence(futures,
                        getContext().system().dispatcher());
```

```
                    //once the replies comes back, we loop through the
              // Iterable to get the replies in same order
              final Future<OrderHistory> aggResult =
                      aggregate.map(new Mapper<Iterable<Object>,
                      OrderHistory>() {
                  public OrderHistory apply(Iterable<Object> coll) {
                          final Iterator<Object> it =
                          coll.iterator();
                          final Order order = (Order) it.next();
                          final Address address = (Address)
                          it.next();
                          return new OrderHistory(order,
                          address);
                          }
                  });
              //aggregated result is piped to another actor
              pipe(aggResult).to(orderAggregateActor);
          }
      }
  }
```

Scala:

```
import akka.pattern.ask
import akka.pattern.pipe
import akka.util.Timeout
import akka.util.duration._
import akka.dispatch.Future

class ProcessOrderActor extends Actor {
  implicit val timeout = Timeout(5 seconds)
  val orderActor = context.actorOf(Props[OrderActor])
  val addressActor = context.actorOf(Props[AddressActor])
  val orderAggregateActor = context.actorOf(
                          Props[OrderAggregateActor])
  def receive = {
    case userId: Integer =>
              val aggResult: Future[OrderHistory] =
              for {
                   // call pattern directly
                  order <- ask(orderActor, userId).mapTo[Order]
                  // call by implicit conversion
                  address <- addressActor ask userId mapTo
                  manifest[Address]
              } yield OrderHistory(order, address)
          aggResult pipeTo orderAggregateActor
  }
}
```

In the preceding example, we saw the use case where a message comes in with user ID and we need to get the user's order and address details. We make use of the `ask()` pattern to invoke the actors concurrently, and their future results are composed into a new `future` construct for comprehension. On completion of the `future`, we pipe the aggregated results (`OrderHistory`) into the third actor. All the preceding calls are non-blocking and asynchronous.

[Fire and forget will always give a very good performance, as there is no waiting for a reply.]

Receiving messages

An actor needs a mechanism for receiving messages being sent by other threads or actors. All actors extend the `UntypedActor` class and implement the method as follows:

```
void onReceive(Object message)
```

This method is the entry point for all the messages that are received by the actor. Let's see an example of the actor and the `onReceive()` method implementation.

Java:

```java
public class DemoActor extends UntypedActor {
  LoggingAdapter log = Logging.getLogger(
                       getContext().system(), this);
  public void onReceive(Object message) throws Exception {
    if (message instanceof String)
      log.info("Message Received by Actor ->{}", message);
    else
      unhandled(message);
  }
}
```

Scala:

```scala
class DemoActor extends Actor with ActorLogging {
  def receive = {
      case message:String =>
       log.info("Message Received by Actor -> {}",message)
      case _ => log.info("unknown message")
    }
}
```

The messages are passed as a base object, which is mapped based on the type of instance, and appropriate actions are tagged.

Replying to messages

One of the key aspects of communicating via messages is the ability to reply back to the actors. When an actor receives a message and a reply is expected back, the actor can make use of the sender available within the actor to reply back.

Java:

```
public void onReceive(Object request) {
    if (message instanceof String)
                getSender().tell(message + "world");
    }
}
```

Scala:

```
def receive = {
    case message:String =>
            sender ! (message + "world")
}
```

In case, no sender is specified or available, the reply is sent back to the `DeadLetterActorRef`. Non-availability of a sender can be because of various reasons, such as the sender dies before the message could be sent back, or the caller is a non-actor.

Forwarding messages

At times, the actor might be acting as a forwarding agent. When writing an actor that provides functionality such as routing or load balancing or replication, the incoming messages will get forwarded to the target actors. In this case, it is very important that the original sender reference is maintained and passed on to the target actors. This makes sure that the replies go to the original sender and not the mediator actor.

Java:

```
actor.forward(message, getContext());
```

Scala:

```
actor.forward(message)
```

In case of Java, we need to pass the context variable too.

Stopping actors

Once the actors have processed the messages, it may be imperative to stop them. Stopping of actors may be required because we have created a large number of actors and now the load has come down, so we can stop some to conserve resources. In this section, we will see the various options available to stop actors.

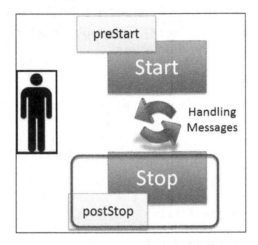

Actor termination involves multiple steps. Once the STOP signal is received by the actor, the following actions take place:

1. Actor stops processing the mailbox messages.
2. Actor sends the STOP signal to all the children.
3. Actor waits for termination message from all its children.
4. Next, Actor starts the self-termination process that involves the following:
    - Invoking the postStop() method
    - Dumping the attached mailbox
    - Publishing the terminated message on DeathWatch
    - Informing the supervisor about self-termination

Each actor at any level will follow the same set of steps when it receives the STOP signal. The stop action is performed asynchronously. In case of an actor system shutting down, the preceding set of activities is performed for the top-level actors initiated as part of the actor system.

Actors are stopped in the following ways:

- When the actor system calls the `shutdown()` method, this technique shuts down all the actors and the actor system.

- By sending a `PoisonPill` message to an actor—`PoisonPill` is like any message that goes and sits in the mailbox of the actor. A `PoisonPill` message is processed by initiating the shutdown of the actor.

- By calling `context.stop(self)` for stopping itself and calling `context.stop(child)` to stop the child actors.

Java:

```
//first option of shutting down the actors by shutting down
//the ActorSystem
system.shutdown();
//second option of shutting down the actor by sending a
//poisonPill message
actor.tell(poisonPill());
//third option of shutting down the actor
getContext().stop(getSelf());
//or
getContext().stop(childActorRef);
```

Scala:

```
//first option of shutting down the actors by shutting down
//the ActorSystem
system.shutdown()
//second option of shutting down the actor by sending a
//poisonPill message
actor ! PoisonPill
//third option of shutting down the actor
context.stop(self)
//or
context.stop(childActorRef)
```

As part of the actor shutdown, the `postStop()` method is invoked, which can be used to free up any resources held by the actor. Other actors in a different supervisor hierarchy can also be informed about actor shutdown.

Java:

```
@Override
public void postStop() {
// free up the resources held by actor e.g. db connection
//closing
}
```

Scala:

```
override def postStop() = {
// free up the resources held by actor e.g. db connection
//closing
}
```

Killing actors

An actor can be killed when a `kill()` message is sent to it. Unlike `PoisonPill`, which is an asynchronous way to shut down the actor, `kill()` is a synchronous way. The killed actor sends `ActorKilledException` to its parent.

Java:

```
actor.tell(kill());
```

Scala:

```
actor ! Kill
```

Actor lifecycle monitoring

Akka provides a mechanism to monitor the lifecycle of an actor. An actor is automatically the supervisor for all its children and manages their error conditions. Monitoring provides the ability to monitor the health of any actor other than its own children so that you can manage the impact on your own processing logic. Monitoring is observation of error, while supervision is management of error.

For example, if the Monitor actor wants to be notified of another actor's (worker) termination, the Monitor actor will watch for the reception of the terminated message dispatched by the worker actor upon termination. When the message is received, the Monitor actor can take appropriate action (including trying to instantiate and create another instance of the worker actor):

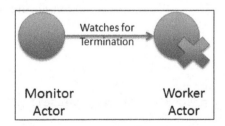

We will cover lifecycle monitoring in more detail in *Chapter 6, Supervision and Monitoring*.

HotSwap

Another key functionality of Akka is the ability to HotSwap an actor's message loop functionality at runtime. The functionality is provided via the getContext(). become() and getContext().unbecome() methods. The HotSwapped code is kept in a stack, which can be pushed and popped when the become() or unbecome() methods are invoked.

Let's see a simple Ping Pong example, where we develop a logic to handle the messages swapped at runtime.

Java:

```
public class PingPongActor extends UntypedActor {
    static String PING = "PING";
    static String PONG = "PONG";
    int count = 0;

    public void onReceive(Object message) throws Exception {
        if (message instanceof String) {
            if (((String) message).matches(PING)) {
                    System.out.println("PING");
                count += 1;
                Thread.sleep(100);
                getSelf().tell(PONG);
                getContext().become(new Procedure<Object>() {
                    public void apply(Object message) {
                        if (message instanceof String) {
                            if (((String) message).
                            matches(PONG)) {
                                System.out.println("PONG");
                                count += 1;
                                try {     Thread.sleep(100); }
                                                        catch
    (Exception e) {     }

                                getSelf().tell(PING);
                                getContext().unbecome();
                            }
                        }
                    }
                });
                if (count > 10)
                    getContext().stop(getSelf());
            }
        }
    }
}
```

Scala:

```scala
case class PING
case class PONG

class PingPongActor extends Actor {
  import context._
  var count = 0
  def receive: Receive = {
    case PING =>
      println("PING")
      count = count + 1
      Thread.sleep(100)
      self ! PONG
            become {
                    case PONG =>
                    println("PONG")
                    count = count + 1
                    Thread.sleep(100)
                    self ! PING
                    unbecome()
                }
        if(count > 10) context.stop(self)
  }
}
```

We defined the `PingPongActor` class with two message types—PING and PONG. In the message loop, we checked for PING messages. When a PING message is received, the following actions are performed:

1. Print a message.
2. Increment the counter.
3. Send a PONG message to self.
4. Call the `become()` method where we swap the message loop for handling the PONG message.

When the PONG message comes, similar steps are performed, but in the end, the `unbecome()` method is invoked, which restores the original message handling loop for PING messages.

In case of Java, we use `akka.japi.Procedure` to write the message receive function, which makes the code look a little complex. All this complexity will vanish with the Lambda feature of Java 8.

Next, we will invoke the actor and see the output.

- **Java**:

```
ActorSystem _system = ActorSystem.create("BecomeUnbecome");
ActorRef pingPongActor = _system
        .actorOf(new Props(PingPongActor.class));
pingPongActor.tell(PingPongActor.PING);
Thread.sleep(2000);
_system.shutdown();
```

- **Scala**:

```
val _system = ActorSystem("BecomeUnbecome")
val pingPongActor = _system.actorOf(Props[PingPongActor])
pingPongActor ! PING
Thread.sleep(2000)
_system.shutdown
```

The output of the program is simple as follows:

PING

PONG

PING

PONG

PING

Summary

This completes the overview of actors. We saw the lifecycle of the actor, how to create actors, how to pass and process messages, and how to stop or kill the actor. In addition, we saw the HotSwap feature of Actors, which allows us to swap the message loop of the actor at runtime and replace with another procedure.

In the next chapter, we will cover typed actors, which are a special case of actors. Typed actors are especially useful when you have an existing POJO-based application, which you want to migrate to the Akka world.

4
Typed Actors

In this chapter, we will cover typed actors, how to define them, how to create instances of them, how to send/receive messages, how to reply to messages, how to forward messages, and how to stop actors. We will also cover the use of dispatchers and routers with respect to typed actors.

In the previous chapter, we saw how the actors are defined and created, and how they process the messages. In the case of untyped actors, any message can be passed, meaning the service-level contracts are not strictly defined. So, if a message is passed to an untyped actor, and if the actor does not have any handling mechanism, then the message is relegated as an unhandled message.

In order to define strict contracts for actors that can respond to only the predefined set of messages, the Typed Actor Model is used. In this case, every message need not be encapsulated as one object; typed actors allow us to define separate methods that accept multiple inputs as defined by the contract. In Java parlance, typed actors provide the Java interface in the object-oriented world.

 Untyped actors respond to messages sent, while typed actors respond to method calls.

What are typed actors?

A typed actor has two parts—a publicly defined interface, and secondly, an implementation of the interface. Calls to the publicly defined interface are delegated asynchronously to the private instance of the implementation. In effect, the public interface provides the service contract that bridges the Actor Model to the object-oriented paradigm.

The explicit public interface makes the actors more clear and concise, lending an object-oriented design paradigm to the Actor Model, as opposed to an event-driven design paradigm. So, if you have existing **Plain Old Java Object (POJO)** code or are writing an object-oriented application, typed actors allow you to integrate the Actor Model within the existing object-oriented paradigm.

For converting the POJO bean objects into asynchronous actors that process method calls, or writing strict contract-based, object-oriented applications, typed actors can be used. Typed actors are on the cusp where the Actor Model meets the POJO world.

In Akka, typed actors have been implemented using the Active Object pattern. We will cover the basics of the Active Object pattern which will provide us with the understanding of how the typed actors are implemented.

 The Active Object Design pattern decouples method execution from method invocation, which reside in their own threads of control. The goal is to introduce concurrency and fault tolerance, by using asynchronous method invocation and a scheduler for handling requests.

The key objective of the Active Object pattern is to decouple the method execution from the method invocation. We have to move the method execution and invocation to separate threads. Having invocation and execution in separate threads allows us to provide concurrent and synchronized access to the object state.

How do we decouple?

To decouple the method invocation and execution, the Active Object pattern uses the proxy pattern (interface) to separate the interface and implementation of the object. The idea is to run the proxy and the implementation in separate threads, as shown in the following diagram:

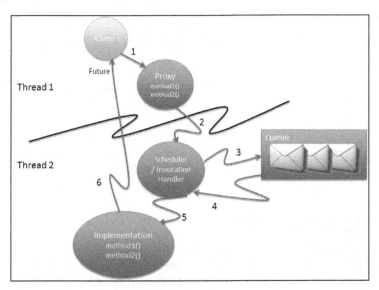

Let's go ahead and see how the Active Object pattern decouples the method invocation from method execution as follows:

1. At runtime, the client calls the proxy object and invokes the method.
2. The proxy in turn passes the method calls as method requests to a scheduler or invocation handler that intercepts the call.
3. Scheduler or invocation handler enqueues the method requests on a queue.
4. The scheduler continuously monitors the queue and determines which method request(s) have become runnable, that is when their synchronization constraints are met. At this point, the scheduler or invocation handler dequeues the requests from the queue.
5. Scheduler or invocation handler dispatches the requests to the implementation object.
6. The implementation object, running on the same thread as the scheduler, processes the request and returns any value to the client as `Future`.

In Akka, the proxy pattern is implemented using the JDK proxies, which allow us to use the class interface to be specified as a proxy at runtime. Method invocations through the interface of the class are dispatched to another object implementing that interface.

Each proxy instance has an associated invocation handler. Method invocation on the proxy instance is dispatched to the invoke method of the instance's invocation handler. The invoke method takes in the proxy instance, a `java.lang.reflect.Method` object identifying the method invoked, and lastly an array of the `Object` type containing the arguments.

You can read more about implementation of dynamic proxy classes in JDK at `http://docs.oracle.com/javase/6/docs/technotes/guides/reflection/proxy.html`

 Typed actors are implemented as an extension in Akka.

Defining an actor

To define a typed actor, two things are required—a public interface, and secondly, an implementation of the interface. Let's create a simple calculator interface that does some simple tasks such as addition, subtraction, and counter updating.

Java:

```java
public interface CalculatorInt {
    public Future<Integer> add(Integer first, Integer second);
    public Future<Integer> subtract(Integer first,
                            Integer second);
    public void incrementCount();
    public Option<Integer> incrementAndReturn();
}
```

Scala:

```scala
trait CalculatorInt {
    def add(first: Int, second: Int): Future[Int]
    def subtract(first: Int, second: Int): Future[Int]
    def incrementCount(): Unit
    def incrementAndReturn(): Option[Int]
}
```

An important thing to note here is the method return types as follows:

- Methods with the void return type are dispatched in a fire and forget manner similar to tell() for untyped actors.

- Methods with the Future return type are dispatched in a request-reply manner similar to the ask() method for untyped actors. There calls are non-blocking.

- Methods with the Option return type are also dispatched in a request-reply manner, but these calls are blocking. The calling thread will wait for an answer or the call will return "None" in case of timeout where the answer is not received within the defined time period (default timeout period is 5 seconds).

- Methods with any other return type make use of the request-reply dispatcher. In case of timeout, the java.util.concurrent.TimeoutException is thrown.

Next, let's go ahead and implement the interface.

Java:

```java
public class Calculator implements CalculatorInt {
    Integer counter = 0;

    //Non-blocking request response
    public Future<Integer> add(Integer first, Integer second) {
        return Futures.successful(first + second,
                        TypedActor.dispatcher());
    }
    //Non-blocking request response
    public Future<Integer> subtract(Integer first,
                                Integer second) {
        return Futures.successful(first - second,
                    TypedActor.dispatcher());
    }
    //fire and forget
    public void incrementCount() {
        counter++;
    }
    //Blocking request response
    public Option<Integer> incrementAndReturn() {
        return Option.some(++counter);
    }
}
```

Scala:

```scala
class Calculator extends CalculatorInt {

    var counter: Int = 0

    import TypedActor.dispatcher

    def add(first: Int, second: Int): Future[Int] =
                    Promise successful first + second

    def subtract(first: Int, second: Int): Future[Int] =
                    Promise successful first - second

    def incrementCount(): Unit = counter += 1

    def incrementAndReturn(): Option[Int] = {
        counter += 1
        Some(counter)
    }
}
```

The `Calculator` class implements the interface and provides the concrete implementation of the methods defined in the interface. The method based on the return type makes use of the explicit `Future` or `Option` calls to return the appropriate type back to the calling thread. Here `Future` is `akka.dispatch.Future<?>` and `Option` is `akka.japi.Option<?>`. In Scala, you can also make use of `scala.Option`.

In addition, we make use of `Futures.successful` or `Promise successful`, which creates an already completed promise with the specified result. `Futures.successful` takes in a strict value and blocks till the call is finished. However, the call to the `TypedActor` method is asynchronous.

With this, we saw how to define a typed actor having a public interface and corresponding implementation class.

Although typed actors can be extended to work and behave like normal actors, such behavior is not inherent in them. Actors are entities that change their state by processing the incoming messages and generating other messages in response. Typed actors are not modeled on the same premise. Use typed actors sparingly and avoid blocking behavior by writing methods that either return `Unit` or `Future`.

Creating actors

Next we will go ahead and try creating the `TypedActor` objects within the `ActorSystem` context.

An actor with a default constructor

When the typed actor implementation has a default constructor, it is constructed using the following syntax.

Java:

```
ActorSystem _system = ActorSytem.create("TypedActorsExample");
CalculatorInt calculator = TypedActor.get(_system)
  .typedActorOf(new TypedProps<Calculator>(
  CalculatorInt.class, Calculator.class));
```

Scala:

```
val _system = ActorSystem("TypedActorsExample")
val calculator1: CalculatorInt =
TypedActor(_system).typedActorOf(TypedProps[Calculator]())
```

The typed actor has been implemented as an Akka extension. So to get hold of the extension, the following call gets the extension object—TypedActor.get(_system).

Once we get the TypedActor extension handle, we invoke the typedActorOf() call by passing the TypedProps parameter. The TypedProps class takes in the interface and the implementation class name. The typedActorOf() method call returns the instance of the dynamic proxy object for the Calculator class.

An actor with a non-default constructor

In case we have typed actor implementation with a non-default constructor, it is constructed using the following syntax.

Java:

```
ActorSystem _system = ActorSytem.create("TypedActorsExample");

CalculatorInt calculator = TypedActor.get(_system)
.typedActorOf(new TypedProps<Calculator>(CalculatorInt.class,
new Creator< Calculator >() {
    public Calculator create() {
        return new Calculator ("foo");
    }
  }
));
```

Scala:

```
val _system = ActorSystem("TypedActorsExample")

val calculator1: CalculatorInt =
TypedActor(_system).typedActorOf(
 TypedProps(classOf[CalculatorInt],
            new Calculator("foo")))
```

In this case, we use the `Creator()` method to create the object of the implementation class by calling the non-default constructor and passing on to the `TypedProps` method.

Messaging model

The basic premise of the Typed Actor Model is communication via method calls. The parameter values are the messages and these need to be immutable. The actor's state responds or reacts based on the method that is invoked onto it.

Sending messages

Once the actor reference is available, messages can be passed to an actor in two modes, as follows:

- **Fire and forget**: This is a one-way method call model, where the caller of the method does not expect any reply. All methods with return types `void` or `Unit` belong to this category.

- **Send and receive**: In this mode, the caller of the method expects a reply from the implementation class and will wait for that reply. In this mode, the method may be invoked asynchronously and a `Future` is returned representing a potential reply. In the case of send and receive method calls with blocking mode, caller threads wait for the response.

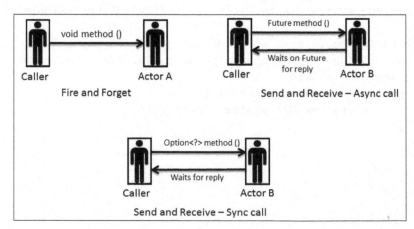

Fire and forget messages

To invoke the fire and forget messages, get the dynamic proxy object and invoke the call.

Java:

```
CalculatorInt calculator = TypedActor.get(_system)
  .typedActorOf(new TypedProps<Calculator>(
  CalculatorInt.class,Calculator.class));
```

```
calculator.incrementCount();
```

Scala:

```
val calculator: CalculatorInt =
TypedActor(_system).typedActorOf(TypedProps[Calculator]())
```

```
calculator.incrementCount()
```

Invoking the method here is as simple as invoking the method on the proxy interface.

Send and receive messages

To invoke the send and receive messages in the blocking or non-blocking mode, once again get the dynamic proxy object and invoke the respective call.

Java:

```
Timeout timeout = new Timeout(Duration.parse("5 seconds"));
```

```
CalculatorInt calculator = TypedActor.get(_system)
  .typedActorOf(new TypedProps<Calculator>(
  CalculatorInt.class, Calculator.class));
```

```
// Invoke the method and wait for result
Future<Integer> future = calculator.add(Integer.valueOf(14),
                Integer.valueOf(6));
Integer result = Await.result(future, timeout.duration());
```

Scala:

```
val calculator: CalculatorInt =
    TypedActor(_system).typedActorOf(TypedProps[Calculator]())
// Invoke the method and wait for result
val future = calculator.add(14,6);
val result = Await.result(future, 5 second);
```

In the preceding example, we invoked the method that returns a Future object. Subsequently, we wait for the reply from the Future object.

For the blocking method calls, the calls to the methods are in a straightforward manner.

Java:

```
CalculatorInt calculator = TypedActor.get(_system)
.typedActorOf(new TypedProps<Calculator>(
CalculatorInt.class, Calculator.class));

//Method invocation in a blocking way
Option<Integer> counterResult = calculator.incrementAndReturn();
```

Scala:

```
val calculator: CalculatorInt =
    TypedActor(_system).typedActorOf(TypedProps[Calculator]())

//Method invocation in a blocking way
val result = calculator.incrementAndReturn()
```

Stopping actors

Typed actors can be stopped via calling the Stop or PoisonPill method on the TypedActor extension and passing the reference of the dynamic proxy instance.

Java:

```
//To shut down the typed actor, call the stop method on the //
TypedActor extension and providing the proxy instance
TypedActor.get(system).stop(calculator);

//Other way to stop the actor is invoke the Poisonpill method //on the
TypedActor extension and passing the proxy instance
TypedActor.get(system).poisonPill(calculator);
```

Scala:

```
//To shut down the typed actor, call the stop method on the //
TypedActor extension and providing the proxy instance
TypedActor(system).stop(calculator)

//Other way to stop the actor is invoke the Poisonpill method //on the
TypedActor extension and passing the proxy instance
TypedActor(system).poisonPill(calculator)
```

Actor lifecycle monitoring

We saw the typed actor being defined and created, methods getting invoked, and how to stop the actors. In the case of untyped actors we saw support for the preStart() and postStop() methods where any resource initialization and subsequent cleaning could be handled.

So, in the case of typed actors, additional hooks can be implemented by making the implementation class implement additional interfaces. These interfaces can be overridden to initialize resources on actor start and clean up resources on actor stop.

Lifecycle callbacks

Typed actors can implement the TypedActor.PreStart and TypedActor.PostStop interfaces to add the additional hooks into the code.

Java:

```java
public class Calculator implementsCalculatorInt, PreStart, PostStop {

    LoggingAdapter log = Logging.getLogger(
                    TypedActor.context().system(), this);
    //Allows to tap into the Actor PreStart hook
    public void preStart() {
        log.info("Actor Started !");
    }
    //Allows to tap into the Actor PostStop hook
    public void postStop() {
        log.info("Actor Stopped !");
    }
}
```

Scala:

```scala
class Calculator extends CalculatorInt with PreStart
                    with PostStop {
import TypedActor.context
val log = Logging(context.system,
                    TypedActor.self.getClass())
    def preStart(): Unit = {
        log.info ("Actor Started")
    }

    def postStop(): Unit = {
        log.info ("Actor Stopped")
    }
}
```

By implementing the `TypedActor.PreStart` and `TypedActor.PostStop` interfaces, we can add the required functionality before the actor starts responding to the method calls:

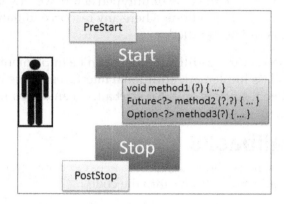

Similarly, we can also implement the `TypedActor.PreRestart` and `TypedActor.PostRestart` interfaces to add functionality on actor restart as part of the supervision.

Now, we have added hooks to manage the typed actor's lifecycle, but how do we extend the typed actor for receiving messages similar to actors or how are the typed actors managed in case of a fault or an exception. For this, the typed actor provides additional interfaces that can be implemented to add the requisite functionality to the actor.

Receiving messages

Typed actors can implement the `akka.actor.TypedActor.Receiver` interface in order to process messages coming to them. Now, the typed actor can handle the arbitrary messages in addition to the method calls. Adding this interface is useful when the typed actor is managing standard child actors and it wants to be notified of their termination (`DeathWatch`).

By implementing this interface, typed actors can receive any arbitrary message, like the standard actors.

Java:

```
public class Calculator implements Receiver, CalculatorInt {
    LoggingAdapter log = Logging.getLogger(
            TypedActor.context().system(), this);
    public void onReceive(Object msg, ActorRef actor) {
        log.info("Received Message -> {}", msg);
    }
}
```

Scala:

```scala
class Calculator extends CalculatorInt {
 import TypedActor.context
 val log = Logging(context.system,
                    TypedActor.self.getClass())
   def onReceive(message: Any, sender: ActorRef): Unit = {
       log.info("Message received->{}", message)
   }
}
```

In case of Java, the implementation class needs to implement the interface and the method to be able to receive any arbitrary messages. For Scala, the existing trait—CalculatorInt extends the Receiver trait, which is subsequently implemented in the Calculator class. This allows the typed actor to handle messages:

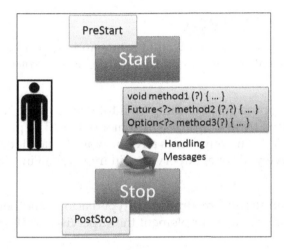

To pass a message to the typed actor, we need to get hold of the ActorRef associated with the dynamic proxy interface. We can get access to the ActorRef with the following code snippet.

Java:

```java
ActorSystem _system = ActorSystem.create("TypedActorsExample",
            ConfigFactory.load().getConfig("TypedActorExample"));

CalculatorInt calculator = TypedActor.get(_system)
        .typedActorOf(new TypedProps<Calculator>(
            CalculatorInt.class, Calculator.class));
//Get access to the ActorRef
ActorRef calActor = TypedActor.get(_system)
                .getActorRefFor(calculator);
//pass a message
calActor.tell("Hi there");
```

Scala:

```scala
val _system = ActorSystem("TypedActorsExample")

val calculator: CalculatorInt =
TypedActor(_system).typedActorOf(TypedProps[Calculator]())

//Get access to the ActorRef
val calActor:ActorRef = TypedActor(_system)
                        .getActorRefFor(calculator)

//pass a message
calActor.tell("Hi there")
```

Supervisor strategy

When the typed actor is dealing with child actors and the parent actor needs to manage the faults or failures of the child actors, the supervisor strategy needs to be defined.

Remember, Akka's approach to handling fault tolerance, or the "Let It Crash" model, is implemented by linking actors in a hierarchy. Akka promotes that instead of each actor trying to figure out who is alive or who is dead, let somebody else handle my failure. We will cover supervisors in more detail in *Chapter 6, Supervision and Monitoring*.

For implementing the supervisor strategy in typed actors, another interface/trait has been provided that allows us to implement the supervisor strategy applicable for the child actors.

Java:

```java
public class Calculator implements Supervisor {

    public SupervisorStrategy supervisorStrategy() {
        return strategy;
    }

    private static SupervisorStrategy strategy =
    new OneForOneStrategy(10, Duration.parse("10 second"),
    new Function<Throwable, Directive>() {
        public Directive apply(Throwable t) {
            if (t instanceof ArithmeticException) {
                    return resume();
            } else if (t instanceof IllegalArgumentException) {
                    return restart();
```

```
            } else if (t instanceof NullPointerException) {
                    return stop();
            } else {
                    return escalate();
            }
        }
    });
}
```

Scala:

```scala
class Calculator extends CalculatorInt with Supervisor {

  def supervisorStrategy(): SupervisorStrategy =
    OneForOneStrategy(maxNrOfRetries = 10,
          withinTimeRange = 10 seconds) {
    case _: ArithmeticException => Resume
    case _: IllegalArgumentException => Restart
    case _: NullPointerException => Stop
    case _: Exception => Escalate
  }
}
```

The defined supervisor strategy will be applicable to the actors created within the context of the actor.

Creating an actor hierarchy

To create child actors under a typed actor, we need to get the TypedActor context and then invoke the actorOf method.

Java:

```java
//create a child actor under the Typed Actor context
ActorRef childActor = TypedActor.context().actorOf(
            new Props(ChildActor.class), "childActor");
```

Scala:

```scala
import TypedActor.context
//create a child actor under the Typed Actor context
val childActor:ActorRef = context.actorOf(Props[ChildActor],
name="childActor")
```

> Remember, TypedActor.context() is only valid within methods of a TypedActor implementation.

Dispatchers and routers

A dispatcher controls and coordinates the message dispatching to the actors that is mapped on the underlying threads. Akka provides multiple dispatch policies that can be customized according to the underlying hardware resource (number of cores or memory available) and type of application workload.

In Akka, a router is also a type of actor, which routes the incoming messages to the outbound actors. When a large number of actors are working in parallel to process the incoming stream of messages, the router actor directs the message from the source to the destination actor.

Refer to *Chapter 5, Dispatchers and Routers* for more details on dispatchers and routers. Here we will cover how to make use of dispatchers and routers with typed actors.

Using dispatchers

In simple terms, the dispatcher controls and coordinates the message dispatching to the actors that are mapped on the underlying threads. For using the dispatcher with typed actors, use the following syntax.

Java:

```
ActorSystem _system = ActorSystem.create("TypedActorsExample",
    ConfigFactory.load().getConfig("TypedActorExample"));

CalculatorInt calculator = TypedActor.get(_system).typedActorOf(
    new TypedProps<Calculator>(CalculatorInt.class,
        Calculator.class).withDispatcher("defaultDispatcher"));
```

Scala:

```
val _system = ActorSystem("TypedActorsExample",ConfigFactory.load().
getConfig("TypedActorExample"))

val calculator: CalculatorInt =
    TypedActor(_system).typedActorOf(TypedProps[Calculator]()
        .withDispatcher("defaultDispatcher"))
```

For a definition of the dispatcher, look at the following section.

application.conf

For the `application.conf` class, look at the following code snippet:

```
TypedActorExample{
  defaultDispatcher {
      type = Dispatcher
      executor = "fork-join-executor"
      fork-join-executor {
          parallelism-min = 2
          parallelism-factor = 2.0
          parallelism-max = 4
      }
  }
}
```

Using routers

Ideally, typed actors are used at the intersection of POJO and the Actor Model. At times, there are situations where we may want to spread the number of messages being passed across in a round robin way. Unlike actors, routing is not available as a method on `TypedProps`.

We need to get `ActorRef` for all the typed actors, combine those in a vector, and use that to create the router.

Java:

```
ActorSystem _system = ActorSytem.create("TypedActorsExample");

CalculatorInt calculator1 = TypedActor.get(_system)
    .typedActorOf(new TypedProps<Calculator>(
    CalculatorInt.class,    Calculator.class));

CalculatorInt calculator2 = TypedActor.get(_system)
    .typedActorOf(new TypedProps<Calculator>(
    CalculatorInt.class, Calculator.class));

// Create a router with Typed Actors
ActorRef actor1 = TypedActor.get(_system)
            .getActorRefFor(calculator1);

ActorRef actor2 = TypedActor.get(_system)
            .getActorRefFor(calculator2);
```

```
Iterable<ActorRef> routees = Arrays.asList(new ActorRef[] {
actor1,actor2 });

//Create the router actor
ActorRef router = _system.actorOf(new Props()
        .withRouter(BroadcastRouter.create(routees)));

router.tell("Hello there");
```

Scala:

```
val _system = ActorSystem("TypedActorsExample")

val calculator1: CalculatorInt2 =
    TypedActor(_system).typedActorOf(TypedProps[Calculator]())

val calculator2: CalculatorInt2 =
    TypedActor(_system).typedActorOf(TypedProps[Calculator]())

// Create a router with Typed Actors
val actor1: ActorRef = TypedActor(_system).getActorRefFor(calculator1)

val actor2: ActorRef = TypedActor(_system).getActorRefFor(calculator2)

val routees = Vector[ActorRef](actor1, actor2)

//Create the router actor
val router = _system.actorOf(new Props().withRouter(
        BroadcastRouter(routees = routees)))

router.tell("Hello there")
```

Summary

This completes the overview of typed actors. We saw the lifecycle of the actor, how
to create actors, how to pass and process messages, how to stop or kill the actors.
We also saw how typed actors can be extended for additional hooks—preStart,
postStop, Receiver, and Supervisor, which allow extending their functionality
and becoming a bridge between the Actor Model and the object-oriented application.

In the next chapter, we shall cover the dispatchers and routers. Dispatchers are the
heart of the Akka application and this is what makes it humming. Routers on the
other hand, route incoming messages to the outbound actors.

5
Dispatchers and Routers

Dispatchers are the heart of the Akka application and this is what makes it humming. Routers on the other hand, route incoming messages to outbound actors. In this chapter we will cover the following:

- What a dispatcher is and how it works, various types of dispatchers and their usage and configuration settings
- Different types of mailboxes, and their usage and configuration
- What a router is, and different types of routers and their usage
- How to write a custom router

Dispatcher is the engine that powers the Akka application. It is very important to understand the switches and knobs that need to be tuned to extract the maximum concurrency and scalability out of the application.

Dispatchers

In the real world, **dispatchers** are the communication coordinators that are responsible for receiving and passing messages. For the emergency services (for example, in U.S. – 911), the dispatchers are the people responsible for taking in the call, and passing on the message to the other departments (medical, police, fire station, or others). The dispatcher coordinates the route and activities of all these departments, to make sure that the right help reaches the destination as early as possible.

Another example is how the airport manages airplanes taking off. The **air traffic controllers** (**ATCs**) coordinate the use of the runway between the various planes taking off and landing. On one side, air traffic controllers manage the runways (usually ranging from 1 to 3), and on the other, aircrafts of different sizes and capacity from different airlines ready to take off and land. An air traffic controller coordinates the various airplanes, gets the airplanes lined up, and allocates the runways to take off and land:

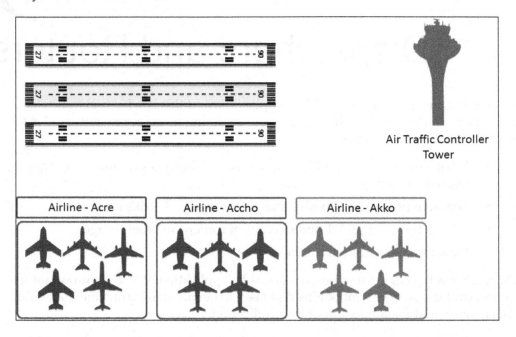

As we can see, there are multiple runways available and multiple airlines, each having a different set of airplanes needing to take off. It is the responsibility of air traffic controller(s) to coordinate the take-off and landing of planes from each airline and do this activity as fast as possible.

Dispatcher as a pattern

Dispatcher is a well-recognized and used pattern in the Java world. Dispatchers are used to control the flow of execution. Based on the dispatching policy, dispatchers will route the incoming message or request to the business process. Dispatchers as a pattern provide the following advantages:

- **Centralized control**: Dispatchers provide a central place from where various messages/requests are dispatched. The word "centralized" means code is re-used, leading to improved maintainability and reduced duplication of code.

- **Application partitioning**: There is a clear separation between the business logic and display logic. There is no need to intermingle business logic with the display logic.

- **Reduced inter-dependencies**: Separation of the display logic from the business logic means there are reduced inter-dependencies between the two. Reduced inter-dependencies mean less contention on the same resources, leading to a scalable model.

Dispatcher as a concept provides a centralized control mechanism that decouples different processing logic within the application, which in turn reduces inter-dependencies.

Executor in Java

Before we jump into the Akka dispatchers, it is important to understand the underlying constructs provided by the language (Java) to support the dispatcher features and functionality.

In Akka, dispatchers are based on the Java Executor framework (part of `java.util.concurrent`). Executor provides the framework for the execution of asynchronous tasks. It is based on the producer–consumer model, meaning the act of task submission (producer) is decoupled from the act of task execution (consumer). The threads that submit tasks are different from the threads that execute the tasks.

Two important implementations of the Executor framework are as follows:

- **ThreadPoolExecutor**: It executes each submitted task using thread from a predefined and configured thread pool.

- **ForkJoinPool**: It uses the same thread pool model but supplemented with work stealing. Threads in the pool will find and execute tasks (work stealing) created by other active tasks or tasks allocated to other threads in the pool that are pending execution.

 Fork/join is based a on fine-grained, parallel, divide-and-conquer style, parallelism model. The idea is to break down large data chunks into smaller chunks and process them in parallel to take advantage of the underlying processor cores.

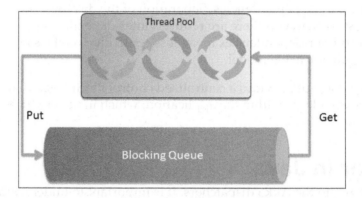

Executor is backed by constructs that allow you to define and control how the tasks are executed. Using these Executor constructor constructs, one can specify the following:

- How many threads will be running? (thread pool size)
- How are the tasks queued until they come up for processing?
- How many tasks can be executed concurrently?
- What happens in case the system overloads, when tasks to be rejected are selected?
- What is the order of execution of tasks? (LIFO, FIFO, and so on)
- Which pre- and post-task execution actions can be run?

 In the book *Java Concurrency in Practice, Addison-Wesley Publishing*, the authors have described the Executor framework and its usage very nicely. It will be useful to read the book for more details on the concurrency constructs provided by Java language.

Dispatchers in Akka

In the Akka world, the dispatcher controls and coordinates the message dispatching to the actors mapped on the underlying threads. They make sure that the resources are optimized and messages are processed as fast as possible. Akka provides multiple dispatch policies that can be customized according to the underlying hardware resource (number of cores or memory available) and type of application workload.

If we take our example of the airport and map it to the Akka world, we can see that the runways are mapped to the underlying resources — threads. The airlines with their planes are analogous to the mailbox with the messages. The ATC tower employs a dispatch policy to make sure the runways are optimally utilized and the planes are spending minimum time on waiting for clearance to take off or land:

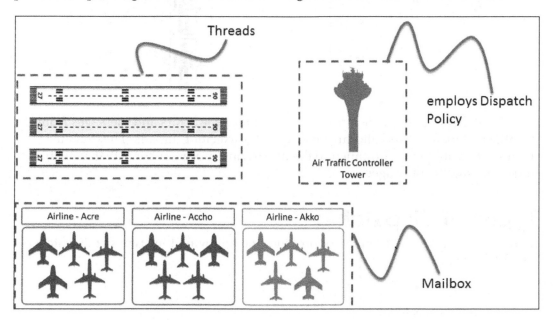

For Akka, the dispatchers, actors, mailbox, and threads look like the following diagram:

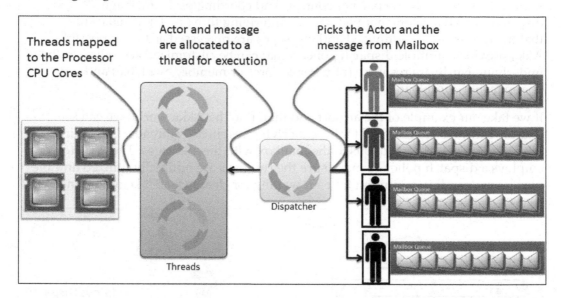

The dispatchers run on their threads; they dispatch the actors and messages from the attached mailbox and allocate on heap to the executor threads. The executor threads are configured and tuned to the underlying processor cores that available for processing the messages.

Types of dispatcher

In the case of Akka, the framework provides the following four types of dispatchers out of the box:

- Dispatcher
- Pinned dispatcher
- Balancing dispatcher
- Calling thread dispatcher

Similarly, there are four default mailbox implementations provided as follows:

- Unbounded mailbox
- Bounded mailbox
- Unbounded priority mailbox
- Bounded priority mailbox

Threads are the underlying resources and they are optimized based on the available CPU cores and the type of application workload. The number of threads is configured in conjunction with the dispatcher policy employed for the application.

 Akka allows you to write your own dispatcher implementation or your own mailbox implementation.

Dispatcher

This is the default dispatcher used by the Akka application in case there is nothing defined. This is an event-based dispatcher that binds a set of actors to a thread pool backed up by a `BlockingQueue` method.

The following are the characteristics of the default dispatcher:

- Every actor is backed by its own mailbox
- The dispatcher can be shared with any number of actors
- The dispatcher can be backed by either thread pool or fork join pool
- The dispatcher is optimized for non-blocking code

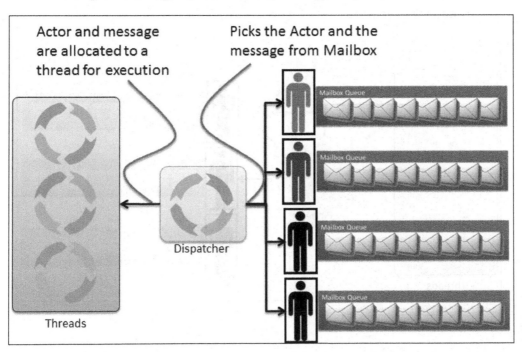

Pinned dispatcher

This dispatcher provides a single, dedicated thread (pinned) for each actor. This dispatcher is useful when the actors are doing I/O operations or performing long-running calculations. The dispatcher will deallocate the thread attached to the actor after a configurable period of inactivity.

The following are the characteristics of the pinned dispatcher:

- Every actor is backed by its own mailbox.
- A dedicated thread for each actor implies that this dispatcher cannot be shared with any other actors.
- The dispatcher is backed by the thread pool executor.
- The dispatcher is optimized for blocking operations. For example, if the code is making I/O calls or database calls, then such actors will wait until the task is finished. For such blocking operation, the pinned dispatcher performs better than the default dispatcher.

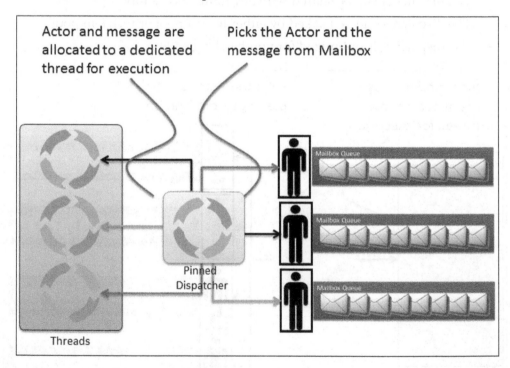

Balancing dispatcher

The balancing dispatcher, as the name suggests is an event-based dispatcher that tries to redistribute work from busy actors and allocate it to idle ones. Redistribution of tasks can only work if all actors are of the same type (requirement). This task redistribution is similar to the work-stealing technique, as described in the fork join pool. The dispatcher looks for actors that are idle and dispatches the message(s) to them for processing.

The following are the characteristics of the balancing dispatcher:

- There is only one mailbox for all actors
- The dispatcher can be shared only with actors of the same type
- The dispatcher can be backed by a either thread pool or fork join pool

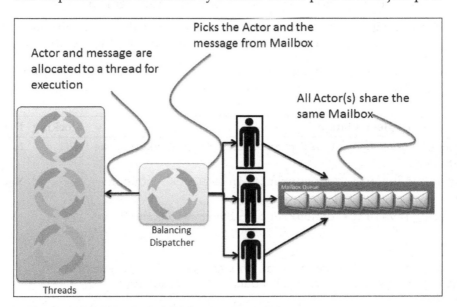

Calling thread dispatcher

The calling thread dispatcher is primarily used for testing. This dispatcher runs the task execution on the current thread only. It does not create any new threads and provides a deterministic execution order. The dispatch strategy is to run on the current thread, unless the target actor is either suspended or already running on the current thread. If the invocation is not run immediately, the task is queued in a thread-local queue to be executed once the active invocation(s) further up in the call stack are finished. If you make use of blocking code with calling thread dispatcher, then the blocking code will hold the thread for processing, leaving other messages in the queue for a long time.

The following are the characteristics of the calling thread dispatcher:

- Every actor is backed by its own mailbox
- The dispatcher can be shared with any number of actors
- The dispatcher is backed by the calling thread

Types of mailboxes

Mailboxes are backed by queue implementation from the Java concurrent package. The queues are characterized by two factors as follows:

- **Blocking queue**: Blocking queue means a queue that waits for space to become available before putting in an element and similarly waits for the queue to become non-empty before retrieving an element
- **Bounded queue**: Bounded queue means a queue that limits the size of the queue; meaning you cannot add more elements than the specified size

In Akka, the following queue implementations are based on the blocking/bounded factors available:

Types	Implementation	Blocking	Bounded
Unbounded mailbox	`java.util.concurrent.ConcurrentLinkedQueue`	No	No
Bounded mailbox	`java.util.concurrent.LinkedBlockingQueue`	Yes	Yes
Unbounded priority mailbox	`java.util.concurrent.PriorityBlockingQueue`	Yes	No
Bounded priority mailbox	`java.util.concurrent.PriorityBlockingQueue` wrapped in `akka.util.BoundedBlockingQueue`	Yes	Yes

You can choose between the unbounded and bounded mailbox via the configuration. In the case of a priority mailbox (unbounded or bounded), a simple implementation needs to be provided to for use by the dispatcher.

Dispatcher usage

The Executor contexts supported by Akka are as follows:

- **Thread pool executor**: Here, the idea is to create a pool of worker threads. Tasks are assigned to the pool using a queue. If the number of tasks exceeds the number of threads, then the tasks are queued up until a thread in the pool is available. Worker threads minimize the overhead of allocation/deallocation of threads.

- **Fork join executor**: This is based on the premise of divide-and-conquer. The idea is to divide a large task into smaller tasks whose solution can then be combined for the final answer. The tasks need to be independent to be able run in parallel.

For each of these execution contexts, Akka allows us to specify the configuration parameters that will define and construct the underlying resources. The parameters define the following:

- Minimum number of threads that will be allocated

- Maximum number of threads that will be allocated

- Multiplier factor to be used (based on number of CPU cores available)

For example, if the minimum number is defined as 3 and the multiplier factor is 2, then the dispatcher starts with a minimum of 3 x 2 = 6 threads. The maximum number defines the upper limit on the number of threads. If the maximum number is 8, then the maximum number of threads will be 8 x 2 = 16 threads.

Next, we will see which key configuration parameters are used for each of the executors.

Thread pool executor

The following are the key parameters that need to be configured for the thread pool executor:

```
# Configuration for the thread pool
thread-pool-executor {
  # minimum number of threads
  core-pool-size-min = 2
  # available processors * factor
  core-pool-size-factor = 2.0
  # maximum number of threads
  core-pool-size-max = 10
}
```

Fork join executor

The following are the key parameters that need to be configured for the fork join executor:

```
# Configuration for the fork join pool
  fork-join-executor {
    # Min number of threads
    parallelism-min = 2
    # available processors * factor
    parallelism-factor = 2.0
    # Max number of threads
    parallelism-max = 10
}
```

Depending on the type of dispatcher being used and support provided for the executor, the preceding configuration parameters can be used in conjunction with other settings.

To define the dispatcher for a set of actors, the following are the important configuration parameters:

Parameter name	Description	Potential values
type	Identifies the name of the event-type dispatcher being used	Dispatcher or PinnedDispatcher or BalancingDispatcher or FQCN of a class extending MessageDispatcherConfigurator
executor	Decides what kind of Executor service to use	fork-join-executor or thread-pool-executor or FQCN of a class extending ExecutorServiceConfigurator
fork-join-executor	Section for defining the fork-join-executor parameters as defined above	
thread-pool-executor	Section for defining the thread-pool-executor parameters as defined previously	
throughput	Identifies the maximum number of messages to be processed per actor before the thread jumps to the next actor	One (to be fair for everyone)

Parameter name	Description	Potential values
mailbox-capacity (optional)	Specifies the mailbox capacity to be used for the actor queue	Negative (or zero) implies usage of an unbounded mailbox (default). A positive number implies bounded mailbox and with the specified size.
mailbox-type (optional)	Specifies the mailbox type to be used	Bounded or unbounded mailbox used if nothing is specified (dependent on mailbox capacity) or FQCN of the mailbox implementation (for example, priority mailbox implementations if defined, need to be specified here)

The sample `Dispatcher` parameter's definition in `application.conf` looks something like the following code snippet:

```
my-dispatcher {
    type = Dispatcher
    executor = "fork-join-executor"
    fork-join-executor {
      parallelism-min = 2
      parallelism-factor = 2.0
      parallelism-max = 10
    }
    throughput = 100
    mailbox-capacity = -1
    mailbox-type =""
}
```

Or another example can be the `PinnedDispatcher` parameter's definition along with the `thread-pool-executor` parameter as follows:

```
my-dispatcher {
    type = PinnedDispatcher

    executor = "thread-pool-executor"
    thread-pool-executor {
      core-pool-size-min = 2
      core-pool-size-factor = 2.0
      core-pool-size-max = 10
    }
    throughput = 100

    mailbox-capacity = -1

    mailbox-type =""
}
```

We define the dispatcher identifier that will be used to inform the underlying actors about the dispatcher policy to be used. Next we define the type of the dispatcher being used, executor policy being used, the parameters required for the executor policy, and the `throughput` parameter. In case we are using a bounded mailbox, we will define the mailbox size. When using custom-defined mailboxes, we will specify the FQCN of the mailbox class.

The following are the key parameters for your application performance:

- **Choice of dispatcher**: Based on the type of activity being performed by your actor, the right dispatcher needs to be selected. Look at parameters such as blocking versus non-blocking operations, homogeneity versus heterogeneity of actors, to determine the right choice of dispatcher.

- **Choice of executor**: Choosing between thread pool or fork join depends upon the characteristics of your application logic. The choice of executor comes into play in the case of default dispatcher and balancing dispatcher. For most cases, fork join is excellent when large numbers of tasks can be forked (started).

- **Number of threads (min/max) factored to the CPU cores**: The number of min/max threads that are deployed for the dispatcher and mapped to the underlying cores determine the processing power of the application. Define it too high and threads might end up doing a lot of context switching; define too low and the processing power is not fully optimized.

- **Throughput factor**: This determines the number of messages that are processed by one actor as a batch or in one go. For example, if the throughput is 50, then the actor will process 50 messages (if available in the queue) before returning the thread to the pool. On the flip side, other actors will wait for the thread (using the same dispatcher) to be available before they begin to process their set of messages. The optimal value depends upon the processing time taken by your message.

Once the dispatcher configuration has been defined in `application.conf`, the application needs to specify which dispatcher policy is used for which actors. Using the combination of the right type of dispatcher and supported executor, the various combinations of the dispatcher policy are realized. Remember, you can define a different dispatcher policy for a different set of actors depending upon the functionality of the actors.

Java:

```
ActorSystem _system = ActorSystem.create("dispatcher",
        ConfigFactory.load().getConfig("MyDispatcherExample"));

ActorRef actor = _system.actorOf(new Props(MsgEchoActor.class)
        .withDispatcher("my-dispatcher"));
```

Scala:

```
val _system = ActorSystem("dispatcher", ConfigFactory.load().getConfig
("MyDispatcherExample"))

val actor = _system.actorOf(Props[MsgEchoActor].withDispatcher
("my-dispatcher"))
```

When defining the actor, the `Props` class provides the `withDispatcher()` method, which is invoked by passing the string name of the dispatcher configuration defined in `application.conf`.

You can define multiple instances of an actor of the same type and pass the dispatcher policy. The dispatcher is mostly used in conjunction with the router functionality provided by Akka. We will see routers in the next section of the chapter.

Routers

In the previous section, we saw how we can use dispatchers to increase the message processing throughput by using the right dispatching policy. When a large number of actors are working in parallel to process the incoming stream of messages, there is need of an entity that directs the message from the source to the destination actor. This entity is called the **router**.

In Akka, a router is also a type of actor, which routes the incoming messages to the outbound actors. For the router, the outbound actors are also called **routees**. The router employs a different set of algorithms to route the messages to the routee actors:

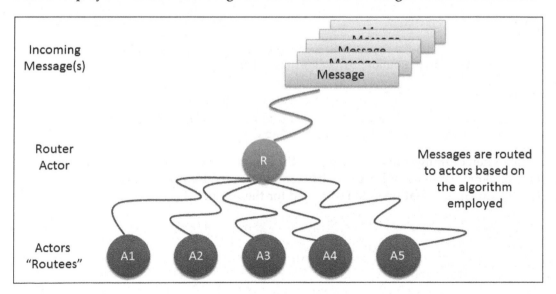

In order to avoid the single point of bottleneck, the router actors are of a special type—`RouterActorRef`. `RouterActorRef` does not make use of the store-and-forward mechanism to route the messages to it routees. Instead, routers dispatch the incoming messages directly to the routee's mailboxes and avoid the router's mailbox.

By default, the Akka router supports the following router mechanisms:

- **Round robin router**: It routes the incoming messages in a circular order to all its routees

- **Random router**: It randomly selects a routee and routes the message to the same

- **Smallest mailbox router**: It identifies the actor with the least number of messages in its mailbox and routes the message to the same

- **Broadcast router**: It forwards the same message to all the routees

- **Scatter gather first completed router**: It forwards the message to all its routees as a `future`, then whichever routee actor responds back, it takes the results and sends them back to the caller

Router usage

In order to create the router and set the number of routee actors, we need to have the following information—the router mechanism to be used and the number of instances of routee actors.

Java:

```
ActorRef router = system.actorOf(new Props(MyActor.class).
withRouter(new RoundRobinRouter(nrOfInstances)),"myRouterActor");
```

Scala:

```
val router = system.actorOf(Props[MyActor].withRouter(RoundRobinRouter
(nrOfInstances = 5)) , name = "myRouterActor")
```

Here, when defining the actor, we pass the router instance, which in this case is `RoundRobinRouter`, whose constructor takes in the number of instances (`nrOfInstances`) that need to be created for the routees.

When we defined the router actor, we provided a name—`myRouterActor`. As one actor can only have one given name within the parent context, the router actor becomes the parent (head) and the routees are the child actors spawned by the parent. The parent actor is now the supervisor for the routees (there's more on supervisors in the next chapter) and manages the lifecycle—creation, restarting, and termination—of the actors.

All of the router types are used in a similar manner; we pass the `router` object along with the necessary constructor parameters.

We will examine router-type definitions and their usage as follows:

Router type	Usage

RoundRobinRouter	**Java:**
	
	 ```ActorRef router = system.actorOf(new Props (MyActor.class).withRouter(new RoundRobinRouter (nrOfInstances)));```
	
	 Scala:
	
	 ```val router = system.actorOf(Props[MyActor]. withRouter(RoundRobinRouter(nrOfInstances = 5)))```

RandomRouter	**Java:**
	
	 ```ActorRef router = system.actorOf(new Props(MyActor.class).withRouter(new RandomRouter(nrOfInstances)));```
	
	 Scala:
	
	 ```val router = system.actorOf(Props[MyActor]. withRouter(RandomRouter(nrOfInstances = 5)))```

SmallestMailbox Router	**Java:**
	
	 ```ActorRef router = system.actorOf(new Props(MyActor. class).withRouter(new SmallestMailboxRouter (nrOfInstances)));```
	
	 Scala:
	
	 ```val router = system.actorOf(Props[MyActor]. withRouter(SmallestMailboxRouter (nrOfInstances = 5)))```

Router type	Usage

BroadcastRouter	**Java:**
	
	```\nActorRef router = system.actorOf(new Props\n(MyActor.class).withRouter(new BroadcastRouter\n(nrOfInstances)));\n```
	Scala:
	
	```\nval router = system.actorOf(Props[MyActor].\nwithRouter(BroadcastRouter (nrOfInstances = 5)))\n```

ScatterGatherFirst CompletedRouter	**Java:**
	
	```\nActorRef router = system.actorOf(new Props(MyActor.\nclass).withRouter(new ScatterGatherFirstCompletedRo\nuter(nrOfInstances, Duration.parse("5 seconds"))));\n```
	Scala:
	
	```\nval router = system.actorOf(Props[MyActor].\nwithRouter(ScatterGatherFirstCompletedRouter\n(nrOfInstances = 5, within = 5 seconds)))\n```
	In this case, in addition to the number of instances, we also pass the future duration timeout period.

Router usage via application.conf

The router for the actor can also be described using the configuration file—application.conf. In application.conf, we describe the router configuration as follows:

```
MyRouterExample{
    akka.actor.deployment {
      /myRandomRouterActor {
        router = random
        nr-of-instances = 5
      }
    }
}
```

Next, in the code, we load the application.conf file using ActorSystem.

Java:

```
ActorSystem _system = ActorSystem.create("RandomRouterExample",
        ConfigFactory.load().getConfig("MyRouterExample"));

ActorRef randomRouter = _system.actorOf(
    new Props(MsgEchoActor.class).withRouter(new FromConfig()),
"myRandomRouterActor");
```

Scala:

```
val _system = ActorSystem.create("RandomRouterExample",
ConfigFactory.load()
            .getConfig("MyRouterExample"))

val randomRouter = _system.actorOf(Props[MsgEchoActor].
withRouter(FromConfig()), name = "myRandomRouterActor")
```

When defining the router to be used, we pass on the `FromConfig()` parameter and the name of the router actor—`myRandomRouterActor`, which is used to read the `config` file settings for the router information.

Router usage for distributed actors

It is possible that we may want to make use of distributed actors and route the incoming message to them. In this case, each actor has a different address. For handling such cases, we first need to create the different `Address` objects with the remote node details and add them to an array. Subsequently the array of the addresses is passed as a parameter to the router.

Java:

```
Address addr1 = new Address("akka", "remotesys", "host1", 1234);
Address addr2 = new Address("akka", "remotesys", "host2", 1234);

Address[] addresses = new Address[] { addr1, addr2 };

ActorRef routerRemote = system.actorOf(new Props(MyEchoActor.class)
  .withRouter(new RemoteRouterConfig(new RoundRobinRouter(5),
addresses)));
```

Scala:

```
val addresses = Seq( Address("akka", "remotesys", "host1",
1234),Address("akka", "remotesys", "host2", 1234))

val routerRemote = system.actorOf(Props[MyEchoActor].withRouter(
  RemoteRouterConfig(RoundRobinRouter(5), addresses)))
```

The remote nodes' addresses can also be read via `application.conf`. So, in addition to defining the router configuration, we can also define the target nodes' address for each of the participating remote nodes:

```
akka.actor.deployment {
  /myRandomRouterActor  {
    router = round-robin
```

```
        nr-of-instances = 5
        target {
              nodes = ["akka://app@192.168.0.5:2552",
"akka://app@192.168.0.6:2552"]
            }
    }
}
```

Dynamically resizing routers

To handle the variability of the incoming message traffic, it might be important
to increase the number of actors available to handle the load at runtime. For this,
routers provide a construct called `resize`, which allows us to define the range
bound in terms of minimum and maximum instances.

Java:

```
int lowerBound = 2;
int upperBound = 15;
DefaultResizer resizer = new DefaultResizer(lowerBound, upperBound);

ActorRef randomRouter = _system.actorOf(new Props(MsgEchoActor.class).
withRouter(new RandomRouter(resizer)));
```

Scala:

```
val resizer = DefaultResizer(lowerBound = 2, upperBound = 15)

val randomRouter = system.actorOf(Props[MsgEchoActor].withRouter(
  RandomRouter (resizer = Some(resizer))))
```

The range can also be specified in `application.conf` as follows:

```
akka.actor.deployment {
  /myRandomRouterActor  {
    router = round-robin
    nr-of-instances = 5
    resizer {
      lower-bound = 2
      upper-bound = 15
    }
  }
}
```

Custom router

In case the default router types are not sufficient, Akka also allows you to write your own custom router. Akka provides the `RouterConfig` interface, which can be used to write your own router. Akka also provides the `ScatterGatherFirstCompletedLike` interface, which can be used to implement your own implementation of the scatter gather first completed router model. In our custom router, we will make use of `RouterConfig`.

Let's go ahead and create a custom router. We will create a bursty message router — meaning the router will route a predefined number of messages to one actor before moving to the next one.

If we define 10 as the message burst size and if there are five instances of actors running, then 1 to 10 messages will go to actor 1, 11 to 20 messages will go to actor 2, and so on:

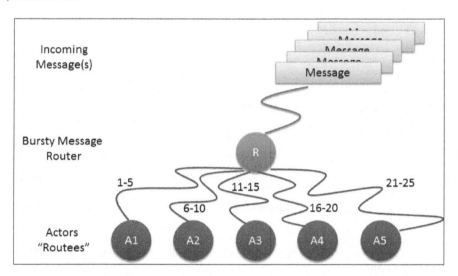

We define the `BurstyMessageRouter` class and create a constructor that takes in two parameters. First is the number of instances that needs to be created for the actor and second is the `messageBurst` rate, which identifies the number of messages that need to be passed on to one actor before moving to next.

Java:

```java
public class BurstyMessageRouter extends CustomRouterConfig {

    int noOfInstances;
    int messageBurst;
```

```java
        public BurstyMessageRouter(int inNoOfInstances, int
inMessageBurst) {
            noOfInstances = inNoOfInstances;
            messageBurst = inMessageBurst;
        }
    }
```

Scala:

```scala
    class BurstyMessageRouter(noOfInstances: Int, messageBurst: Int)
    extends RouterConfig {

    }
```

Next, we define the dispatcher and supervisor policy for the router. In our case we are using the default policies only.

Java:

```java
    public String routerDispatcher() {
        return Dispatchers.DefaultDispatcherId();
    }

    public SupervisorStrategy supervisorStrategy() {
        return SupervisorStrategy.defaultStrategy();
    }
```

Scala:

```scala
    def routerDispatcher: String = Dispatchers.DefaultDispatcherId

    def supervisorStrategy: SupervisorStrategy = SupervisorStrategy.
    defaultStrategy
```

Next is the key piece of the router, which is defining the routing mechanism of our bursty message router.

Java:

```java
    public CustomRoute createCustomRoute(Props props,
            RouteeProvider routeeProvider) {

        //create the routee actors and register with routeeprovider

        //return CustomRoute()

    }
```

Scala:

```
def createRoute(props: Props, routeeProvider: RouteeProvider):
Route = {

}
```

In this, we override the createCustomRoute() method. There are two distinct parts of this method. First, we need to create the number of instances passed for the routee actors. We create the list of routee actors and register it with routeeProvider.

Java:

```
// create the arraylist for holding the actors
final List<ActorRef> routees = new ArrayList<ActorRef>(noOfInstances);

for (int i = 0; i < noOfInstances; i++) {
        // initialize the actors and add to the arraylist
        routees.add(routeeProvider.context().actorOf(props));
}

// register the list
routeeProvider.registerRoutees(routees);
```

Scala:

```
def createRoute(props: Props, routeeProvider: RouteeProvider): Route =
{

        routeeProvider.createAndRegisterRoutees(props,
noOfInstances, Nil)


}
```

Next, we return the CustomRoute() method, which needs to be used for routing the messages to the routee actors.

Java:

```
return new CustomRoute() {
        public Iterable<Destination>
        destinationsFor(ActorRef sender,
                        Object message) {
                        //logic for routing goes here
        }
};
```

Scala:

```
{
        case (sender, message) =>
            List(Destination(sender, actor))
}
```

Here we created the `CustomRoute` class and implemented the `destinationsFor()` method, which returns the `Iterable<Destination>` object with the destination logic implemented.

Here is the complete code for `BurstyMessageRouter`, for your reference.

Java:

```java
public class BurstyMessageRouter extends CustomRouterConfig {

    int noOfInstances;
    int messageBurst;

    public BurstyMessageRouter(int inNoOfInstances,
    int inMessageBurst) {
        noOfInstances = inNoOfInstances;
        messageBurst = inMessageBurst;
    }

    public String routerDispatcher() {
        return Dispatchers.DefaultDispatcherId();
    }

    public SupervisorStrategy supervisorStrategy() {
        return SupervisorStrategy.defaultStrategy();
    }

    @Override
    public CustomRoute createCustomRoute(Props props,
            RouteeProvider routeeProvider) {

        // create the arraylist for holding the actors
        final List<ActorRef> routees =
        new ArrayList<ActorRef>(noOfInstances);
        for (int i = 0; i < noOfInstances; i++) {
            // initialize the actors and add to the arraylist
            routees.add(routeeProvider.context().actorOf(props));
        }
        // register the list
        routeeProvider.registerRoutees(routees);
```

```java
        return new CustomRoute() {
            int messageCount = 0;
            int actorSeq = 0;


            public Iterable<Destination>
            destinationsFor(ActorRef sender,
                    Object message) {
                ActorRef actor = routees.get(actorSeq);
                List<Destination> destinationList = Arrays
                        .asList(new Destination[]
                        { new Destination(sender,
                                actor) });
                //increment message count
                messageCount++;
                //check message count
                if (messageCount == messageBurst) {
                    actorSeq++;
                    //reset the counter
                    messageCount = 0;
                    //reset actorseq counter
                    if (actorSeq == noOfInstances) {
                        actorSeq = 0;
                    }
                }
                return destinationList;
            }
        };
    }
}
```

Scala:

```scala
class BurstyMessageRouter(noOfInstances: Int, messageBurst: Int)
extends RouterConfig {
    var messageCount = 0
    var actorSeq = 0

    def routerDispatcher: String = Dispatchers.DefaultDispatcherId

    def supervisorStrategy: SupervisorStrategy =
    SupervisorStrategy.defaultStrategy

    def createRoute(props: Props, routeeProvider:
    RouteeProvider): Route = {
        routeeProvider.createAndRegisterRoutees(props,
        noOfInstances, Nil)
```

```
        {
            case (sender, message) =>
                var actor = routeeProvider.routees(actorSeq)
                //increment message count
                messageCount += 1
                //check message count
                if (messageCount == messageBurst) {
                    actorSeq += 1
                    //reset the counter
                    messageCount = 0
                    //reset actorseq counter
                    if (actorSeq == noOfInstances) {
                        actorSeq = 0
                    }
                }
                List(Destination(sender, actor))
        }
    }
}
```

That's it. We have written our own custom router. We can invoke the custom router as any other router call.

Java:

```
ActorSystem _system = ActorSystem.create("CustomRouterExample");

ActorRef burstyPacketRouter = _system.actorOf(new Props(
    MsgEchoActor.class).withRouter(new BurstyMessageRouter(5,2)));
```

Scala:

```
val _system = ActorSystem.create("CustomRouterExample")

val burstyMessageRouter = _system.actorOf(Props[MsgEchoActor].
withRouter(new BurstyMessageRouter(5,2)))
```

The message burst size can be configured along with the dispatcher throughput setting to get the optimal throughput.

This brings us to the completion of the router usage within an Akka application.

Summary

We saw the role played by dispatchers and how they can be chosen and configured based on the type of application. Dispatcher's tuning will have maximum impact on the application throughput, so make sure you tune your engine to extract the maximum power. On the other hand, routers allow us to load-balance the incoming message traffic and distribute the same to the routee actors. Application scalability is achieved by using the appropriate router type. Together, dispatchers and routers are responsible for achieving the maximum throughput and scalability of the application.

In the next chapter, we will cover techniques for building fault tolerance and actor supervision strategies when writing large-scale concurrent programs. We will look at the "Let It Crash" paradigm and how it is managed in the Actor Model using the various supervision strategies.

Supervision and Monitoring

This chapter will cover fault tolerance lifecycle, supervision strategies, and linking strategies when writing large-scale concurrent programs. The reader is introduced to the "Let It Crash" paradigm and how it is managed in the Actor Model using the various supervision strategies, which are as follows:

- One-For-One strategy
- All-For-One strategy

In addition, we will cover actor state transitions that are not bound by parent-child relationship via lifecycle monitoring.

Let It Crash

When an actor crashes or throws an exception, who is responsible to catch the exception?

One way to look at it is to make sure that every actor knows how to handle failures, but then it becomes more defensive programming. The actor keeps adding code for handling various exceptions and soon, instead of lightweight units, they become large, bloated actors that do not scale very well.

What if the actors are dependent on each other? Meaning the data processing is done in a series of steps, as shown in the following image:

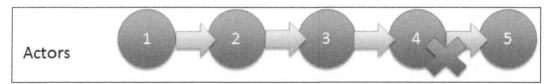

As we see in the previous image, when actor number 4 fails, the other actors may be in an unstable state and we may need to reset the state of all the actors (1-5) to process the message correctly. So, the question arises, how is the failure of one actor handled, how the other actors are made aware of the failure of one actor, and how consistent state is maintained across the actors.

To keep the actors as small computation units and still provide a mechanism to handle actor failures, Akka organizes the actors into a hierarchy model. Let's go ahead and delve into what actor hierarchy is and why it is needed.

Actor hierarchy

Actors are the computational units in their purest form. The whole design idea of the Actor Model is to break down the large task into smaller tasks to the point where the task is granular and structured enough to be performed by one specialized actor.

To manage these specialized actors, we have Supervisor actors that coordinate and manage the lifecycle of the specialized actors. As the complexity of the problem grows, the hierarchy also expands to manage the complexity. This allows the system to be as simple or as complex as required based on the tasks that need to be performed. As we see in the following image, the depth of the actor hierarchy is determined by the complexity of the problem:

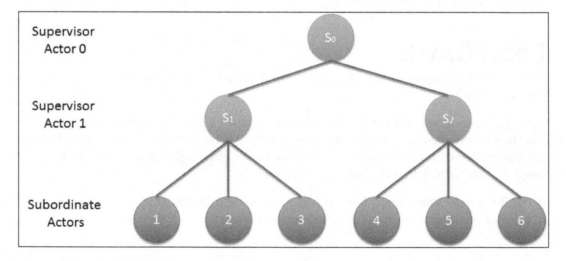

Each actor knows what kind of message it will process and how to react in terms of failure. So, if the actor does not know how to handle a particular message or an abnormal runtime behavior, it asks its supervisor for help. The recursive actor hierarchy allows the problem to be propagated upwards to the point where it can be handled. Remember, every actor in Akka will have one and only one supervisor. This actor hierarchy forms the basis of the Akka's "Let It Crash" fault-tolerance model:

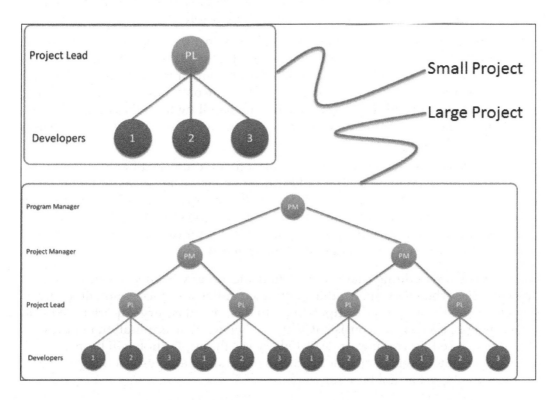

To use a simple analogy, when we have a small IT project, we usually staff the project with a couple of developers reporting to a project lead. The developers design and architect the solution components. The project lead supervises and manages the developer team. In a large program, you will have multiple teams (lead + developers) that report to a project manager, and multiple project managers will report to a program manager, and so on. So, the developers are the main computational workers (we all agree to that) and **project leads** (**PLs**) and **project managers** (**PMs**) form the supervisor hierarchy. PLs and PMs know how to manage the team and how to respond to situations.

The Akka fault-tolerance model is built upon the actor hierarchy and supervisors. Akka provides a default supervisor – "user"–under whose context all the application-specific actor hierarchy is created. The whole concept of fault tolerance is built on the following principles:

- Any actor that creates another actor becomes the parent of that actor. The parent actor is expected to know what the child actor is doing and how to handle failures or exceptions from the child actor.

- The actor hierarchy is formed in such a way that the actors at the bottom of the hierarchy are performing the computational tasks. The Supervisor actor concerns itself with the child actor's failure or exception scenarios. By splitting the computational task and failure handling, the actors become lean and focused. This separation of fault handling from the computational task, allows the Supervisor actor to retry or handle runtime failures scenarios more elegantly.

- If two actors are dependent upon each other but under different supervisors, then the dependent actor should watch the other actor's liveliness and watch out for termination notices from the other actor. This is different from supervision, as the dependent actor watching the other actor has no effect on the other actor's lifecycle. The dependent actor can only change its own behavior based on termination of the watched actor.

So, when you are building a large application, the actors will have implicit dependencies when they are handling or implementing a service, maintaining user session, or performing some computations. In this case, it is very important to have actor linkages, because for consistent state and behavior, an application requires all actors to be either running or dead. Otherwise, the application will be in an inconsistent state where some actors process or persist messages when the entire computation logic has not been finished.

Akka promotes the idea that instead of each actor trying to figure out who is alive or who is dead, let somebody else handle my failure. Inform somebody who oversees all the actors and knows how to handle failure of any actor under its hierarchy.

Remember, if you keep starting actors that are not managed, how will you ever know whether they are working or not, or how many are running. Initializing new actors blindly will soon lead to resource crunch scenarios. If you cannot control and measure something, the whole idea of somebody working for you is missing.

To help manage the fault tolerance and manage the actors, Akka provides a concept called **supervisors**.

Supervision

Supervision in simple terms means overseeing the performance or operations of a group. In our case, we are creating hundreds of actors to do work for us, it is possible that some of these actors might fail or throw exceptions in certain situations.

Supervisors provide a dependency relationship between the actors – in the sense that every actor has a supervisor attached to it. The supervisor is responsible for delegating the tasks to the actors – called **subordinates** and manage the lifecycle of the Subordinate actors. This is shown in the following image:

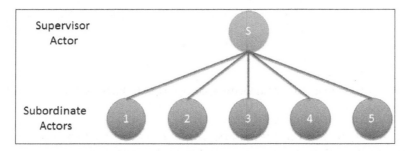

If any of the subordinates report a failure or exception, the supervisor is informed and is expected to know how to handle the failure:

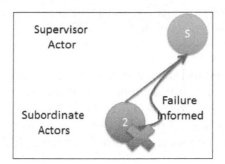

When the supervisor is informed of the failure of a Subordinate actor, the possible choices for the supervisor are as follows:

1. Restart the Subordinate actor – means kill the current actor instance and instantiate a new actor instance.

2. Resume the Subordinate actor – means the actor keeps its current state and goes back to its current state as though nothing has happened.

3. Terminate the Subordinate actor permanently.

4. Escalate the failure to its own supervisor.

These steps are shown in the following image:

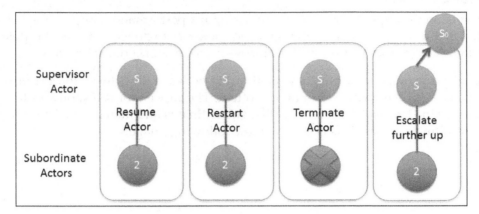

We can see how the supervisor has multiple options to handle the Subordinate actor's failure(s).

But at times, a large computation may be implemented via actors that are bound in a series of steps and all need to be restarted to make sure that they are all in a stable and consistent state:

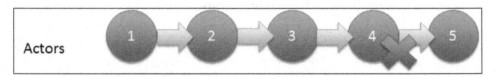

For this we need to understand that each actor is part of the overall supervision hierarchy, meaning for a Subordinate there is always a supervisor higher up. So, in this case, having a supervisor for managing these steps will automatically allow us to handle their failures. It is good practice to group actors together in a hierarchy that work together or are dependent on each other, shown as follows:

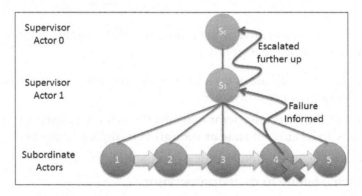

Supervisor actor 1 manages all the Subordinate actors. Supervisor actor 0 in turn manages Supervisor actor 1. When Subordinate actor 4 reports a failure, the same is reported to Supervisor actor 1. Supervisor actor 1 further escalates to Supervisor actor 0 for handling the failure. Now Supervisor actor 0 has the same choices as earlier mentioned:

1. Restart actor S1, which in turn will definitely stop all the Subordinate actors (1-5).
2. Resume actor S1, which in turn will resume actor 4.
3. Terminate actor S1, which in turn will terminate all the actors (1-5).
4. Still escalate the failure further up.

Every supervisor is capable of taking a decision to handle the failure scenarios and translate it into an action as described in the previous steps. Based on how the scenarios need to be handled, the actor-supervisor hierarchy can be suitably defined. For example, if a particular supervisor hierarchy needs to be restarted versus another supervisor hierarchy that only needs to be resumed, the super-supervisor can make an appropriate decision based on where the failure is originating. This allows us to handle failures in a recursive way and without adding additional burden on each and every actor.

Shut down of the actor system becomes very clean. Each of the actors will wait for the actors in its own hierarchy to terminate before terminating itself. Actors will be left dangling in the absence of this hierarchical process. This tree structure of the actor hierarchy provides a convenient and elegant way to organize, run, and shut down the actors:

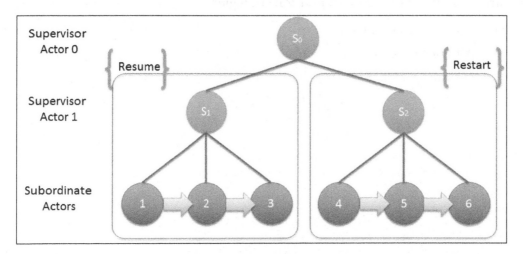

Unlike resume, where the actors go back to the current state when the failure happened, the restart of the actors is a little different. Restart of the actor means:

- All the child actors in the hierarchy will undergo the restart process. All the child actors are sent the termination request. The parent actor waits for all the child actors to stop before terminating itself.

- As part of the restart, the parent-child will be restarted, the child actors get stopped and restarted. The mailbox attached to the child actors is retained and they start processing the next message from their mailbox. If you want to destroy the child actors' mailboxes as well, then the child actors need to be terminated and recreated via the supervisor.

- In case the child actors need to carry across the initialized state, the `Actor` instance restarts. Then they need to tap into the `postStop` and `postRestart` lifecycle hooks of the actor.

Akka by default provides a parental supervisor – "user". This parental supervisor creates the rest of the actors and the actor hierarchy. Having the system define a parental supervisor makes sure there is no orphan actors and there is one top-level supervisor that handles the entire actor hierarchy. It is bad practice to create too many top-level actors, as you end up losing fine-grained control over the actor hierarchy.

Supervision strategies

We saw how every Supervisor actor has four choices when it comes to handling failures. Akka provides two supervision strategies:

- One-For-One strategy
- All-For-One strategy

Supervision strategies define how the failure of the child actors are handled, how often the child is allowed to fail, and how long to wait before the child actor is recreated. As the name suggests, One-For-One strategy means the supervision strategy is applied only to the failed child. All-For-One strategy means that the supervision strategy is applied to all the actor siblings as well:

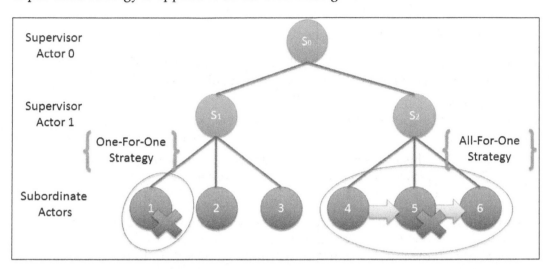

 One-For-One strategy is the default strategy if a strategy is not defined explicitly. This strategy works fine in most use cases.

All-For-One strategy is used when the actor and its children have tight inter-dependencies. For example, if you are processing stock feed data, the data processing is a series of steps, and a failure on one step leads to an inconsistency of state in the other actors. In this case, it becomes pertinent to restart all the actors to make sure that they all have a consistent state. When your actor hierarchy is using this strategy, failure of one actor will lead to the supervisor sending a command to stop and restart. But this does not mean that all the sibling actors will restart. The sibling actors will need to be restarted explicitly by the supervisor.

Akka implements the two strategies via two classes:

- `akka.actor.OneForOneStrategy`
- `akka.actor.AllForOneStrategy`

Constructing the `Strategy` object is straightforward, shown as follows:

- `OneForOneStrategy(maxNrOfRetries: int, withinTimeRange: Duration, decider: Decider)`
- `AllForOneStrategy(maxNrOfRetries: int, withinTimeRange: Duration, decider: Decider)`

It takes in the following three arguments:

- `maxNrOfRetries`: This defines the number of times an actor is allowed to be restarted before it is assumed to be dead. A negative number implies no limits.
- `withinTimeRange`: This defines the duration of the time window for `maxNrOfRetries`. The value – `Duration.Inf` means no window defined.
- `decider`: This is the function defined where the `Throwable` are mapped to the directives that allow us to specify the actions – `resume()`, `restart()`, `stop()`, or `escalate()`.

Ideally, you should not define a large number for maximum number of retries (`maxNrOfRetries`) within a given time range (`withinTimeRange`). If the actor is encountering a large number of retries very rapidly, then it could point towards a problem in the logic or the external resource not being available. For example, if the socket connection is not opening, then trying again and again within the time period may not help, and we may need to handle the socket unavailable condition differently. The whole idea behind limiting `maxNrOfRetries` is to prevent a situation where an actor repeatedly dies for the same reason, only to be restarted again.

Let's go ahead and see examples of both the strategies to understand how the supervision works.

One-For-One strategy

Let's take the previous example and see how we can implement the same. The
One-For-One strategy implies that in case of failure of any one actor under the
supervisor, the strategy will apply to that actor alone. Meaning, if a Supervisor
actor is managing actor 1 and actor 2 and employing the One-For-One strategy,
then failure of actor 1 will have no impact on the lifecycle of actor 2, and vice versa:

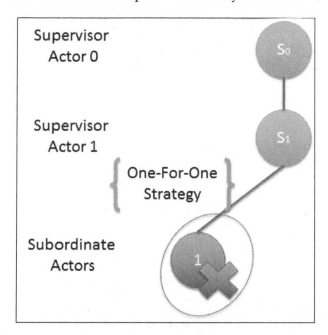

Let's implement the actors and see how the supervisor strategy works. Let's start
with `WorkerActor`.

Java:

```java
public class WorkerActor extends UntypedActor {
    LoggingAdapter log = Logging.getLogger(
                        getContext().system(), this);
    private int state = 0;
    public static class Result {}
```

```java
    @Override
    public void preStart() {
        log.info("Starting WorkerActor instance hashcode # {}",
            this.hashCode());
    }

    public void onReceive(Object o) throws Exception {
        if (o == null) {
            throw new NullPointerException("Null Value Passed");
        } else if (o instanceof Integer) {
            Integer value = (Integer) o;
            if (value <= 0) {
                throw new ArithmeticException("Number equal or
                                        less than zero");
            } else
                state = value;
        } else if (o instanceof Result) {
            getSender().tell(state);
        } else {
            throw new IllegalArgumentException("Wrong
            Argument");
        }
    }

    @Override
    public void postStop() {
        log.info("Stopping WorkerActor instance hashcode # {}",
            this.hashCode());
    }
}
```

Scala:

```scala
case class Result
class WorkerActor extends Actor with ActorLogging {
  var state: Int = 0

  override def preStart() {
    log.info("Starting WorkerActor instance hashcode # {}",
            this.hashCode())
  }
  override def postStop() {
    log.info("Stopping WorkerActor instance hashcode # {}",
            this.hashCode())
  }
```

```scala
def receive: Receive = {
  case value: Int =>
    if (value <= 0)
      throw new ArithmeticException("Number equal or less
                                    than zero")
    else
      state = value
  case result: Result =>
    sender ! state
  case ex: NullPointerException =>
    throw new NullPointerException("Null Value Passed")
  case _ =>
    throw new IllegalArgumentException("Wrong Argument")
}
}
```

If we see the code for `WorkerActor`, we have created an actor that holds its state using the `int state` variable.

Java:

```java
public class WorkerActor extends UntypedActor {
    private int state = 0;
}
```

Scala:

```scala
class WorkerActor extends Actor with ActorLogging {
      var state: Int = 0
}
```

We have overloaded `preStart()` and `postStop()` in order to keep track of when the actor is getting created or destroyed.

In the `OnReceive()` method, we implement the following checks:

- Check whether the message is not NULL, if yes, then throw a `NullPointerException ()`
- If the message is of type integer but its value is less than or equal to zero, we throw `ArithmeticException()`
- If the message is of instance `Result()`, then we return the current state of the actor
- Any other message sent is responded back with `IllegalArgumentException()`

Java:

```java
public void onReceive(Object o) throws Exception {
    if (o == null) {
        throw new NullPointerException("Null Value Passed");
    } else if (o instanceof Integer) {
        Integer value = (Integer) o;
        if (value <= 0) {
            throw new ArithmeticException("Number equal or
                                    less than zero");
        } else
            state = value;
    } else if (o instanceof Result) {
        getSender().tell(state);
    } else {
        throw new IllegalArgumentException("Wrong
        Argument");
    }
}
```

Scala:

```scala
def receive: Receive = {
  case value: Int =>
    if (value <= 0)
      throw new ArithmeticException("Number equal or less
                                than zero")
    else
      state = value
  case result: Result =>
    sender ! state
  case ex: NullPointerException =>
    throw new NullPointerException("Null Value Passed")
  case _ =>
    throw new IllegalArgumentException("Wrong Argument")
}
```

Next, let's move to the `SupervisorActor`. `SupervisorActor` will be the parent of the `WorkerActor` and also implement the `SupervisorStrategy`.

Java:

```java
public class SupervisorActor extends UntypedActor {

    private ActorRef childActor;
```

```java
        public SupervisorActor() {
                childActor = getContext().actorOf(new Props(WorkerActor.
    class),
                        "workerActor");
        }

        private static SupervisorStrategy strategy =
            new OneForOneStrategy(10,Duration.parse("10 second"),
            new Function<Throwable, Directive>() {
                        public Directive apply(Throwable t) {
                                if (t instanceof ArithmeticException) {
                                        return resume();
                                } else if (t instanceof
    NullPointerException) {
                                        return restart();
                                } else if (t instanceof
    IllegalArgumentException) {
                                        return stop();
                                } else {
                                        return escalate();
                                }
                        }
                });

        @Override
        public SupervisorStrategy supervisorStrategy() {
                return strategy;
        }

        public void onReceive(Object o) throws Exception {
                if (o instanceof Result) {
                        childActor.tell(o, getSender());
                } else
                        childActor.tell(o);
        }
}
```

Scala:

```scala
    class SupervisorActor extends Actor with ActorLogging {


      val childActor = context.actorOf(Props[WorkerActor],
                                  name = "workerActor")
```

```
    override val supervisorStrategy = OneForOneStrategy(
            maxNrOfRetries = 10, withinTimeRange = 10 seconds) {

      case _: ArithmeticException => Resume
      case _: NullPointerException => Restart
      case _: IllegalArgumentException => Stop
      case _: Exception => Escalate
    }
    def receive = {
      case result: Result =>
        childActor.tell(result, sender)
      case msg: Object =>
        childActor ! msg
    }
  }
```

We create the `SupervisorActor` and it holds the reference to the `WorkerActor`. We create the `WorkerActor` as part of the `Supervisor` constructor.

Java:

```java
public class SupervisorActor extends UntypedActor {

    private ActorRef childActor;

    public SupervisorActor() {
            childActor = getContext().actorOf(new Props(WorkerActor.
class),
                        "workerActor");
    }
}
```

Scala:

```scala
class SupervisorActor extends Actor with ActorLogging {

    val childActor = context.actorOf(Props[WorkerActor],
                            name = "workerActor")

}
```

Next, we define the `SupervisorStrategy` that will be applicable for supervising the `WorkerActor`.

Java:

```java
private static SupervisorStrategy strategy =
    new OneForOneStrategy(10,Duration.parse("10 second"),
    new Function<Throwable, Directive>() {
                public Directive apply(Throwable t) {
                        if (t instanceof ArithmeticException) {
                                return resume();
                        } else if (t instanceof
NullPointerException) {
                                return restart();
                        } else if (t instanceof
IllegalArgumentException) {
                                return stop();
                        } else {
                                return escalate();
                        }
                }
        });

    @Override
    public SupervisorStrategy supervisorStrategy() {
        return strategy;
    }
```

Scala:

```scala
override val supervisorStrategy = OneForOneStrategy(
        maxNrOfRetries = 10, withinTimeRange = 10 seconds) {

  case _: ArithmeticException => Resume
  case _: NullPointerException => Restart
  case _: IllegalArgumentException => Stop
  case _: Exception => Escalate
}
```

Let's examine the key components of the SupervisorStrategy. The first two arguments define the maximum number of tries and time limit within which the maximum number of tries are valid. For our SupervisorStrategy, the third argument is important. Let's examine the decider for more details.

Java:

```java
public Directive apply(Throwable t) {
        if (t instanceof ArithmeticException) {
            return resume();
        } else if (t instanceof NullPointerException) {
            return restart();
        } else if (t instanceof IllegalArgumentException) {
            return stop();
        } else {
            return escalate();
        }
}
```

Scala:

```scala
case _: ArithmeticException => Resume
case _: NullPointerException => Restart
case _: IllegalArgumentException => Stop
case _: Exception => Escalate
```

What we have done for each of the exceptions we have identified, we have mapped the strategy for the actor. For example, if the actor throws ArithmeticException(), our SupervisorStrategy is to resume() the processing as though nothing has happened. In case IllegalArgumentException() is thrown, our strategy is to stop() the actor, so that it can process no messages.

So, we have created WorkerActor and SupervisorActor, let's see how the whole thing works. Let's put together ActorSystem and see SupervisorStrategy working. Let's pass the messages and see what is displayed on the console.

Java:

```java
ActorSystem system = ActorSystem.create("faultTolerance");

LoggingAdapter log = Logging.getLogger(system, system);

Integer originalValue = Integer.valueOf(0);

ActorRef supervisor = system.actorOf(new
        Props(SupervisorActor.class),    "supervisor");
```

```
log.info("Sending value 8, no exceptions should be thrown! ");
supervisor.tell(Integer.valueOf(8));

Integer result = (Integer) Await.result(
        Patterns.ask(supervisor, new Result(), 5000),
        Duration.create(5000, TimeUnit.MILLISECONDS));

log.info("Value Received-> {}", result);
```

Scala:

```
val system = ActorSystem("faultTolerance")
val log = system.log
val originalValue: Int = 0

val supervisor = system.actorOf(Props[SupervisorActor],
                    name = "supervisor")

log.info("Sending value 8, no exceptions should be thrown! ")
var mesg: Int = 8
supervisor ! mesg

implicit val timeout = Timeout(5 seconds)
var future = (supervisor ? new Result).mapTo[Int]
var result = Await.result(future, timeout.duration)

log.info("Value Received-> {}", result)
```

The output on console is as follows:

```
[INFO] [09/22/2012 08:19:30.12] [main] [ActorSystemImpl(akka://faultTolerance)]
Sending value 8, no exceptions should be thrown!
[INFO] [09/22/2012 08:19:30.287] [faultTolerance-akka.actor.default-dispatcher-2]
[akka://faultTolerance/user/supervisor/workerActor] Starting WorkerActor instance
hashcode # 32959941
[INFO] [09/22/2012 08:19:30.339] [main] [ActorSystemImpl(akka://faultTolerance)]
Value Received-> 8
```

We create an instance of Supervisor actor, in whose constructor WorkerActor gets instantiated. On the console we can see the preStart() method of the WorkerActor indicating the start of the WorkerActor instance.

We pass on the Integer value of 8, which is then passed on to the WorkerActor. The Integer value is correct and is set as the state of the actor.

Next, we get the state of WorkerActor by sending the message Result() and asking for the result.

As we can see, the result returned is 8.

Next, lets try sending a negative value for which our WorkerActor should throw an exception – ArithmeticException().

Java:

```
log.info("Sending value -8, ArithmeticException should be thrown!
        Our Supervisor strategy says resume !");
supervisor.tell(Integer.valueOf(-8));

result = (Integer) Await.result(
            Patterns.ask(supervisor, new Result(), 5000),
            Duration.create(5000, TimeUnit.MILLISECONDS));

log.info("Value Received-> {}", result);
```

Scala:

```
log.info("Sending value -8, ArithmeticException should be thrown!
        Our Supervisor strategy says resume!")
mesg = -8
supervisor ! mesg

future = (supervisor ? new Result).mapTo[Int]
result = Await.result(future, timeout.duration)

log.info("Value Received-> {}", result)
```

The output on console is as follows:

```
[INFO] [09/22/2012 08:19:30.339] [main] [ActorSystemImpl(akka://faultTolerance)]
Sending value -8, ArithmeticException should be thrown! Our Supervisor strategy
says resume !
[ERROR] [09/22/2012 08:19:30.340] [faultTolerance-akka.actor.default-dispatcher-3]
[akka://faultTolerance/user/supervisor/workerActor] Number equal or less than zero
java.lang.ArithmeticException: Number equal or less than zero
        at org.akka.essentials.supervisor.example1.WorkerActor.onReceive
(WorkerActor.java:24)
        at akka.actor.UntypedActor$$anonfun$receive$1.apply(UntypedActor.scala:154)
        at akka.actor.UntypedActor$$anonfun$receive$1.apply(UntypedActor.scala:153)
        at akka.actor.Actor$class.apply(Actor.scala:290)
        at akka.actor.UntypedActor.apply(UntypedActor.scala:93)
        at akka.actor.ActorCell.invoke(ActorCell.scala:617)
        at akka.dispatch.Mailbox.processMailbox(Mailbox.scala:179)
        at akka.dispatch.Mailbox.run(Mailbox.scala:161)
        at akka.dispatch.ForkJoinExecutorConfigurator$MailboxExecutionTask.exec
(AbstractDispatcher.scala:505)
        at akka.jsr166y.ForkJoinTask.doExec(ForkJoinTask.java:259)
        at akka.jsr166y.ForkJoinPool$WorkQueue.runTask(ForkJoinPool.java:997)
        at akka.jsr166y.ForkJoinPool.runWorker(ForkJoinPool.java:1495)
        at akka.jsr166y.ForkJoinWorkerThread.run(ForkJoinWorkerThread.java:104)

[INFO] [09/22/2012 08:19:30.496] [main] [ActorSystemImpl(akka://faultTolerance)]
Value Received-> 8
```

We send the message with the value -8, and as expected the WorkerActor throws the exception – ArithmeticException. Now, our SupervisorStrategy for handling ArithmeticException was resume(), which means the actor can continue with its current state.

Next, we get the state of WorkerActor by sending the message Result() and asking for the result.

As we can see the result returned is 8, which is consistent because we asked the Actor to resume. As a result, the previous state of WorkerActor should be retained.

Java:

```
log.info("Sending value null, NullPointerException should be thrown!
        Our Supervisor strategy says restart !");
supervisor.tell(null);

result = (Integer) Await.result(
        Patterns.ask(supervisor, new Result(), 5000),
        Duration.create(5000, TimeUnit.MILLISECONDS));

log.info("Value Received-> {}", result);
```

Scala:

```
log.info("Sending value null, NullPointerException should be thrown!
        Our Supervisor strategy says restart !")
supervisor ! new NullPointerException

future = (supervisor ? new Result).mapTo[Int]
result = Await.result(future, timeout.duration)

log.info("Value Received-> {}", result)
```

The output on console is as follows:

```
[INFO] [09/22/2012 08:19:30.496] [main] [ActorSystemImpl(akka://faultTolerance)]
Sending value null, NullPointerException should be thrown! Our Supervisor strategy
says restart !
[ERROR] [09/22/2012 08:19:30.496] [faultTolerance-akka.actor.default-dispatcher-2]
[akka://faultTolerance/user/supervisor/workerActor] Null value Passed
java.lang.NullPointerException: Null value Passed
        at org.akka.essentials.supervisor.example1.WorkerActor.onReceive
(WorkerActor.java:20)
        at akka.actor.UntypedActor$$anonfun$receive$1.apply(UntypedActor.scala:154)
        at akka.actor.UntypedActor$$anonfun$receive$1.apply(UntypedActor.scala:153)
        at akka.actor.Actor$class.apply(Actor.scala:290)
        at akka.actor.UntypedActor.apply(UntypedActor.scala:93)
        at akka.actor.ActorCell.invoke(ActorCell.scala:617)
        at akka.dispatch.Mailbox.processMailbox(Mailbox.scala:179)
        at akka.dispatch.Mailbox.run(Mailbox.scala:161)
        at akka.dispatch.ForkJoinExecutorConfigurator$MailboxExecutionTask.exec
(AbstractDispatcher.scala:505)
        at akka.jsr166y.ForkJoinTask.doExec(ForkJoinTask.java:259)
        at akka.jsr166y.ForkJoinPool$WorkQueue.runTask(ForkJoinPool.java:997)
        at akka.jsr166y.ForkJoinPool.runWorker(ForkJoinPool.java:1495)
        at akka.jsr166y.ForkJoinWorkerThread.run(ForkJoinWorkerThread.java:104)

[INFO] [09/22/2012 08:19:30.497] [faultTolerance-akka.actor.default-dispatcher-2]
[akka://faultTolerance/user/supervisor/workerActor] Stopping WorkerActor instance
hashcode # 32959941
[INFO] [09/22/2012 08:19:30.497] [faultTolerance-akka.actor.default-dispatcher-2]
[akka://faultTolerance/user/supervisor/workerActor] Starting WorkerActor instance
hashcode # 8652307
[INFO] [09/22/2012 08:19:30.497] [main] [ActorSystemImpl(akka://faultTolerance)]
Value Received-> 0
```

Next, we try sending a null object to `WorkerActor`. `WorkerActor` will throw a `NullPointerException` when the passed message is null.

The `SupervisorStrategy` configured for `NullPointerException` is to restart. We can see that `WorkerActor` is stopped and restarted.

Next, we get the state of `WorkerActor` by sending the message `Result()` and asking for the result.

As we can see the result returned is `0`, which is the original default state value of `WorkerActor` because we asked the actor to restart.

Java:

```
log.info("Sending value \"String\", IllegalArgumentException should be
thrown! Our Supervisor strategy says Stop !");

supervisor.tell(String.valueOf("Do Something"));
```

Scala:

```
log.info("Sending value \"String\", IllegalArgumentException should be
thrown! Our Supervisor strategy says Stop !")

supervisor ? "Do Something"
```

The output on console is as follows:

```
[INFO] [09/22/2012 08:19:30.497] [main] [ActorSystemImpl(akka://faultTolerance)]
Sending value "String", NullPointerException should be thrown! Our Supervisor
strategy says Stop !
[INFO] [09/22/2012 08:19:30.497] [main] [ActorSystemImpl(akka://faultTolerance)]
Worker Actor shutdown !
[ERROR] [09/22/2012 08:19:30.498] [faultTolerance-akka.actor.default-dispatcher-2]
[akka://faultTolerance/user/supervisor/workerActor] Wrong Argument
java.lang.IllegalArgumentException: Wrong Argument
        at org.akka.essentials.supervisor.example1.workerActor.onReceive
(WorkerActor.java:30)
        at akka.actor.UntypedActor$$anonfun$receive$1.apply(UntypedActor.scala:154)
        at akka.actor.UntypedActor$$anonfun$receive$1.apply(UntypedActor.scala:153)
        at akka.actor.Actor$class.apply(Actor.scala:290)
        at akka.actor.UntypedActor.apply(UntypedActor.scala:93)
        at akka.actor.ActorCell.invoke(ActorCell.scala:617)
        at akka.dispatch.Mailbox.processMailbox(Mailbox.scala:179)
        at akka.dispatch.Mailbox.run(Mailbox.scala:161)
        at akka.dispatch.ForkJoinExecutorConfigurator$MailboxExecutionTask.exec
(AbstractDispatcher.scala:505)
        at akka.jsr166y.ForkJoinTask.doExec(ForkJoinTask.java:259)
        at akka.jsr166y.ForkJoinPool$WorkQueue.runTask(ForkJoinPool.java:997)
        at akka.jsr166y.ForkJoinPool.runWorker(ForkJoinPool.java:1495)
        at akka.jsr166y.ForkJoinWorkerThread.run(ForkJoinWorkerThread.java:104)

[INFO] [09/22/2012 08:19:30.498] [faultTolerance-akka.actor.default-dispatcher-2]
[akka://faultTolerance/user/supervisor/workerActor] Stopping WorkerActor instance
hashcode # 8652307
```

Next, we try sending an invalid message object to `WorkerActor`. `WorkerActor` will throw an `IllegalArgumentException` when the passed message is invalid or not recognized.

The `SupervisorStrategy` configured for `IllegalArgumentException` is to stop. We can see that `WorkerActor` is stopped.

This completes the example. We saw how the supervisor handles the actor's failure and how the supervisor can take the right calls to deal with those failures.

All-For-One strategy

The **All-For-One** strategy implies that in case of failure of any one actor under the supervisor, the strategy will apply to all the actors under its supervision. Meaning, if we as `SupervisorActor` are managing actor 1 and actor 2 and employing the All-For-One strategy, then the supervisor strategy will be applicable to both actor 1 and actor 2:

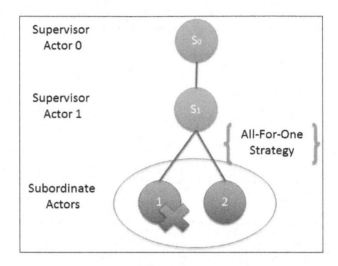

This example is similar to the example we saw in the One-For-One strategy, except that `SupervisorActor` here manages two actors – `WorkerActor1` and `WorkerActor2`.

Java:

```
public class SupervisorActor2 extends UntypedActor {

    public ActorRef workerActor1;
    public ActorRef workerActor2;

    public SupervisorActor2() {
        workerActor1 = getContext().actorOf(
            new Props(WorkerActor1.class),"workerActor1");
        workerActor2 = getContext().actorOf(
            new Props(WorkerActor2.class),"workerActor2");
    }
```

```java
    private static SupervisorStrategy strategy =
        new AllForOneStrategy(10,
            Duration.parse("10 second"),
        new Function<Throwable, Directive>() {
                public Directive apply(Throwable t) {
                        if (t instanceof ArithmeticException) {
                                return resume();
                        } else if (t instanceof
NullPointerException) {

                                return restart();
                        } else if (t instanceof
IllegalArgumentException) {

                                return stop();
                        } else {
                                return escalate();
                        }
                }
        });

    @Override
    public SupervisorStrategy supervisorStrategy() {
        return strategy;
    }

    public void onReceive(Object msg) throws Exception {
        if (msg instanceof Result) {
                workerActor1.tell(msg, getSender());
        } else
                workerActor1.tell(msg);
    }
}
```

Scala:

```scala
class SupervisorActor extends Actor with ActorLogging {
  import akka.actor.OneForOneStrategy
  import akka.actor.SupervisorStrategy._
  import akka.util.duration._
  import org.akka.essentials.supervisor.example2.Result

  val workerActor1 = context.actorOf(Props[WorkerActor1],
                    name = "workerActor1")
  val workerActor2 = context.actorOf(Props[WorkerActor2],
                    name = "workerActor2")

  override val supervisorStrategy = AllForOneStrategy(
        maxNrOfRetries = 10, withinTimeRange = 10 seconds) {
```

```
    case _: ArithmeticException => Resume
    case _: NullPointerException => Restart
    case _: IllegalArgumentException => Stop
    case _: Exception => Escalate
  }

def receive = {
  case result: Result =>
    workerActor1.tell(result, sender)
  case msg: Object =>
    workerActor1 ! msg

  }
}
```

The Worker actors are similar to each other. The key difference in SupervisorActor is SupervisorStrategy.

Java:

```
private static SupervisorStrategy strategy =
        new AllForOneStrategy(10,
              Duration.parse("10 second"),
        new Function<Throwable, Directive>() {
                      public Directive apply(Throwable t) {
                              if (t instanceof ArithmeticException) {
                                      return resume();
                              } else if (t instanceof
NullPointerException) {
                                      return restart();
                              } else if (t instanceof
IllegalArgumentException) {
                                      return stop();
                              } else {
                                      return escalate();
                              }
                      }
              });

@Override
public SupervisorStrategy supervisorStrategy() {
        return strategy;
}
```

Scala:

```scala
override val supervisorStrategy = AllForOneStrategy(
    maxNrOfRetries = 10, withinTimeRange = 10 seconds) {

  case _: ArithmeticException => Resume
  case _: NullPointerException => Restart
  case _: IllegalArgumentException => Stop
  case _: Exception => Escalate
}
```

Here we define AllForOneStrategy() with similar arguments as defined in the previous one.

Let's put together ActorSystem and see SupervisorStrategy working. Let's pass the messages and see what is displayed on the console.

Java:

```java
ActorSystem system = ActorSystem.create("faultTolerance");

LoggingAdapter log = Logging.getLogger(system, system);

Integer originalValue = Integer.valueOf(0);

ActorRef supervisor = system.actorOf(
    new Props(SupervisorActor2.class),"supervisor");

log.info("Sending value 8, no exceptions should be thrown! ");
supervisor.tell(Integer.valueOf(8));

Integer result = (Integer) Await.result(
        Patterns.ask(supervisor, new Result(), 5000),
        Duration.create(5000, TimeUnit.MILLISECONDS));

log.info("Value Received-> {}", result);
```

Scala:

```scala
val system = ActorSystem("faultTolerance")
val log = system.log
val originalValue: Int = 0

val supervisor = system.actorOf(Props[SupervisorActor],
                name = "supervisor")
```

```
log.info("Sending value 8, no exceptions should be thrown! ")
var mesg: Int = 8
supervisor ! mesg

implicit val timeout = Timeout(5 seconds)
var future = (supervisor ? new Result).mapTo[Int]
var result = Await.result(future, timeout.duration)

log.info("Value Received-> {}", result)
```

The output on console is as follows:

```
[INFO] [09/22/2012 08:28:03.994] [main] [ActorSystemImpl(akka://faultTolerance)]
Sending value 8, no exceptions should be thrown!
[INFO] [09/22/2012 08:28:04.164] [faultTolerance-akka.actor.default-dispatcher-1]
[akka://faultTolerance/user/supervisor/workerActor1] Starting WorkerActor1 instance
hashcode # 2322880
[INFO] [09/22/2012 08:28:04.191] [faultTolerance-akka.actor.default-dispatcher-2]
[akka://faultTolerance/user/supervisor/workerActor2] Starting WorkerActor2 instance
hashcode # 8169880
[INFO] [09/22/2012 08:28:04.192] [main] [ActorSystemImpl(akka://faultTolerance)]
Value Received-> 8
```

We create an instance of `ActorSupervisor`, in whose constructor `WorkerActor1` and `WorkerActor2` gets instantiated. On the console we can see the `preStart()` method of `WorkerActor1` and `WorkerActor2` indicating the start of the `WorkerActor` instance.

We pass on the `Integer` value of 8, which is then passed on to `WorkerActor1`. The `Integer` value is correct and is set as the state of the actor.

Next, we get the state of `WorkerActor1` by sending the message `Result()` and asking for the result.

As we can see the result returned is 8.

Next, let's try sending a negative value for which our `WorkerActor1` should throw an exception – `ArithmeticException()`.

Java:

```
log.info("Sending value -8, ArithmeticException should be thrown!
        Our Supervisor strategy says resume !");
supervisor.tell(Integer.valueOf(-8));

result = (Integer) Await.result(
        Patterns.ask(supervisor, new Result(), 5000),
        Duration.create(5000, TimeUnit.MILLISECONDS));
```

```
log.info("Value Received-> {}", result);
```

Scala:

```
log.info("Sending value -8, ArithmeticException should be thrown!
         Our Supervisor strategy says resume !")
mesg = -8
supervisor ! mesg

future = (supervisor ? new Result).mapTo[Int]
result = Await.result(future, timeout.duration)

log.info("Value Received-> {}", result)
```

The output on console is as follows:

```
[INFO] [09/22/2012 08:28:04.193] [main] [ActorSystemImpl(akka://faultTolerance)]
Sending value -8, ArithmeticException should be thrown! Our Supervisor strategy
says resume !
[ERROR] [09/22/2012 08:28:04.195] [faultTolerance-akka.actor.default-dispatcher-3]
[akka://faultTolerance/user/supervisor/workerActor1] Number equal or less than zero
java.lang.ArithmeticException: Number equal or less than zero
        at org.akka.essentials.supervisor.example2.WorkerActor1.onReceive
(WorkerActor1.java:25)
        at akka.actor.UntypedActor$$anonfun$receive$1.apply(UntypedActor.scala:154)
        at akka.actor.UntypedActor$$anonfun$receive$1.apply(UntypedActor.scala:153)
        at akka.actor.Actor$class.apply(Actor.scala:290)
        at akka.actor.UntypedActor.apply(UntypedActor.scala:93)
        at akka.actor.ActorCell.invoke(ActorCell.scala:617)
        at akka.dispatch.Mailbox.processMailbox(Mailbox.scala:179)
        at akka.dispatch.Mailbox.run(Mailbox.scala:161)
        at akka.dispatch.ForkJoinExecutorConfigurator$MailboxExecutionTask.exec
(AbstractDispatcher.scala:505)
        at akka.jsr166y.ForkJoinTask.doExec(ForkJoinTask.java:259)
        at akka.jsr166y.ForkJoinPool$WorkQueue.runTask(ForkJoinPool.java:997)
        at akka.jsr166y.ForkJoinPool.runWorker(ForkJoinPool.java:1495)
        at akka.jsr166y.ForkJoinWorkerThread.run(ForkJoinWorkerThread.java:104)

[INFO] [09/22/2012 08:28:04.305] [main] [ActorSystemImpl(akka://faultTolerance)]
Value Received-> 8
```

We send the message with the value -8, as expected WorkerActor throws the exception – ArithmeticException. Now, our SupervisorStrategy for handling ArithmeticException was resume(), which means the actor can continue with its current state.

Next, we get the state of WorkerActor by sending the message Result() and asking for the result.

As we can see the result returned is 8, which is consistent because we asked the actor to resume. As a result, the previous state of WorkerActor should be retained.

Java:

```
log.info("Sending value null, NullPointerException should be thrown!
        Our Supervisor strategy says restart !");
supervisor.tell(null);

result = (Integer) Await.result(
    Patterns.ask(supervisor, new Result(), 5000),
    Duration.create(5000, TimeUnit.MILLISECONDS));

log.info("Value Received-> {}", result);
```

Scala:

```
log.info("Sending value null, NullPointerException should be thrown!
Our Supervisor strategy says restart !")
supervisor ! new NullPointerException

future = (supervisor ? new Result).mapTo[Int]
result = Await.result(future, timeout.duration)

log.info("Value Received-> {}", result)
```

The output on console is as follows:

```
[INFO] [09/22/2012 08:28:04.306] [main] [ActorSystemImpl(akka://faultTolerance)]
Sending value null, NullPointerException should be thrown! Our Supervisor strategy
says restart !
[ERROR] [09/22/2012 08:28:04.306] [faultTolerance-akka.actor.default-dispatcher-3]
[akka://faultTolerance/user/supervisor/workerActor1] Null Value Passed
java.lang.NullPointerException: Null Value Passed
        at org.akka.essentials.supervisor.example2.WorkerActor1.onReceive
(WorkerActor1.java:21)
        at akka.actor.UntypedActor$$anonfun$receive$1.apply(UntypedActor.scala:154)
        at akka.actor.UntypedActor$$anonfun$receive$1.apply(UntypedActor.scala:153)
        at akka.actor.Actor$class.apply(Actor.scala:290)
        at akka.actor.UntypedActor.apply(UntypedActor.scala:93)
        at akka.actor.ActorCell.invoke(ActorCell.scala:617)
        at akka.dispatch.Mailbox.processMailbox(Mailbox.scala:179)
        at akka.dispatch.Mailbox.run(Mailbox.scala:161)
        at akka.dispatch.ForkJoinExecutorConfigurator$MailboxExecutionTask.exec
(AbstractDispatcher.scala:505)
        at akka.jsr166y.ForkJoinTask.doExec(ForkJoinTask.java:259)
        at akka.jsr166y.ForkJoinPool$WorkQueue.runTask(ForkJoinPool.java:997)
        at akka.jsr166y.ForkJoinPool.runWorker(ForkJoinPool.java:1495)
        at akka.jsr166y.ForkJoinWorkerThread.run(ForkJoinWorkerThread.java:104)

[INFO] [09/22/2012 08:28:04.613] [faultTolerance-akka.actor.default-dispatcher-3]
[akka://faultTolerance/user/supervisor/workerActor1] Stopping workerActor1 instance
hashcode # 2322880
[INFO] [09/22/2012 08:28:04.613] [faultTolerance-akka.actor.default-dispatcher-6]
[akka://faultTolerance/user/supervisor/workerActor2] Stopping workerActor2 instance
hashcode # 8169880
[INFO] [09/22/2012 08:28:04.660] [faultTolerance-akka.actor.default-dispatcher-6]
[akka://faultTolerance/user/supervisor/workerActor2] Starting workerActor2 instance
hashcode # 26807853
[INFO] [09/22/2012 08:28:04.664] [faultTolerance-akka.actor.default-dispatcher-3]
[akka://faultTolerance/user/supervisor/workerActor1] Starting workerActor1 instance
hashcode # 24237095
[INFO] [09/22/2012 08:28:04.667] [main] [ActorSystemImpl(akka://faultTolerance)]
Value Received-> 0
```

Next, we try sending a null object to `WorkerActor1`. `WorkerActor1` will throw a `NullPointerException` when the passed message is null.

The `SupervisorStrategy` configured for `NullPointerException` is to restart. We can see that both `WorkerActor1` and `WorkerActor2` are stopped and restarted. Failure of one actor meant that `SupervisorStrategy` applied to all the actors, leading to the restart of both the actors.

Next, we get the state of `WorkerActor1` by sending the message `Result()` and asking for the result.

As we can see the result returned is `0`, which is the original default state value of `WorkerActor1` because we asked the actor to restart.

Java:

```
log.info("Sending value \"String\", IllegalArgumentException should be
thrown! Our Supervisor strategy says Stop !");

supervisor.tell(String.valueOf("Do Something"));
```

Scala:

```
log.info("Sending value \"String\", IllegalArgumentException should be
thrown! Our Supervisor strategy says Stop !")

supervisor ? "Do Something"
```

The output on console is as follows:

```
[INFO] [09/22/2012 08:28:04.668] [main] [ActorSystemImpl(akka://faultTolerance)]
Sending value "String", NullPointerException should be thrown! Our Supervisor
strategy says Stop !
[INFO] [09/22/2012 08:28:04.668] [main] [ActorSystemImpl(akka://faultTolerance)]
Worker Actor shutdown !
[ERROR] [09/22/2012 08:28:04.669] [faultTolerance-akka.actor.default-dispatcher-2]
[akka://faultTolerance/user/supervisor/workerActor1] Wrong Argument
java.lang.IllegalArgumentException: Wrong Argument
        at org.akka.essentials.supervisor.example2.WorkerActor1.onReceive
(WorkerActor1.java:31)
        at akka.actor.UntypedActor$$anonfun$receive$1.apply(UntypedActor.scala:154)
        at akka.actor.UntypedActor$$anonfun$receive$1.apply(UntypedActor.scala:153)
        at akka.actor.Actor$class.apply(Actor.scala:290)
        at akka.actor.UntypedActor.apply(UntypedActor.scala:93)
        at akka.actor.ActorCell.invoke(ActorCell.scala:617)
        at akka.dispatch.Mailbox.processMailbox(Mailbox.scala:179)
        at akka.dispatch.Mailbox.run(Mailbox.scala:161)
        at akka.dispatch.ForkJoinExecutorConfigurator$MailboxExecutionTask.exec
(AbstractDispatcher.scala:505)
        at akka.jsr166y.ForkJoinTask.doExec(ForkJoinTask.java:259)
        at akka.jsr166y.ForkJoinPool$WorkQueue.runTask(ForkJoinPool.java:997)
        at akka.jsr166y.ForkJoinPool.runWorker(ForkJoinPool.java:1495)
        at akka.jsr166y.ForkJoinWorkerThread.run(ForkJoinWorkerThread.java:104)

[INFO] [09/22/2012 08:28:04.700] [faultTolerance-akka.actor.default-dispatcher-2]
[akka://faultTolerance/user/supervisor/workerActor1] Stopping WorkerActor1 instance
hashcode # 24237095
[INFO] [09/22/2012 08:28:04.700] [faultTolerance-akka.actor.default-dispatcher-7]
[akka://faultTolerance/user/supervisor/workerActor2] Stopping WorkerActor2 instance
hashcode # 26807853
```

Next, we try sending an invalid message object to `WorkerActor1`. `WorkerActor1` throws an `IllegalArgumentException` when the passed message is invalid or not recognized.

`SupervisorStrategy` configured for `IllegalArgumentException` is to `stop()`. We can see both the Worker actors are stopped, implying that the configured `AllForOneStrategy` is applied to the actors managed by the supervisor.

This completes the second example. We saw how the supervisor handles the actor's failure and how the supervisor can take the right calls to deal with those failures. The strategy employed by the supervisor is applied to all the actors managed.

Lifecycle monitoring

Besides `SupervisorStrategy`, there is another way to monitor the actor lifecycle. The monitoring strategy provides a mechanism where any actor can listen to certain events on another actor. Based on these events, the listening actor can direct another actor or it can take decisions on how to handle the actor termination. Some of the guidelines when lifecycle monitoring is required are as follows:

- The actor monitoring is usually used when the actors in question are not part of your hierarchy. So actors at the horizontal level are primarily the candidates for monitoring.

- When the supervisor wants to terminate the child actors instead of just restarting (in order to clear the mailbox attached to the actors), monitoring on the actor's termination is used.

- When the child actor is terminated because of an external event (such as `PoisonPill` from another actor or a `system.stop()` request), in this case, the supervisor will be required to monitor and take an action.

The listener's events provided are only for actor's termination events, unlike supervisor's where the `SupervisorActor` reacts to the failures also. This service is provided by the `DeathWatch` component of the `ActorSystem`.

In order to monitor an actor for termination, the actor needs to register itself with the Monitoring actor:

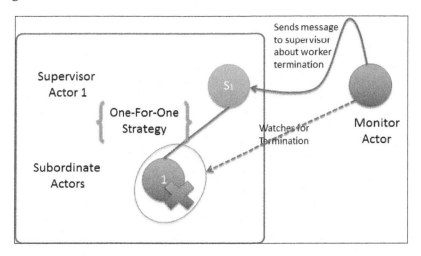

Let's go ahead and create a simple `WorkerActor` that accepts the message of type `instanceof Integer` only. If you send any other message, the `WorkerActor` shuts itself down.

Java:

```
public class Result {}
public class DeadWorker {}public class RegisterWorker {
    ActorRef worker;
    ActorRef supervisor;

    public RegisterWorker(ActorRef worker, ActorRef supervisor) {
        this.worker = worker;
        this.supervisor = supervisor;
    }

    public ActorRef getWorker() {
        return worker;
    }

    public ActorRef getSupervisor() {
        return supervisor;
    }
}
```

```java
public class WorkerActor extends UntypedActor {
    LoggingAdapter log = Logging.getLogger(getContext().system(),
                         this);
    private int state = 0;

    @Override
    public void preStart() {
        log.info("Starting WorkerActor instance hashcode # {}",
                this.hashCode());
    }

    public void onReceive(Object o) throws Exception {
        if (o instanceof Integer) {
            Integer value = (Integer) o;
            state = value;
            log.info("Received a message " + value);
        } else if (o instanceof Result) {
            getSender().tell(state);
        } else {
            throw new IllegalArgumentException("Wrong Argument");
        }
    }

    @Override
    public void postStop() {
        log.info("Stopping WorkerActor instance hashcode # {}",
                this.hashCode());

    }
}
```

Scala:

```scala
case class Result
case class DeadWorker
case class RegisterWorker(val worker: ActorRef,
                          val supervisor: ActorRef)

class WorkerActor extends Actor with ActorLogging {
  import org.akka.essentials.supervisor.example1.Result
  var state: Int = 0

  override def preStart() {
    log.info("Starting WorkerActor instance hashcode # {}",
             this.hashCode())
  }
  override def postStop() {
```

```scala
      log.info("Stopping WorkerActor instance hashcode # {}",
               this.hashCode());
  }
  def receive: Receive = {
    case value: Int =>
      state = value
    case result: Result =>
      sender ! state
    case _ =>
      context.stop(self)
  }
}
```

Next, we will create MonitorActor, that will watch WorkerActor for termination and will be intimated via the Terminated message.

Java:

```java
public class MonitorActor extends UntypedActor {
    LoggingAdapter log = Logging.getLogger(getContext().system(),
                          this);

    Map<ActorRef, ActorRef> monitoredActors =
                    new HashMap<ActorRef, ActorRef>();

    @Override
    public void onReceive(Object message) throws Exception {
          if (message instanceof Terminated) {
                final Terminated t = (Terminated) message;
                if (monitoredActors.containsKey(t.getActor())) {
                        log.info("Received Worker Actor Termination
    Message ->
                        {}", t.getActor().path());
                        log.info("Sending message to Supervisor");
                        monitoredActors.get(t.getActor()).tell(
                        new DeadWorker());
                }
          } else if (message instanceof RegisterWorker) {
                RegisterWorker msg = (RegisterWorker) message;
                getContext().watch(msg.worker);
                monitoredActors.put(msg.worker, msg.supervisor);

          } else {
                unhandled(message);
          }
    }
}
```

Scala:

```scala
class MonitorActor extends Actor with ActorLogging {

  var monitoredActors = new HashMap[ActorRef, ActorRef]

  def receive: Receive = {
    case t: Terminated =>
      if (monitoredActors.contains(t.actor)) {
        log.info("Received Worker Actor Termination Message -> "
          + t.actor.path)
        log.info("Sending message to Supervisor")
        val value: Option[ActorRef] = monitoredActors.get(t.actor)
        value.get ! new DeadWorker()
      }

    case msg: RegisterWorker =>
      context.watch(msg.worker)
      monitoredActors += msg.worker -> msg.supervisor
  }
}
```

In order to monitor `WorkerActor`, the `MonitorActor` needs to be passed the `ActorRef` of the `WorkerActor`. In this case, we have passed the `WorkerActor` reference along with the supervisor reference as a message via `RegisterWorker` to be watched by the `MonitorActor`.

The key here is the statement that registers the actor to watch for termination events.

Java:

```java
this.getContext().watch();
```

Scala:

```scala
getContext().watch()
```

When `WorkerActor` terminates, a `Terminated` event is sent to `MonitorActor`, which can then be used to notify other actors about `WorkerActor` termination.

Let's just run the actor and see how `MonitorActor` receives the `Termination` message when `WorkerActor` dies.

Java:

```java
ActorSystem system = ActorSystem.create("faultTolerance");

ActorRef supervisor = system.actorOf(
            new Props(SupervisorActor.class),"supervisor");

supervisor.tell(Integer.valueOf(10));
supervisor.tell("10");

Thread.sleep(5000);

supervisor.tell(Integer.valueOf(10));

system.shutdown();
```

Scala:

```scala
val system = ActorSystem("faultTolerance")

val supervisor = system.actorOf(Props[SupervisorActor],
                  name = "supervisor")

var mesg: Int = 8
supervisor ! mesg

supervisor ! "Do Something"

Thread.sleep(4000)
supervisor ! mesg

system.shutdown
```

We create `ActorRef` for the two actors – `SupervisorActor` and `MonitorActor`. Then we pass an `Integer` message to the supervisor and, subsequently, we pass a string message to `SupervisorActor`. The first message should process normally; the second message will lead to the shutdown of `WorkerActor`. As part of the actor shutdown process, a `Terminated` message is published.

The output on console is as follows:

```
[INFO] [09/22/2012 08:33:04.303] [faultTolerance-akka.actor.default-dispatcher-2]
[akka://faultTolerance/user/supervisor/workerActor] Starting WorkerActor instance
hashcode # 32165947
[INFO] [09/22/2012 08:33:04.655] [faultTolerance-akka.actor.default-dispatcher-4]
[akka://faultTolerance/user/supervisor/workerActor] Received a message 10
[ERROR] [09/22/2012 08:33:04.656] [faultTolerance-akka.actor.default-dispatcher-4]
[akka://faultTolerance/user/supervisor/workerActor] wrong Argument
java.lang.IllegalArgumentException: wrong Argument
        at org.akka.essentials.supervisor.example3.WorkerActor.onReceive
(WorkerActor.java:24)
        at akka.actor.UntypedActor$$anonfun$receive$1.apply(UntypedActor.scala:154)
        at akka.actor.UntypedActor$$anonfun$receive$1.apply(UntypedActor.scala:153)
        at akka.actor.Actor$class.apply(Actor.scala:290)
        at akka.actor.UntypedActor.apply(UntypedActor.scala:93)
        at akka.actor.ActorCell.invoke(ActorCell.scala:617)
        at akka.dispatch.Mailbox.processMailbox(Mailbox.scala:179)
        at akka.dispatch.Mailbox.run(Mailbox.scala:161)
        at akka.dispatch.ForkJoinExecutorConfigurator$MailboxExecutionTask.exec
(AbstractDispatcher.scala:505)
        at akka.jsr166y.ForkJoinTask.doExec(ForkJoinTask.java:259)
        at akka.jsr166y.ForkJoinPool$WorkQueue.runTask(ForkJoinPool.java:997)
        at akka.jsr166y.ForkJoinPool.runWorker(ForkJoinPool.java:1495)
        at akka.jsr166y.ForkJoinWorkerThread.run(ForkJoinWorkerThread.java:104)

[INFO] [09/22/2012 08:33:05.2] [faultTolerance-akka.actor.default-dispatcher-4]
[akka://faultTolerance/user/supervisor/workerActor] Stopping WorkerActor instance
hashcode # 32165947
[INFO] [09/22/2012 08:33:05.3] [faultTolerance-akka.actor.default-dispatcher-2]
[akka://faultTolerance/user/monitorActor] Received Worker Actor Termination Message
-> akka://faultTolerance/user/supervisor/workerActor
[INFO] [09/22/2012 08:33:05.3] [faultTolerance-akka.actor.default-dispatcher-2]
[akka://faultTolerance/user/monitorActor] Sending message to Supervisor
[INFO] [09/22/2012 08:33:05.4] [faultTolerance-akka.actor.default-dispatcher-1]
[akka://faultTolerance/user/supervisor] Got a DeadWorker message, restarting the
worker
[INFO] [09/22/2012 08:33:05.4] [faultTolerance-akka.actor.default-dispatcher-2]
[akka://faultTolerance/user/supervisor/workerActor] Starting WorkerActor instance
hashcode # 27992831
[INFO] [09/22/2012 08:33:09.123] [faultTolerance-akka.actor.default-dispatcher-3]
[akka://faultTolerance/user/supervisor/workerActor] Received a message 10
[INFO] [09/22/2012 08:33:10.128] [faultTolerance-akka.actor.default-dispatcher-5]
[akka://faultTolerance/user/supervisor/workerActor] Stopping WorkerActor instance
hashcode # 27992831
```

So, we see how when `WorkerActor` shuts down, `MonitorActor` receives the
`Terminated` message. It is able to match the terminated actor to the `ActorRef`
already stored. If it matches, then it publishes the message to the supervisor to
restart `WorkerActor`.

Java:

```java
if (message instanceof Terminated) {
    final Terminated t = (Terminated) message;
    if (monitoredActors.containsKey(t.getActor())) {
        log.info("Received Worker Actor Termination Message ->
            {}", t.getActor().path());
```

```
            log.info("Sending message to Supervisor");
        monitoredActors.get(t.getActor()).tell(
            new DeadWorker());
    }
```

Scala:

```
case t: Terminated =>
    if (monitoredActors.contains(t.actor)) {
        log.info("Received Worker Actor Termination Message -> {}",
         t.actor.path)
        log.info("Sending message to Supervisor")
        val value: Option[ActorRef] = monitoredActors.get(t.actor)
        value.get ! new DeadWorker()
    }
```

Fault tolerance

The key to a fault-tolerant application is to make use of the supervisors and lifecycle monitoring techniques. These techniques can be used to manage not only the local actors, but also remote actors. The supervisor hierarchy can be composed of local and remote actors. Similarly, the application can monitor remote actors for `Termination` messages. We cover remote actors in more detail in *Chapter 9, Remote Actors*.

In a large, distributed application, actors can fail when:

* There is a logic programming error when the message is received (for example, you received a message with incomplete data)
* There is a failure of an external resource on which the actor is dependent (for example, database connection, socket connection, file connection, and so on)
* The actor's internal state is corrupted over a period of time (especially when the cause of the corruption is not known)

In any of the previous conditions, the actor may need to be resumed, restarted, or stopped.

Let's take an example of a Master–Slave kind of application where the Master node passes messages to the Slave nodes for processing. The Master node uses a RoundRobin Router to pass the messages to the remote actors on the Slave nodes. The Master node and the Slave nodes are running in their JVM instances, shown as follows:

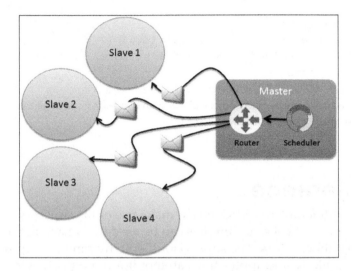

Now, if we have to design such an application, the role of the supervisors and lifecycle monitoring is very important. Let's go ahead and see how the actor hierarchy is designed to handle failures in such a kind of application:

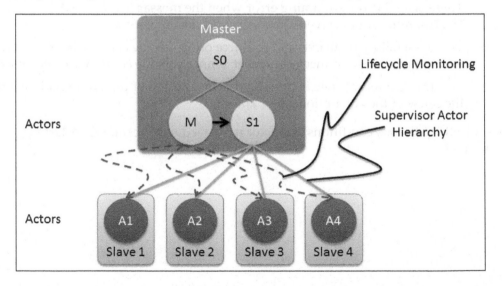

In the previous solution, we have the Supervisor actor (S1) on the Master node, which creates the actor references to each of the actors (A1-A4) on the Slave nodes. Now the supervisor strategy in this case will be One-For-One, because the remote actors on the Slave nodes are independent of each other and their failures are isolated from each other. So in the case of any failure, the respective remote actors can be restarted or resumed.

In addition, we have one Monitoring actor (M) that monitors the lifecycle of the remote actors. So, in the case of any failure conditions, Monitor actor gets notified of the remote actor's termination. Subsequently, the supervisor is informed of the remote actor's failure. The idea is to make sure we do not pass any message to the remote actor that is not available, and meanwhile we try to restart the remote actor.

To manage and monitor the lifecycle of the Monitoring actor (M) and Supervisor actor (S1), we may create another Supervisor actor (S0) to manage both.

The more we monitor and respond to actor failures, the more our application will be resistant to failures.

Summary

In this chapter, we have seen how we can use the supervisor strategy to build linkages between the actors and handle failure of the actors in the hierarchy. The actor hierarchy can go to any level of depth. In case the actors are not managed via the same supervisor hierarchy, we can make use of lifecycle monitoring that allows us to be notified when the actor terminates, so that the application can take corrective action.

In the next chapter, we will examine how to have concurrency control using the **software transactional memory** (**STM**). We will cover how to apply the transactional concepts (begin/commit/rollback semantics) within the Actor Model.

7
Software Transactional Memory

In this chapter, we shall cover the transactional model applicable to the actors. We will see the various Akka constructs provided for the transactional concepts (begin/commit/rollback semantics).

We will cover the following topics:

- Basics of transaction management and examine what is software transactional memory
- Explore the Akka constructs provided for STM — transactors and agents

Transaction management

Transactions provide a mechanism to manage the application access to data (read or write) in a multiuser environment. In a multiuser environment, concurrent access to the data needs to be controlled to ensure data integrity. The transaction is designated as a unit of work that contains a sequence of reads and writes.

The application must ensure that a transaction is fully committed if successful or the entire unit is fully rolled back in case of failure. A very important characteristic of transactions is that they are atomic, meaning that the user will assume either all the actions that are part of the transaction are executed or none are executed. The transaction should leave the data in a consistent state. Another important characteristic of a transaction is isolation. **Isolation** mandates that each transaction sees a consistent view of the data while manipulating the same. Other transactions might be running in parallel, but each transaction should not see intermediate data manipulations unless those transactions have successfully completed and committed their actions.

In traditional applications where the data is stored in an underlying file system, the transaction should also ensure durability. **Durability** means that transactional changes persist in the data store once commit has been issued and any subsequent failure will allow us to recover to the last commit. All in all, these are called the **ACID** (**atomicity, consistency, isolation,** and **durability**) capabilities that guarantee the reliable processing of a transaction. ACID is routinely used in the context of database operations. A single logical operation on the data is called a transaction. The transaction provides a reliable mechanism to ensure the concurrency control of the shared access data. Data managed in storage (using DBMS or other mechanisms) have well defined transaction mechanisms.

For the data/state held in memory, the concurrent programs generally need to manipulate mutable data, and it may not be possible to roll back the set of actions. Since the rollbacks are not easy, the handling of concurrency control in programming languages means relying on conflict avoidance instead of conflict resolution. Java supports concurrent access to the MUTABLE state by allowing multiple threads to be created and executed simultaneously. In Java, every object has a synchronization lock that can be held by only one thread at a time and be used to control access to the object's state.

What is software transactional memory?

The whole concept of threads is based on the model of synchronized access to the shared mutable state. **Shared state** means the same instance variables will be accessed by multiple threads. **Mutable** means the value of the instance will change over the lifetime and that change in the value needs to be managed.

For example, when two threads running simultaneously read a certain variable and try to update the shared object. If the operations are not atomic and access to the shared state is not mutually exclusive, the threads' execution tends to get interleaved, leaving the mutable state in an incorrect state. Usage of locks may guarantee the correct behavior, but it is likely to affect threads running into a deadlock problem, with each acquiring locks in a different order and waiting for each other. As the complexity of the application increases, the number of shared state variables along with the number of locks required to manage those state variables keeps increasing. Soon you end up with a situation where every thread or task requires some subset of locks, and very soon you are facing the deadlock situation.

To abstract the threading and locking hardships, **software transactional memory** (**STM**), a concurrency-control mechanism for managing access to shared memory in a concurrent environment has gained a lot of acceptance.

STM makes use of two concepts – optimism and transactions to manage the shared concurrency control. **Optimism** means that we run multiple atomic blocks in parallel, assuming there will be no errors. When we are done, we check for any problems. If no problems are found, we update the state variables in the atomic block. If we find problems then we roll back and retry. Optimistic concurrency typically provides better scalability options than any other alternate approaches. Secondly, STM is modeled on similar lines of database transaction handling. In the case of STM, the Java heap is the transactional data set with begin/commit and rollback constructs. As the objects hold the state in memory, the transaction only implements the following characteristics – atomicity, consistency, and isolation.

 STM as a concept has been implemented by multiple languages and at times multiple implementations are available for one language. Refer to the following website for more details: http://en.wikipedia.org/wiki/Software_ transactional_memory#Implementations

Akka uses the ScalaSTM for implementing the STM model within Akka. STM treats the entire Java heap as the transaction data set. If every memory location had to be tracked and managed, even when not required, for access and update, that would demand a huge amount of resources. So memory locations that need to be managed are marked, resulting in a smaller number of memory locations to be managed. **ScalaSTM** makes use of Refs (transactional references) that are bound to a single memory location for its lifetime. Ref is a mutable cell that should only contain IMMUTABLE data.

The Refs ensure that these mutable storage locations can only be modified within a transaction. So, whenever there is a need to manage and track multiple pieces of state variables and to perform operations that update these state variables all at once, using Refs is the key. Whenever a state needs to be synchronized between threads, we can use Refs.

Refs use **Compare and Swap (CAS)** semantics to enforce coordinated changes across all Refs participating in the transaction:

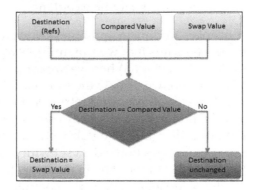

The concept of optimistic concurrency is implemented using the CAS semantics. We compare the values at a particular memory location to a given value, and if they are the same, then we can modify the values at that particular location. The whole idea is, before we enter the transaction, we read the values of the location we want to modify. We go through the logic to modify the values. Once the logic is over, we verify our initially read values against the current memory location value. If the values are the same, we go ahead and update the memory locations. If not, we roll back the transaction.

Let's take a simple example of ScalaSTM and see how the whole transactional model works. The following is a ScalaSTM example, where we have two variables x and y that have been declared as Ref and initialized to values 10 and 0 respectively:

```
val (x, y) = (Ref(10), Ref(0))

def swap = atomic { implicit txn =>
    x = x + y
    y = x - y
    x = x - y
}

def transfer(n: Int) {
  atomic { implicit txn =>
    x -= n
    y += n
  }
}
```

We define two methods: `swap()` that takes in x and swaps their values; and `transfer()` that takes in an integer n and removes the same from x and adds it into y. The set of instructions that need to be performed as a transaction are grouped with the atomic block.

When the two methods are executed in parallel by two threads, both the threads read the initial values of the variables x and y. At the time of commit, the values of x and y that were read originally are compared with the current values of x and y. In the case of Thread 2, the values match. Thread 2 goes ahead and updates the x and y values. When Thread 1 tries to commit the transaction, at that time, the values of x and y do not match, making the transaction roll back, shown as follows:

	Initial Values x = 10, y =0	
Steps		
1	atomic {	atomic {
2	begin txn attempt	begin txn attempt
3	read x -> 10	read x -> 10
4	read y -> 0	write x <- 8
5	write x -> 10	read y -> 0
6	write y -> 10	write y <- 2
7	write x -> 0	commit
8	commit fails -> x,y read is invalid	}
9	roll back	
10	}	
	Thread 1	**Thread 2**

For more details on ScalaSTM, please refer to the following website:
`http://nbronson.github.com/scala-stm/index.html`

Coordinated transactions

The Actor Model is based on the premise of small independent processes working in isolation and where the state can be updated only via message passing. The actors hold the state within themselves, but the asynchronous message passing means there is no guarantee that a stable view of the state can be provided to the calling components. For transactional systems like banking where account deposit and withdrawal need to be atomic, this is a bad fit with an Actor Model.

So, if your Akka applications need to be implementing a shared state model and providing a consensual, stable view of the state across the calling components, STM provides the answer.

To manage multiple transactions running on separate threads as a single atomic block, the concept of CommitBarrier is used. CommitBarrier is a synchronization aid that is used as a single, common barrier point by all the transactions across multiple threads. Once the barrier is reached, all the transactions commit automatically. It is based on the Java's CountDownLatch.

> Read more details on CountDownLatch here:
> http://docs.oracle.com/javase/6/docs/api/
> java/util/concurrent/CountDownLatch.html

Akka transactors are based on CommitBarrier, where the atomic blocks of each actor (member) participating are treated as one, big single unit. Each actor will block until everyone participating in the transaction has completed. This means that all the actions executed as part of the atomic blocks by members of the CommitBarrier will appear to occur as a single atomic action even though the members may be spread across multiple threads. If any of the atomic blocks throw an exception or a conflict happens, all the CommitBarrier members will roll back.

Akka provides a construct for coordinating transactions across actors called coordinated.coordinated, which is used to define the transaction boundary in terms of where the transaction starts, and the coordinated.coordinate() method is used to add all the members that will participate in the same transaction context. The following image shows how the actor's atomic blocks get added to the coordinated block:

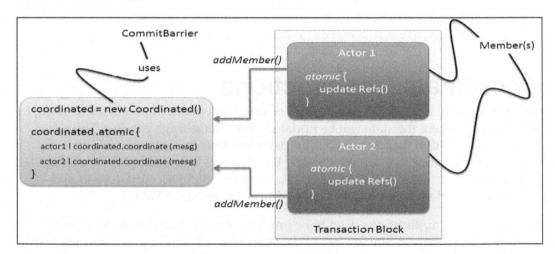

Money transfer between two accounts

Let's take an example and see how the actors can participate in the transactions. We will use the classic example of transfer of funds between two bank accounts. We have an `AccountActor` that holds the account balance and account number information. It has two operations – credit (add money to the account) and debit (take money away from the account). In addition, we have the `TransferActor` object that will hold the two `AccountActor` objects and then invoke the debit and credit operations on the account objects. `TransferActor` is supervised by `BankActor`. From the supervisor hierarchy perspective, the actors are aligned as follows:

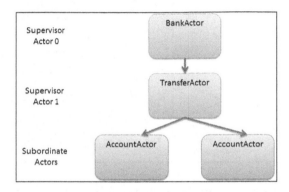

To make sure that the money transfer in the account happens in a synchronized way, we need to implement the following:

- In the account object, the state variable that needs to participate in the transaction should be of type `Ref` (transaction reference). In our case, the account balance will be Refs.

- The credit and debit operations in the account object need to be atomic.

- In the transfer object, the transaction boundary needs to be defined and the account objects need to participate in the same transaction context.

- In addition, we define the supervisor policy in `TransferActor` and `BankActor` to handle the transaction exceptions:

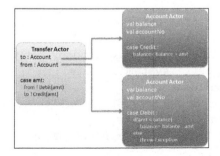

`TransferActor` on receiving the transfer message will begin the transaction context to transfer the amount from one account to another. The two account objects will then join the `coordinated` transaction so that the atomic methods of each of the account objects will join the same transaction context. The following diagram depicts the changes that need to be made for each of the objects:

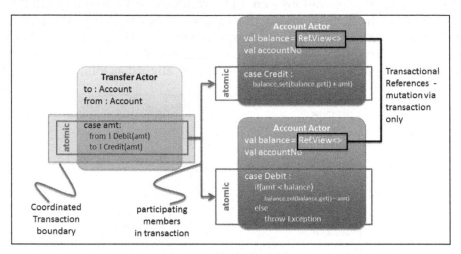

To use transactors within your application, the following dependency needs to be added to the maven `pom.xml` file:

```
<dependency>
          <groupId>com.typesafe.akka</groupId>
          <artifactId>akka-transactor</artifactId>
          <version>2.0.1</version>
</dependency>
```

Let's jump into the code for these two actors and see how the transactor mechanism works.

First, let's go through the `AccountActor`.

Java:

```java
public class AccountActor extends UntypedActor {

    LoggingAdapter log = Logging.getLogger(getContext()
                         .system(), this);
    String accountNumber;
    //Use the scala STM Ref for state variables that need to
    //participate in transactions
    Ref.View<Float> balance = STM.newRef(Float.parseFloat("0"));
```

```java
        public AccountActor(String accNo, Float bal) {
            this.accountNumber = accNo;
            balance.set(bal);
        }


        @Override
        public void onReceive(Object o) throws Exception {
            if (o instanceof Coordinated) {
                Coordinated coordinated = (Coordinated) o;
                final Object message = coordinated.getMessage();
                if (message instanceof AccountDebit) {
                    coordinated.atomic(new Runnable() {
                        public void run() {
                            AccountDebit accDebit =
                            (AccountDebit) message;
                            //check for funds availability
                            if (balance.get() > accDebit.
                            getAmount()) {
                                Float bal = balance.get()
                            - accDebit.getAmount();
                                balance.set(bal);
                            } else {
                                throw new
                                IllegalStateException(
                                "Insufficient Balance");
                            }
                        }
                    });
                } else if (message instanceof AccountCredit) {
                    coordinated.atomic(new Runnable() {
                        public void run() {
                            AccountCredit accCredit =
                            (AccountCredit) message;
                            Float bal = balance.get()
                            + accCredit.getAmount();
                            balance.set(bal);
                        }
                    });
                }
            } else if (o instanceof AccountBalance) {
                // reply with the account balance
                sender().tell(new AccountBalance(accountNumber,
                    balance.get()));
            }
        }
    }
}
```

Scala:

```scala
class AccountActor(accountNumber: String, inBalance: Float)
             extends Actor {
  val balance = Ref(inBalance)
  def receive = {
    case value: AccountBalance =>
      sender ! new AccountBalance(accountNumber,
              balance.single.get)
    case coordinated @ Coordinated(message: AccountDebit) =>
      // coordinated atomic ...
      coordinated atomic { implicit t =>
        //check for funds availability
        if (balance.get(t) > message.amount)
          balance.transform(_ - message.amount)
        else
            throw new IllegalStateException(
            "Insufficient Balance")
      }
    case coordinated @ Coordinated(message: AccountCredit) =>
      // coordinated atomic ...
      coordinated atomic { implicit t =>
        balance.transform(_ + message.amount)
      }
  }
}
```

In the `AccountActor`, the first thing is the account balance state value that needs to be implementing `Ref`. In this case, we have defined balance using the STM library `Ref.View<>`.

Java:

```java
Ref.View<Float> balance = STM.newRef(Float.parseFloat("0"));
```

Scala:

```scala
val balance = Ref(inBalance)
```

Next thing to define in the `AccountActor` are the atomic blocks for the credit and debit operations.

For the credit operation, the change to the balance `Ref` is updated with the new value within the atomic block.

Java:

```
coordinated.atomic(new Runnable() {
    public void run() {
        AccountCredit accCredit = (AccountCredit) message;
        Float bal = balance.get() + accCredit.getAmount();
        balance.set(bal);
    }
});
```

Scala:

```
case coordinated @ Coordinated(message: AccountCredit) =>
    // coordinated atomic ...
    coordinated atomic { implicit t =>
      balance.transform(_ + message.amount)
    }
```

For the debit operation, the check is done to make sure that the amount to be withdrawn is less than the balance amount of the account. If not, an exception is thrown.

Java:

```
coordinated.atomic(new Runnable() {
    public void run() {
        AccountDebit accDebit = (AccountDebit) message;
        //check for funds availability
        if (balance.get() > accDebit.getAmount()) {
            Float bal = balance.get()
                - accDebit.getAmount();
            balance.set(bal);
        } else {
            throw new IllegalStateException(
                "Insufficient Balance");
        }
    }
});
```

Scala:

```
coordinated atomic { implicit t =>
//check for funds availability
    if (balance.get(t) > message.amount)
      balance.transform(_ - message.amount)
    else
      throw new IllegalStateException(
      "Insufficient Balance")
}
```

Moving on to the `TransferActor`, where we will start the transaction and pass the messages on to the account actors for making the transfer. In the `TransferActor`, we need to perform the following:

1. Initialize the two `AccountActor` objects with appropriate balances.

2. When the `TransferMsg` is received, start a new `coordinated` transaction and pass the message to the two account actors in an atomic block.

3. If any of the account actors throw an exception, we capture the exception in a try-catch block and cancel the transaction, leading to the rollback of the account actor's state.

4. `TransferActor` also employs a fault-tolerant supervisor policy to handle the account actors throwing exceptions.

First, we initialize the account actors with appropriate amounts.

Java:

```java
String fromAccount = "XYZ";
String toAccount = "ABC";
// sets the from account with initial balance of 5000
ActorRef from = context().actorOf(new Props(
    new UntypedActorFactory() {
        public UntypedActor create() {
                return new AccountActor(fromAccount,
                    Float.parseFloat("5000"));
        }
}), fromAccount);
// sets the to account with initial balance of 1000
ActorRef to = context().actorOf(new Props(
    new UntypedActorFactory() {
        public UntypedActor create() {
                return new AccountActor(toAccount,
                    Float.parseFloat("1000"));
        }
}), toAccount);
```

Scala:

```scala
val fromAccount = "XYZ";
val toAccount = "ABC";

val from = context.actorOf(Props(new AccountActor(
            fromAccount, 5000)), name = fromAccount)
val to = context.actorOf(Props(new AccountActor(
            toAccount, 1000)), name = toAccount)
```

Next, we define the block to receive messages. Once we receive the message, we start the `coordinated` transaction and send the messages to the account actors in an atomic block.

Java:

```java
            if (message instanceof TransferMsg) {
                final TransferMsg transfer = (TransferMsg) message;
                final Coordinated coordinated =
                        new Coordinated(timeout);
                coordinated.atomic(new Runnable() {
                    public void run() {
                            // credit amount - will always be
    //successful
                            to.tell(coordinated.coordinate(
                    new AccountCredit(transfer
                    .getAmtToBeTransferred())));
                            // debit amount - throws an exception if
            // funds insufficient
                            from.tell(coordinated.coordinate(
                    new AccountDebit(transfer

    .getAmtToBeTransferred())));
                    }
                });
            }
```

Scala:

```scala
    case message: TransferMsg =>
      val coordinated = Coordinated()
      coordinated atomic { implicit t =>
        to ! coordinated(new AccountCredit(
          message.amtToBeTransferred))
        from ! coordinated(new AccountDebit(
          message.amtToBeTransferred))
      }
```

The last and most important part is the fault tolerance strategy to handle the exceptions thrown when the transaction fails. We are tracking two different transactions here – one is `IllegalStateException`, which is thrown by the `AccountActor` in case of insufficient funds, and the second is `CoordinatedTransactionException`, which is thrown when one of the `CommitBarrier` members is unable to go through the transaction.

Java:

```java
//catch the exceptions and apply the right strategy, in this
//case resume()
private static SupervisorStrategy strategy =
    new AllForOneStrategy(10,Duration.parse("10 second"),
    new Function<Throwable, Directive>() {
        public Directive apply(Throwable t) {
            if (t instanceof CoordinatedTransactionException) {
                return resume();
            } else if (t instanceof IllegalStateException) {
                return resume();
            } else if (t instanceof IllegalArgumentException) {
                return stop();
            } else {
                return escalate();
            }
        }
    });
@Override
public SupervisorStrategy supervisorStrategy() {
    return strategy;
}
```

Scala:

```scala
override val supervisorStrategy =
    AllForOneStrategy(maxNrOfRetries = 10,
    withinTimeRange = 10 seconds) {
    case _ : CoordinatedTransactionException => Resume
    case _ : IllegalStateException => Resume
    case _ : IllegalArgumentException => Stop
    case _ : Exception => Escalate
  }
```

We are using the Resume directive here, which allows the Subordinate actors
(in this case the account actors) to go back to working mode and keep their existing
accumulated state. This means that, the account actors hold the previous known
stable view of the balance amount before the rolled-back transaction.

The Stop directive means the actors are stopped and they lose their existing state.
To use the actors again, you will need to initialize them again.

The Restart directive means the actors in question are stopped and restarted,
effectively meaning the actors are reinitialized to their original state.

Here is the complete code of the `TransferActor` for reference. In addition, we have included the code to get the current balance of the account after transfer messages.

Java:

```java
public class TransferActor extends UntypedActor {
    LoggingAdapter log = Logging.getLogger(getContext().system(),
                           this);
    String fromAccount = "XYZ";
    String toAccount = "ABC";

    // sets the from account with initial balance of 5000
    ActorRef from = context().actorOf(new Props(
        new UntypedActorFactory() {
            public UntypedActor create() {
                    return new AccountActor(fromAccount,
                        Float.parseFloat("5000"));
            }
    }), fromAccount);
    // sets the to account with initial balance of 1000
    ActorRef to = context().actorOf(new Props(
        new UntypedActorFactory() {
            public UntypedActor create() {
                    return new AccountActor(toAccount,
                        Float.parseFloat("1000"));
            }
    }), toAccount);
    Timeout timeout = new Timeout(5, TimeUnit.SECONDS);

    @Override
    public void onReceive(Object message) throws Exception {

            if (message instanceof TransferMsg) {
                    final TransferMsg transfer = (TransferMsg) message;
                    final Coordinated coordinated =
                            new Coordinated(timeout);
                    coordinated.atomic(new Runnable() {
                        public void run() {
                                // credit amount - will always be
                                successful
                                to.tell(coordinated.coordinate(
                    new AccountCredit(transfer

                    .getAmtToBeTransferred())));
                                // debit amount - throws an exception if
                    // funds insufficient
```

```
                                from.tell(coordinated.coordinate(
                    new AccountDebit(transfer

                    .getAmtToBeTransferred())));
                        }
                });
            } else if (message instanceof AccountBalance) {
                    AccountBalance accBalance = (AccountBalance) message;
                    // check the account number and return the balance
                    if (accBalance.getAccountNumber().
                    equals(fromAccount)) {
                        from.tell(accBalance, sender());
                    }
                    if (accBalance.getAccountNumber().equals(toAccount))
{
                        to.tell(accBalance, sender());
                    }
            }else if(message instanceof AccountMsg){
                    from.tell(message);
            }
        }


    // catch the exceptions and apply the right strategy,
    // in this case resume()
    private static SupervisorStrategy strategy =
        new AllForOneStrategy(10,Duration.parse("10 second"),
        new Function<Throwable, Directive>() {
            public Directive apply(Throwable t) {
                    if (t instanceof CoordinatedTransactionException) {
                        return resume();
                    } else if (t instanceof IllegalStateException) {
                        return resume();
                    } else if (t instanceof IllegalArgumentException) {
                        return stop();
                    } else {
                        return escalate();
                    }
            }
    });

    @Override
    public SupervisorStrategy supervisorStrategy() {
        return strategy;
    }
}
```

Scala:

```scala
class TransferActor extends Actor {

  val fromAccount = "XYZ";
  val toAccount = "ABC";

  val from = context.actorOf(Props(new AccountActor(
                 fromAccount, 5000)), name = fromAccount)
  val to = context.actorOf(Props(new AccountActor(
                 toAccount, 1000)), name = toAccount)
  implicit val timeout = Timeout(5 seconds)
  override val supervisorStrategy =
          AllForOneStrategy(maxNrOfRetries = 10,
                  withinTimeRange = 10 seconds) {
    case _: CoordinatedTransactionException => Resume
    case _: IllegalStateException => Resume
    case _: IllegalArgumentException => Stop
    case _: Exception => Escalate
  }

  def receive: Receive = {
    case message: TransferMsg =>
      val coordinated = Coordinated()
      coordinated atomic { implicit t =>
        to ! coordinated(new AccountCredit(
          message.amtToBeTransferred))
        from ! coordinated(new AccountDebit(
          message.amtToBeTransferred))
      }
    case message: AccountBalance =>
      if (message.accountNumber.equalsIgnoreCase(fromAccount)) {
        from.tell(message, sender)
      } else if (message.accountNumber
                 .equalsIgnoreCase(toAccount)) {
        to.tell(message, sender)
      }
  }
}
```

In `TransferActor`, we saw the actor managing the lifecycle of the account actors created. The `TransferActor` initiates the `coordinated` transaction, which means the exception occurring at the `TransferActor` needs to be managed by its `SupervisorActor`, which in this case is the `BankActor` as defined in the actor hierarchy earlier. This is shown in the following diagram:

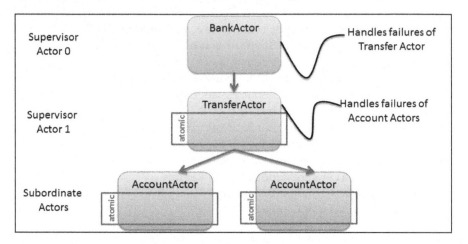

`BankActor` is responsible for initializing `TransferActor`, and has an appropriate supervisor strategy to manage the exceptions or failures coming from `TransferActor`.

Java:

```java
public class BankActor extends UntypedActor {

    ActorRef transfer = getContext().actorOf(
        new Props(TransferActor.class),"TransferActor");

    @Override
    public void onReceive(Object message) throws Exception {
            if (message instanceof TransferMsg) {
                    transfer.tell(message);
            } else if (message instanceof AccountBalance) {
                    AccountBalance account = (AccountBalance) Await.
result(
                            ask(transfer, message, 5000),
                    Duration.parse("5 second"));

                    System.out.println("Account #" +
                    account.getAccountNumber() + " , Balance "
                    + account.getBalance());
                    getSender().tell(account);
```

```java
            }else if(message instanceof AccountMsg){
                    transfer.tell(message);
            }
    }


// catch the exceptions and apply the right strategy, in this case
//resume()
    private static SupervisorStrategy strategy = new
        OneForOneStrategy(10,Duration.parse("10 second"),
        new Function<Throwable, Directive>() {
                public Directive apply(Throwable t) {
                        if (t instanceof
CoordinatedTransactionException) {
                                return resume();
                        } else if (t instanceof IllegalStateException)
{
                                return stop();
                        } else if (t instanceof
                        IllegalArgumentException) {
                                return stop();
                        } else {
                                return escalate();
                        }
                }
        });
    @Override
    public SupervisorStrategy supervisorStrategy() {
            return strategy;
    }
}
```

Scala:

```scala
class BankActor extends Actor with ActorLogging {
    val transferActor = context.actorOf(Props[TransferActor],
                        name = "TransferActor")
    implicit val timeout = Timeout(5 seconds)
    def receive = {
    case transfer: TransferMsg =>
        transferActor ! transfer
    case balance: AccountBalance =>
        val future = ask(transferActor,
                    balance).mapTo[AccountBalance]
        val account = Await.result(future, timeout.duration)
        log.info("Account #{} , Balance {}", account.accountNumber,
            account.accountBalance)
    }
```

```
override val supervisorStrategy = AllForOneStrategy(maxNrOfRetries =
10, withinTimeRange = 10 seconds) {
    case _: CoordinatedTransactionException => Resume
    case _: IllegalStateException => Stop
    case _: IllegalArgumentException => Stop
    case _: Exception => Escalate
  }
}
```

This completes the example where we saw how the actors can participate in a transaction and how STM is used to commit or roll back the transaction.

Transactor

In the previous section, we saw the usage of `coordinated` transactions in untyped actors. Now, it is possible to have scenarios where one operation participates in a transaction if applicable; otherwise, it can perform independently of the transaction as well.

Akka transactors combine the Actor Model and STM to provide the best of both worlds, allowing you to write transactional, asynchronous, event-based message flow applications, and gives you composed ATOMIC, arbitrary, deep message flows.

For example, in the money transfer example, the debit/credit operations for the account can be used outside the client-initiated transactions. So when the user just withdraws money from his account or deposits money in the account, the update to the account balance initiates a new transaction. But the same debit/credit operation can participate as part of the larger transfer transaction.

For this recurrent pattern, Akka provides a construct called `UntypedTransactor` in Java and `Transactor` in Scala. `UntypedTransactor` extends the `UntypedActor`, but provides methods to handle and join `coordinated` transactions.

`Transactor` allows us to segregate the message flow into two parts – one that participates in transactions and needs to execute within the atomic block and one where the messages are normally processed. When we use the transactor model, we need not directly deal with the `coordinated` object. The wrapping of the messages within the `coordinated` object is done transparently by the transactor construct.

Money transfer between two accounts – take two

Let's go back to our previous money transfer example between two accounts and enhance the same to understand how the transactors can be used. In the previous example, `AccountActor` was defined as `UntypedActor` and we had one message loop. Within that message loop, we segregated the messages using `coordinated.atomic()` block for messages that needed to be processed as atomic blocks of transaction versus processing of normal messages.

Transactor provides methods such as:

```
void atomically(Object msg)
```

The message can either be a `coordinated` message or a normal message. When a `coordinated` message comes, the method participates in the incoming `coordinated` transaction context. If a normal message comes, it creates a new `coordinated` transaction context and runs the method within that context.

To completely bypass `coordinated` transactions, override the normal method. Any message matched by normal will not be matched by the other methods, and will not be involved in `coordinated` transactions:

```
boolean normally(Object message)
```

If you want to coordinate with other transactors, then override the `coordinate` method. The `coordinate` method maps a message to a set of `SendTo` objects, pairs of `ActorRef`, and a message:

```
Set<SendTo> coordinate(Object message)
```

Let's go ahead and rewrite the code for `AccountActor` using the transactor model.

Java:

```java
public class AccountActor extends UntypedTransactor {
    String accountNumber;
    // Use the scala STM Ref for state variables that need to
    // participate in transactions
    Ref.View<Float> balance = STM.newRef(Float.parseFloat("0"));

    public AccountActor(String accNo, Float bal) {
        this.accountNumber = accNo;
        balance.set(bal);
    }
```

```java
        // default method to be overridden
        @Override
        public void atomically(Object message) throws Exception {
                if (message instanceof AccountDebit) {
                        AccountDebit accDebit = (AccountDebit) message;
                        // check for funds availability
                        if (balance.get() > accDebit.getAmount()) {
                                Float bal = balance.get() - accDebit.
getAmount();
                                balance.set(bal);
                        } else {
                                throw new IllegalStateException(
                                "Insufficient Balance");
                        }
                } else if (message instanceof AccountCredit) {
                        AccountCredit accCredit = (AccountCredit) message;
                        Float bal = balance.get() + accCredit.getAmount();
                        balance.set(bal);
                }
        }

        // To completely bypass coordinated transactions override the
        //normally method.
        @Override
        public boolean normally(Object message) {
                if (message instanceof AccountBalance) {
                        // reply with the account balance
                        sender().tell(new AccountBalance(accountNumber,
                                balance.get()));
                        return true;
                }
                return false;
        }
}
```

Scala:

```scala
class AccountActor(accountNumber: String, inBalance: Float)
                extends Transactor {

  val balance = Ref(inBalance)
  def atomically = implicit txn => {
    case message: AccountDebit =>
      if (balance.single.get < message.amount)
        throw new IllegalStateException("Insufficient Balance")
      else
        balance transform (_ - message.amount)

    case message: AccountCredit =>
      balance transform (_ + message.amount)
  }
```

```
override def normally: Receive = {
  case value: AccountBalance =>
    sender ! new AccountBalance(accountNumber,
                   balance.single.get)
  }
}
```

In `AccountActor`, we have overridden the methods `atomically(Object msg)` and `normally(Object msg)` to filter out messages according to whether they require transactions or not.

When the messages are received by the transactor (`AccountActor` in this case) for action and are received as part of the atomic block, the transactor will check for an existing `coordinated` transaction. If it exists, then the messages will participate as members in the bigger transactions.

This completes the view of the various constructs provided by the transactor as part of the Akka STM.

Agents

Akka provides another construct called **agents**. As part of the transactors we saw the usage of Refs and how they support and coordinate synchronous change of multiple locations in a transaction. On the other hand, agents provide independent, asynchronous change of individual locations. Agents provide shared access to the immutable state.

Akka agents are modeled on the Clojure agents. Clojure agents are reactive, not autonomous, that is, there is no imperative message loop and no blocking received. Clojure agents are native threads that are managed in thread pools for performance. Agents' primary plus point is that they run on a different thread. One can get the value of the agent without any block calls, and any state changes are effected by applying a function to its value. These state changes are applied in an asynchronous way, so that there is no way to know when the function will run and its changes will be applied.

Akka's Actor Model is based on the message-passing model made popular by Erlang. In an Actor Model, state is encapsulated within an Actor and can only be mutated via the passing of values. In the Actor Model, even for reading the actor state, you need to pass a message and wait before the Actor responds back. Agent is modeled on the premise that reading the state should not be a blocking call.

Agents are integrated with STM. Whenever an agent is used within the context of the transaction, it will participate in the transaction. Any updates made within the transaction are held until the transaction commits or the update is discarded in the case of an aborted transaction. You make use of agents wherever you want parallel reads with serial updates of the immutable state. Agents are used outside the Actor Model.

To use agents within your application, the following dependency needs to be added to the maven file:

```
<dependency>
          <groupId>com.typesafe.akka</groupId>
          <artifactId>akka-agent</artifactId>
          <version>2.0.1</version>
     </dependency>
```

Creating agents

Agent creation is simple and straightforward. Agents are defined by passing the generic type and initialized with the value along with the `ActorSystem`.

Java:

```
ActorSystem system = ActorSystem.create("agent-example");

Agent<String> agent = new Agent<String>(String.valueOf("default-value"), system);
```

Scala:

```
implicit val system = ActorSystem("agent-example ")

val agent = Agent("default-value")
```

Updating agent values

Agent values can be updated by sending the new value or sending a function that transforms the current value. Updates to agents are atomic and asynchronous, meaning that there is no guarantee when the update will be applied, but they will be applied definitely. From a single thread, all updates to the agent occur in the same order as they are applied.

Simply sending the new value is easy.

Java:

```
agent.send("change value");
```

Scala:

```
agent send "change value"
```

Another method to update the agent value is to apply a function.

Java:

```
agent.send(new Function<String, String>() {
    public String apply(String inStr) {
      return inStr.toLowerCase();
    }
});
```

Scala:

```
agent send (_ toLowerCase())
```

There is another method provided – `sendOff` that can be used to pass on long-running functions. In the case of `sendOff`, the functions are computed on a separate thread so as not to block the agent thread. The ability to compose agents using functions, which allows you to send different values depending on context, makes agents shine.

Reading agent values

To read an agent's current value, there is no need to pass any message, and it happens immediately. Agent reads for the state are synchronous.

Java:

```
String result = agent.get();
```

Scala:

```
val result = agent()
```

Read for the agent returns immediately, but at times, you may have to read the agent value after all the updates to that agent have been applied. In that case, you can use the `Timeout` mechanism to wait for a certain period before reading the agent value.

Java:

```
String result = agent.await(new Timeout(5, SECONDS));
```

Scala:

```
implicit val timeout = Timeout(5 seconds)
val result = agent.await
```

Here the SECONDS is imported via `java.util.concurrent.TimeUnit.SECONDS`.

Stopping agents

Once the agent usage is complete, the application can call the `close()` method on the agent, so that garbage collection can take place unless, a reference is held.

Java:

```
agent.close();
```

Scala:

```
agent.close()
```

 In Akka, agent is implemented as a wrapper over ScalaSTM Refs.

Summary

In this chapter, we covered the basics of the transaction management and STM. We explored the Akka construct for STM – transactors that are implemented via Refs, and `UntypedTransactor` instances that provide the automated, coordinated services for managing and updating Refs. Lastly, we explored the agents, modeled on the Clojure agents that provide an uncoordinated, asynchronous change of individual locations.

In the next chapter, we will cover what it takes to make an Akka application ready for production. We will explore how to write unit tests involving actors, managing environment configuration changes and deployment strategy.

8
Deployment Ready

An application, to be ready to go to production, needs to pass certain gating criteria; the criteria are as follows:

- Has the application been tested?
- How is the environment-specific information managed?
- What is the deployment mode or strategy?

In this chapter, we will cover the testing library approach provided by Akka to test your actor-based applications. We will also see how the Akka extension model can be used to extend the configuration (using `application.conf`) to add custom parameter values. Lastly, we will touch upon the microkernel-based and embedded mode of application deployment.

Testing your Akka application

Testing of the application is an integral step of the standard **Software Development Lifecycle (SDLC)**. With the advent of **Continuous Integration (CI)** tools, the test units need to be automated, and every commit to the source control initiates the execution of the test regression suite. This makes sure that none of the code being committed is breaking the application.

Akka provides a comprehensive mechanism to perform unit and integration tests on the application. Akka has a dedicated module, **TestKit**, that provides the requisite libraries with support in writing test cases. The premise of the TestKit is to enable the developers to test the functional code that is written.

The Akka TestKit is geared to support testing at the following two levels:

- **Unit testing**: It is the ability to test the code in an isolated manner. The basic idea is to test the functional logic that is written, since this logic comes with completely deterministic behavior. At this level, we need not worry about actors, threads, ordering of messages, or concurrency.

- **Integration testing**: It is all about testing actors, including the multithreaded scheduling and non-deterministic ordering of message events.

The TestKit is more geared to support Scala development at this point in time. The TestKit provides the basic constructs that can be used to write JUnits in Java. We will cover the various constructs that can be used commonly in both Scala and Java. For the examples, we will be using the JUnit 4.1 library; please refer to http://www.junit.org/ for more details.

To use the Akka TestKit within your application, the following dependency needs to be added to the Maven pom.xml file:

```xml
<dependency>
    <groupId>com.typesafe.akka</groupId>
    <artifactId>akka-testkit</artifactId>
    <version>2.0.1</version>
</dependency>
```

Writing the first unit test with TestActorRef

Let's take the example of an actor that takes in the message, and based on the message received, performs a set of actions.

Java:

```java
public class TickTock extends UntypedActor {
  public static class Tick {
    String message;
    public Tick(String inStr) {
      message = inStr;
    }
  };
  public static class Tock {
    String message;
    public Tock(String inStr) {
      message = inStr;
    }
  };

  public boolean state = false;
```

```java
    @Override
    public void onReceive(Object message) throws Exception {
      if (message instanceof Tick) {
        tick((Tick) message);
      } else if (message instanceof Tock) {
        tock((Tock) message);
      } else
        throw new IllegalArgumentException("boom!");
    }

    public void tock(Tock message) {
      // do some processing here
      if (state == false)
        state = true;
      else
        state = false;
    }

    public void tick(Tick message) {
      // do some processing here
      sender().tell("processed the tick message");
    }
  }
```

Scala:

```scala
  case class Tick(message: String)
  case class Tock(message: String)

  class TickTock extends Actor {
    var state = false

    def receive: Receive = {
      case message: Tick => tick(message)
      case message: Tock => tock(message)
      case _ => throw new IllegalArgumentException("boom!")
    }

    def tock(message: Tock) = {
      // do some processing here
      if (state == false)
        state = true
      else
        state = false
    }

    def tick(message: Tick) = {
      // do some processing here
      sender.tell("processed the tick message")
    }
  }
```

Testing the `TickTock` actor in this case will be a two-step process. In the first step, we need to make sure that the business logic written to process the message works fine. In this case, it means testing whether the methods have been written correctly and are performing the business logic as expected:

```
public void tock(Tock message) {}
public void tick(Tick message) {}
```

The second step would be to test the `TickTock` actor by passing in the message and verifying the behavior of the actor and its state. In this step, the messages will be passed in a variable order, and our actor will need to act on them.

Let's go ahead with the basic business logic testing. For testing the business logic, the TestKit provides `TestActorRef`. The `TestActorRef` is a special type of actor reference that is to be used for testing purposes only.

`TestActorRef` provides access to the actor in two ways, as follows:

- It provides a reference to the underlying `Actor` object reference. This is in contrast to `ActorRef`, which mandates that access to the actor is only via mailbox messages.
- It allows the actor behavior to be invoked/queried.

Access to the underlying actor reference

To get access to the actor reference, we make use of `TestActorRef` to create the instance of our `TickTock` actor. Once we have the `TestActorRef` to the actor, we invoke the method `actorRef.underlyingActor()` to get access to the underlying instance of the `Actor` object. Once we have access to the instance, we can invoke the methods on the object as any Java class and write our unit tests.

Java:

```
TestActorRef<TickTock> actorRef = TestActorRef.apply(new Props(
TickTock.class), _system);

    // get access to the underlying actor object
    TickTock actor = actorRef.underlyingActor();

// access the methods the actor object and directly pass arguments
// and test
actor.tock(new Tock("tock something"));

Assert.assertTrue(actor.state);
```

Scala:

```
val actorRef = TestActorRef[TickTock]

    // get access to the underlying actor object
    val actor: TickTock = actorRef.underlyingActor

// access the methods the actor object and directly pass arguments
// and test
actor.tock(new Tock("some message"))

Assert.assertTrue(actor.state)
```

In the preceding unit test case, we saw how the access to the underlying actor Java class is made, and subsequently we can make method calls on the same. The actor class cannot be instantiated directly using the new() method; the Actor Model does not allow such an initialization method. As a result, we use TestActorRef to provide us access to the underlying Actor object.

Testing actor behavior

The second step in testing the actor is to pass the messages to it and see how it responds back. The TestActorRef reference extends the standard LocalActorRef. In addition to the standard methods available on LocalActorRef, TestActorRef also provides an additional method, namely receive(), that returns the changed state of the actor in response to the message. TestActorRef processes the messages synchronously on the current thread and uses CallingThreadDispatcher for the same purpose. In short, when we use TestActorRef, it sets the dispatcher to CallingThreadDispatcher.global and receiveTimeout to None. This means that all the operations are invoked synchronously, because CallingThreadDispatcher uses the single thread model to execute the Actor Model. We have learned about CallingThreadDispatcher in *Chapter 5, Dispatchers and Routers*.

Let's see how we can use TestActorRef, and pass messages to our TickTock actor instance of TestActorRef.

Java:

```
TestActorRef<TickTock> actorRef = TestActorRef.apply(new Props(
TickTock.class), _system);

    String result = (String) Await.result(ask(actorRef,
      new Tick("msg"), 5000),Duration.parse("5 second"));

    Assert.assertEquals("processed the tick message", result);
```

Scala:

```scala
val actorRef = TestActorRef[TickTock]

implicit val timeout = Timeout(5 seconds)
    val future = (actorRef ? new Tick("")).mapTo[String]
    val result = Await.result(future, timeout.duration)
Assert.assertEquals("processed the tick message", result)
```

In the preceding code snippet, we created an instance of `TestActorRef` and then passed a message to our `TickTock` actor. The `TickTock` actor responds back to the sender with the message. In this case, we receive the message and check for its correctness.

Testing exception scenarios

In our `TickTock` actor, if the message passed is not of type `Tick` or `Tock`, then the actor throws an `IllegalArgumentException`. When we want to test such an exception condition, we can invoke the `receive()` method on `TestActorRef`, which passes the message to the underlying actor and propagates back any exceptions that are thrown.

Java:

```java
TestActorRef<TickTock> actorRef = TestActorRef.apply(new Props(
  TickTock.class), _system);
    try {actorRef.receive("do something");
  //should not reach here
Assert.fail();

}
catch (IllegalArgumentException e) {
    Assert.assertEquals(e.getMessage(), "boom!");
}
```

Scala:

```scala
val actorRef = TestActorRef[TickTock]

try {
   actorRef.receive("do something")
   //should not reach here
   Assert.fail()

} catch {
   case e: IllegalArgumentException =>
           Assert.assertEquals(e.getMessage(), "boom!")
}
```

We have seen three ways where we can use TestActorRef to write the unit tests. These tests can be written utilizing one or all of the approaches simultaneously. Using TestActorRef, we can write individual unit tests to check the business logic of our actors.

Once we have unit tested and confirmed the unit tests, we need to test how our actors interact with each other and how their behavior changes when processing the messages.

Integration testing with TestKit

Unlike the traditional integration testing that tests the various components of the system, in Akka, integration testing means testing the actor functionality. It means that we need to have a test suite with the actors under test and the actors that intend to get the replies. The actor functionality is tested by passing messages, which based on the functionality, are either processed, replied back, or forwarded to another actor.

In order to test the actors, TestKit provides a default TestActor. The test specification extends the TestKit, and the default TestActor() is provided to assist in the testing of the custom-written actor classes. TestActor is implicit within the TestKit and we need not create anything explicitly for.

The TestKit also provides a number of assertions (expectMsg*) that can be used to verify the correctness of the actor's behavior.

In addition, an interface/trait, ImplicitSender, is provided as part of the TestKit. ImplicitSender allows the custom actor messages to be passed to TestActor, on which we can run the various assertions. In case of Java, ImplicitSender does not work; as a result, we need to pass the sender ActorRef as TestActor().

Let's check out some testing code that tests out the following different sets of actors:

- EchoActor: It responds back with whatever has been passed to it
- BoomActor: It responds back with an exception to the string or integer passed
- ForwardingActor: It forwards the message to another actor
- SequencingActor: It replies back in a series of messages, but assumes we are interested in only one message
- SupervisorActor: It manages a worker actor, and based on the exception thrown by it, applies the appropriate supervisor strategy

Let's quickly look at the code for each of these actors, and later we will see how the TestKit helps in writing test cases for such actor scenarios.

EchoActor

Java:

```java
public class EchoActor extends UntypedActor
{
  @Override
  public void onReceive(Object message) throws Exception {
    sender().tell(message);
  }
}
```

Scala:

```scala
class EchoActor extends Actor {
  def receive: Receive = {
    case message => sender ! message
  }
}
```

BoomActor

Java:

```java
public class BoomActor extends UntypedActor {
  @Override
  public void onReceive(Object message) throws Exception {
    if (message instanceof String)
      throw new IllegalArgumentException("boom!");
    else if (message instanceof Integer)
      throw new NullPointerException("caput");
  }
}
```

Scala:

```scala
class BoomActor extends Actor {
  def receive: Receive = {
    case message: String =>
            throw new IllegalArgumentException("boom!")
    case message: Integer =>
            throw new NullPointerException("caput")
  }
}
```

ForwardingActor

Java:

```java
public class ForwardingActor extends UntypedActor {
  ActorRef next;
  public ForwardingActor(ActorRef next) {
    this.next = next;
  }
  @Override
  public void onReceive(Object message) throws Exception {
    next.tell(message);
  }
}
```

Scala:

```scala
class ForwardingActor(next: ActorRef) extends Actor {
  def receive: Receive = {
    case message => next ! message
  }
}
```

SequencingActor

Java:

```java
public class SequencingActor extends UntypedActor {
  ActorRef next;
  List<Integer> head;
  List<Integer> tail;
  public SequencingActor(ActorRef next,
  List<Integer> head, List<Integer> tail)
{
    this.next = next;
    this.head = head;
    this.tail = tail;
  }

  @Override
  public void onReceive(Object message) throws Exception {
    for (Integer value : head) {
      sender().tell(value);
    }
    sender().tell(message);
    for (Integer value : tail) {
      sender().tell(value);
    }
  }
}
```

Scala:

```scala
class SequencingActor(next: ActorRef, head:
        List[Integer], tail: List[Integer]) extends Actor {
  def receive: Receive = {
    case message =>
      head map (next ! _)
      next ! message
      tail map (next ! _)
  }
}
```

SupervisorActor

Java:

```java
public class SupervisorActor extends UntypedActor {
  private ActorRef childActor;
  private static SupervisorStrategy strategy =
          new OneForOneStrategy(10, Duration.parse("10 second"),
          new Function<Throwable, Directive>() {
    public Directive apply(Throwable t) {
      if (t instanceof IllegalArgumentException) {
        return stop();
      } else if (t instanceof NullPointerException) {
        return resume();
      } else
        return escalate();
      }
  });
  @Override
  public SupervisorStrategy supervisorStrategy() {
    return strategy;
  }
  public void onReceive(Object o) throws Exception {
    if (o instanceof Props) {
      this.childActor = getContext()
.actorOf((Props) o, "childActor");
      sender().tell(childActor);
    } else
      childActor.tell(o, sender());
  }
}
```

Scala:

```scala
class SupervisorActor() extends Actor {
  var childActor: ActorRef = _
  def receive: Receive = {
    case message: Props =>
```

```
        childActor = context.actorOf(message, name = "childActor")
        sender ! childActor
      case message =>
        childActor.tell(message, sender)
  }
  override val supervisorStrategy = OneForOneStrategy(
maxNrOfRetries = 10, withinTimeRange = 1 minute) {
      case _: NullPointerException => Resume
      case _: IllegalArgumentException => Stop
      case _: Exception => Escalate
  }
}
```

Let's check the various test cases that can be written to verify the actor integration. In order to use the TestKit, we need to extend our test suite example with TestKit. The TestKit constructor takes in `ActorSystem` as the input.

Java:

```java
public class ExampleUnitTest extends TestKit {
    static ActorSystem _system = ActorSystem.create("TestSys",
                 ConfigFactory.load().getConfig("TestSys"));
  LoggingAdapter log = Logging.getLogger(_system, this);
  public UnitTestExample() {
    super(_system);
  }
}
```

Scala:

```scala
@RunWith(classOf[JUnitRunner])
class ExampleUnitTest(_system: ActorSystem) extends TestKit(_system)
with ImplicitSender with WordSpec with MustMatchers with
BeforeAndAfterAll with ShouldMatchersForJUnit {
    def this() = this(ActorSystem("TestSys",
      ConfigFactory.load().getConfig("TestSys")))

}
```

The following is the code snippet for `application.conf`:

```
TestSys {
    akka {
        mode = test
          event-handlers = ["akka.testkit.TestEventListener"]
        loglevel = DEBUG
        actor {
            debug {
              receive = on
              autoreceive = on
```

```
                 lifecycle = on
               }
          }
       }
   }
```

In the preceding case, there is a small difference when initializing the Scala example. For unit testing Scala code, we are making use of the `ScalaTest` library for providing the extension points to write the unit test cases. For more details, please refer to the Scala test documentation available at `http://www.scalatest.org/`

Once we have initialized the TestKit, we can start writing the test cases. We will go over some of the message passing patterns and see how we can test those patterns using the TestKit.

EchoActor testing

In order to test our first actor, namely `EchoActor`, we write the following test code.

Java:

```java
@Test
public void testEchoActor() {
  ActorRef echoActorRef = _system.actorOf(
                          new Props(EchoActor.class));

    // pass the reference to implicit sender testActor() otherwise
    // message end up in dead mailbox
      echoActorRef.tell("Hi there", super.testActor());
    expectMsg("Hi there");
}
```

Scala:

```scala
"Test Echo actor" must {
  "send back messages unchanged" in {
    val echo = system.actorOf(Props[EchoActor])
      echo ! "Hi there"
        expectMsg("Hi there")
  }
}
```

In the Java case, we create the actor and pass the message along with `super.testActor()` as the implicit sender. Next, we use `expectMsg()` to verify the message received from `EchoActor`. If we do not pass the reference to the implicit sender `testActor()`, the messages end up in the dead mailbox. In the case of Scala code, the implicit sender is automatically passed as `testActor`.

ForwardingActor testing

For testing `ForwardingActor`, we need two actors; the first is our `ForwardingActor` and the second is the forwarded actor, where the message ends up. In this case, we can use the implicit sender `testActor()` as the actor to which the message gets forwarded.

Java:

```java
@Test
public void testForwardingActor() {
  ActorRef forwardingActorRef = _system.actorOf(new Props(
    new UntypedActorFactory() {
    public UntypedActor create() {
      return new ForwardingActor(testActor());
    }
  }));
// pass the reference to implicit sender testActor() otherwise
  // message end up in dead mailbox
    forwardingActorRef.tell("test message", super.testActor());
    expectMsg("test message");
}
```

Scala:

```scala
"Test Forwarding actor" must {
  "forwards the messages unchanged to another actor" in {
    val forwarding = system.actorOf(Props(
        new ForwardingActor(this.testActor)))
    forwarding ! "test message"
    expectMsg("test message")
  }
}
```

SequencingActor testing

In the `SequencingActor` test, we want to test for one particular message in a series of messages passed to the actor.

Java:

```java
@Test
public void testSequencingActor() {
  final List<Integer> headList = new ArrayList<Integer>();
  final List<Integer> tailList = new ArrayList<Integer>();

  int randomHead = new Random().nextInt(6);
  int randomTail = new Random().nextInt(10);

  for (int i = 0; i < randomHead; i++)
    headList.add(i);
```

```
      for (int i = 1; i < randomTail; i++)
        tailList.add(i);

    ActorRef sequencingActorRef = _system.actorOf(new Props(
      new UntypedActorFactory() {
        public UntypedActor create() {
          return new SequencingActor(testActor(),
            headList,tailList);
            }
      }));

    // pass the reference to implicit sender testActor() otherwise
    // message end up in dead mailbox
    sequencingActorRef.tell("do something", super.testActor());

      for (Integer value : headList) {
        expectMsgClass(Integer.class);
    }
      expectMsg("do something");
      for (Integer value : tailList) {
        expectMsgClass(Integer.class);
    }
  expectNoMsg();
  }
```

Scala:

```
"Test Sequencing actor" must {
    "checks for one message" in {
      val randomHead = new Random().nextInt(6)
      val randomTail = new Random().nextInt(10)

      val headList = List().padTo(randomHead, new Integer(0))
      val tailList = List().padTo(randomTail, new Integer(1))

      val sequencing = system.actorOf(Props(
         new SequencingActor(this.testActor, headList, tailList)))
      sequencing ! "test message"
      ignoreMsg {
        case msg: Integer => msg != Integer.valueOf(100)
      }
      expectMsg("test message")
      ignoreMsg {
        case msg: Integer => msg == Integer.valueOf(1)
      }
      expectNoMsg
    }
  }
```

In this case, we are using the following new assertions ignoreMsg() and
expectNoMsg().

SupervisorActor testing

Let's see another example where `SupervisorActor` manages the worker actor and how the supervisor strategy can be tested. In our case, we will use `BoomActor` as the child actor. `BoomActor` throws an `IllegalArgumentException` for a string message and a `NullPointerException` for an integer message. In our `SupervisorActor`, we will trap both the exceptions. In the case of `IllegalArgumentException`, we will stop `BoomActor`, and in the case of `NullPointerException`, we will resume `BoomActor` for processing more messages.

Java:

```
@Test
public void testSupervisorStrategy1() throws Exception {

   ActorRef supervisorActorRef1 = _system.actorOf(new Props(
       SupervisorActor.class), "supervisor1");

   Duration timeout = Duration.parse("5 second");

   // register the BoomActor with the Supervisor
   final ActorRef child = (ActorRef) Await.result(
     ask(supervisorActorRef1, new Props(BoomActor.class),
           5000),timeout);

      child.tell(123);
      Assert.assertFalse(child.isTerminated());
}
```

Scala:

```
"Test Supervisor Strategy 1" must {
   "checks for terminated workers" in {
     implicit val timeout = Timeout(5 seconds)

     val supervisor = system.actorOf(Props[SupervisorActor])
     val future = (supervisor ? Props[BoomActor]).mapTo[ActorRef]
     val child = Await.result(future, timeout.duration)

     child.tell(Integer.valueOf(123))
     Assert.assertFalse(child.isTerminated)
    }
}
```

In this case, we have created `BoomActor` as a child actor of `SupervisorActor`. When we pass an integer to `BoomActor`, it should throw a `NullPointerException`. The `SupervisorActor` will catch hold of and ask the actor to `resume()`.

Let's take the next case, where we will pass a string message that should lead to our
BoomActor getting stopped. In this case, we will make use of TestProbe. It provides
a simple way to filter out the messages being sent to testActor(). TestProbe
keeps a track on the actors for messages, and it can be used along with the assert
statements to validate the expected response. So in case the supervisor is managing
multiple actors, TestProbe can be initialized and made to monitor different actors
for different messages.

Java:

```
@Test
public void testSupervisorStrategy2() throws Exception {

    ActorRef supervisorActorRef2 = _system.actorOf(new Props(
        SupervisorActor.class), "supervisor1");

    final TestProbe probe = new TestProbe(_system);

    // register the BoomActor with the Supervisor
    final ActorRef child = (ActorRef) Await.result(
      ask(supervisorActorRef2, new Props(BoomActor.class), 5000),
      Duration.parse("5 second"));

    probe.watch(child);
    // second check
    child.tell("do something");
    probe.expectMsg(new Terminated(child));

    }
```

Scala:

```
"Test Supervisor Strategy 2" must {
    "checks for terminated workers" in {
    implicit val timeout = Timeout(5 seconds)

    val supervisor = system.actorOf(Props[SupervisorActor])
    val probe = TestProbe()

    val future = (supervisor ? Props[BoomActor]).mapTo[ActorRef]
    val child = Await.result(future, timeout.duration)
    probe.watch(child)
    child.tell("do something")
    probe.expectMsg(Terminated(child))
    }
}
```

In the preceding code, we saw how the TestKit can be used to write test cases for integration testing on the actors.

TestKit by default makes use of the following configuration:

```
akka {
  test {
    # factor by which to scale timeouts during tests
    timefactor =  1.0

   # EventFilter.intercept wait duration
   filter-leeway = 3s

   # expectMsg default wait duration
   single-expect-default = 3s

  # implicit DefaultTimeout
  default-timeout = 5s

  calling-thread-dispatcher {
    type = akka.testkit.CallingThreadDispatcherConfigurator
  }
  }
}
```

Based on the number of tests, the time taken to run the test suite, and the wait time required or used by the actors, you may need to tune the parameters.

This completes the overview of the TestKit functionality, provided as part of the toolkit to help test your actors. In the current version, the Scala support is much better and well documented compared to Java.

In the upcoming Akka 2.1 release, a JavaTestKit will be released. The JavaTestKit will provide a number of assertions (expectMsg*) that can be used to test the assumptions about your program, when writing Java-based tests.

Remote actors testing

One of the key features of the Akka application is its scale-out model. The Akka application can span across multiple nodes. Everything in Akka is designed to work in a distributed setting. Akka's location transparency means there is no specific API for the remoting of actors. We write the application assuming everything is local, and at the time of deployment, we can configure the location of the actors. This means that the writing of the test case for the actors that will be deployed remotely can be written using the same principles as outlined in the previous sections.

But there are times, when you want to distribute your application to run across multiple JVMs, with the actor hierarchy spawning across the distributed JVMs. For these cases, Typesafe has released a multi-JVM SBT plugin. The plugin is available at `http://github.com/typesafehub/sbt-multi-jvm`

Using this plugin, you can write test cases that can test message passing across JVMs. The plugin currently supports writing Scala-based test cases only.

Managing application configuration using Akka extensions

In a typical application, the application configuration settings are managed outside the application. So when the application moves from the development to testing to staging to production environment, the application configuration settings can be updated to match the environment. This allows the core deployable unit to be independent of the underlying environment. Examples of such configuration settings can be the application database connectivity options or service end points.

Akka provides a powerful mechanism called extensions. Extensions are loaded in a static way with only one instance per `ActorSystem`. Extensions are implemented as a factory pattern. Akka extensions are comprised of two parts, given as follows:

- **Extension**: Extension is the interface that needs to be implemented by the class and registered with `ActorSystem`, and `ActorSystem` will register the class and make the result available.

- **ExtensionId**: It is the unique ID of the extension that is used to identify the extension within `ActorSystem`.

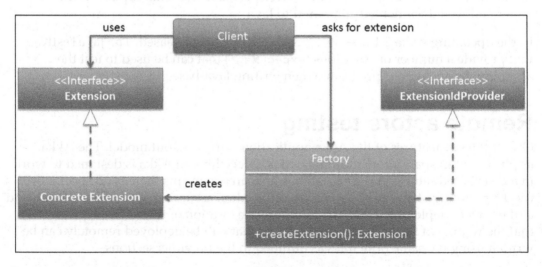

In the real-world application, the environment-specific configuration settings are managed in multiple ways and integrated with your build tool.

One of the common ways is to have specific configuration files depending on each environment. Based on the environment specified in the build file, an appropriate configuration file is chosen. This method requires an application build to be done for every environment.

Another way is to have all the environment configurations in one configuration file. A system variable is used to identify which environment is currently deploying the application, and based on that, the appropriate selection is made. In this case, any wrong system setting means the application can choose the wrong configuration.

Let's go ahead and create an extension to load the configuration settings for connecting to the MySQL database from `application.conf`. Here, we are creating the basic environment configuration usage:

```
TestApp {
  connecton {
    db {
    mysql {
    url = "jdbc:mysql://localhost:3306/"
    dbname = "sampleDB"
    driver = "com.mysql.jdbc.Driver"
    username = "root"
    userpassword = "password"
      }
    }
  }
}
```

Let's go ahead and create the extension.

Java:

```
public class MySQLJDBCSettingsImpl implements Extension {
  public final String DB_URL;
  public final String DB_NAME;
  public final String DB_DRIVER;
  public final String DB_USER_NAME;
  public final String DB_USER_PASSWORD;

    public MySQLJDBCSettingsImpl(Config config) {
    DB_URL = config.getString("connection.db.mysql.url");
```

```
        DB_NAME = config.getString("connection.db.mysql.dbname");
        DB_DRIVER = config.getString("connection.db.mysql.driver");
        DB_USER_NAME =
            config.getString("connection.db.mysql.username");
        DB_USER_PASSWORD =
          config.getString("connection.db.mysql.userpassword");
    }
}
```

Scala:

```
class MySQLJDBCSettingsImpl(config: Config) extends Extension {
  val DB_URL: String = config.getString("connection.db.mysql.url")
  val DB_NAME: String =
        config.getString("connection.db.mysql.dbname")
  val DB_DRIVER: String =
        config.getString("connection.db.mysql.driver")
  val DB_USER_NAME: String =
        config.getString("connection.db.mysql.username")
  val DB_USER_PASSWORD: String =
        config.getString("connection.db.mysql.userpassword")
}
```

We define the class MySQLJDBCSettingsImpl that extends the Extension interface. The class implements the constructor that takes in the config object. The config object provides various methods to read the data. In this case, the example is using config.getString(). We can also write additional custom methods that we may want to expose to the ActorSystem. As Extension is loaded in a static way, this can be an easy reference point for accessing common information across the actors.

Next, we write the Factory class that will provide access to the Extension.

Java:

```
public class MySQLJDBCSettings extends
    AbstractExtensionId<MySQLJDBCSettingsImpl> implements
    ExtensionIdProvider {

  public final static MySQLJDBCSettings SettingsProvider =
                    new MySQLJDBCSettings();
  public MySQLJDBCSettings lookup() {
    return MySQLJDBCSettings.SettingsProvider;
  }
  public MySQLJDBCSettingsImpl createExtension(
                    ExtendedActorSystem system) {
    return new MySQLJDBCSettingsImpl(
                    system.settings().config());
  }
}
```

Scala:

```
object MySQLJDBCSettings extends ExtensionId[MySQLJDBCSettingsImpl]
with ExtensionIdProvider {
  override def lookup = MySQLJDBCSettings
  override def createExtension(system: ExtendedActorSystem) =
            new MySQLJDBCSettingsImpl(system.settings.config)
}
```

In this case, the MySQLJDBCSettings class extends AbstractExtensionId<MySQLJ DBCSettingsImpl> and implements the ExtensionIdProvider interface. The class creates a static instance of MySQLJDBCSettings and implements two methods.

Java:

```
public MySQLJDBCSettings lookup()
public MySQLJDBCSettingsImpl createExtension(ExtendedActorSystem
system)
```

Scala:

```
override def lookup : MySQLJDBCSettings
override def createExtension(system: ExtendedActorSystem)
```

The first method lookup() is used by the ActorSystem to load up the Extension when it is starting up. The second method, createExtension (ExtendedActorSystem) is used by Akka to instantiate the extension class MySQLJDBCSettingsImpl.

The usage of Extension is very easy. Just pass the ActorSystem to the provider and get access to the Extension class. Once you get access to the Extension instance, then it is just a matter of invoking calls on the same.

Java:

```
ActorSystem _system = ActorSystem.create("Extension-Test",
ConfigFactory.load().getConfig("TestApp"));
MySQLJDBCSettingsImpl mysqlSetting = MySQLJDBCSettings.
SettingsProvider.get(_system);

System.out.println(mysqlSetting.DB_NAME);
System.out.println(mysqlSetting.DB_URL);
```

Scala:

```
val system = ActorSystem("Extension-Test",
            ConfigFactory.load().getConfig("TestApp"))
val mysqlSetting = MySQLJDBCSettings(system)

println(mysqlSetting.DB_NAME)
println(mysqlSetting.DB_URL)
```

We create `ActorSystem`, and using `ConfigFactory`, load the configuration, `TestApp` as defined in `application.conf`. We get the `Extension` instance `MySQLJDBCSettingsImpl` from the `extensionprovider` class, `MySQLJDBCSettings`, by passing the `ActorSystem`. Once we get the reference to `Extension`, we can access the methods and variables defined in the `Extension` class.

If you want to access `Extension` within `Actor`, the following method is used.

Java:

```java
public class MyActor extends UntypedActor {
  @Override
  public void onReceive(Object message) throws Exception {
    MySQLJDBCSettingsImpl mysqlSetting =
                MySQLJDBCSettings.SettingsProvider
      .get(getContext().system());
    System.out.println(mysqlSetting.DB_USER_NAME);
    System.out.println(mysqlSetting.DB_USER_PASSWORD);
  }
}
```

Scala:

```scala
class MyActor extends Actor {
  def receive: Receive = {
    case _ =>
      val mysqlSetting = MySQLJDBCSettings(context.system)
      println(mysqlSetting.DB_USER_NAME)
      println(mysqlSetting.DB_USER_PASSWORD)
  }
}
```

In `Actor`, we get `ExtensionId` (in this case, it is `MySQLJDBCSettingsImpl`) and pass the `system()` using the `context()` actor. Once we get the reference to `Extension`, then we can invoke the methods on the same.

As `Extension` is loaded as a singleton object, all state variables in the `Extension` object need to be made thread-safe, in case `Extension` is being read and written. Extensions provide an easy way to load the configuration data from `application.conf`, for use within your Akka application.

Overall, extension is a powerful concept that can be used to provide additional services or functionality to your application. Features such as typed actors, transactor, and ZeroMQ have been implemented using extensions.

Deployment mode

Akka application deployment is available as two options; the first is bundled as a framework JAR within your Java or Scala application, and the second is to be able to deploy the Akka application as a standalone application running within its own microkernel.

The first option of bundling the Akka library JARs in your application is straightforward. You need to add the dependency JARs to the class path using your existing application packaging strategy. The Akka actors can be invoked and used within your application using `ActorSystem`, which is is loaded in a static way, and the actors can be created and invoked using the initialized `ActorSystem`.

The second option for running the Akka application using the microkernel provides a smart way to run the actor application, without incurring any additional overheads of a server container. The microkernel module provides a lightweight and free *application server* bundle, so it's easy to distribute and run your Akka application.

When creating a large, distributed application, which makes use of remote nodes, the remote node logic is the perfect candidate to be packaged as a microkernel application. The microkernel application gets deployed on the remote nodes, and on startup, they can connect to the server/master node to start working. Remote actors can be packaged and deployed as a microkernel application that can be created or invoked from the master node.

It means, when you want to scale out your application processing across JVMs and nodes, there should be an easy way to deploy the code, without the additional overheads of any additional application server licensing.

Microkernel

Akka, by default, is bundled with a microkernel. When you download the Akka library and extract it into a folder, you will find the **bin** directory, as shown in the following screenshot, which holds the executable script (`akka.sh` or `akka.bat`) to run the microkernel:

In order to make your Akka application deployable within the microkernel, the application needs to create a `Bootable` class, which handles the startup and shutdown for the application.

Java:

```java
public class ServerSystem implements Bootable {
  private ActorSystem system = ActorSystem.create("ServerSys");
  public void shutdown() {
    system.shutdown();

  }
  public void startup() {
    // create the actor
    ActorRef actor = system.actorOf(
        new Props(ServerActor.class),"serverActor");
    actor.tell("do something");
  }
}
```

Scala:

```scala
object ServerSystem extends Bootable {
  val system = ActorSystem("ServerSys")
  def startup = {
    val serverActor = system.actorOf(Props[ServerActor],
```

```
                              name = "serverActor")
        actor.tell("do something")
    }
    def shutdown = {
     system.shutdown()
    }
}
```

When the class extends the `Bootable`, there are two methods that need to be implemented.

Java:

```
public void startup()
public void shutdown()
```

Scala:

```
def startup():Unit
def shutdown():Unit
```

In the `startup`, we initialize `ActorSystem` and actors that need to be started, and start the processing of the application. In the `shutdown` method, we write the code to clean up of any of the resources and then shut down `ActorSystem`. Once we have written this class, we bundle the same within the application and create the required deployable unit, which in this case is the JAR file. Once we have the JAR file, we drop it in the `deploy` folder in the Akka deployment path. After dropping the JAR file, we go to the `akka` folder and run `akka.sh` or `akka.bat` to start the application by providing the complete path of the `Bootable` class.

For Windows users, the following path is used:

```
bin/akka.bat   org.akka.essentials.server.ServerSystem
```

For Unix users, the following path is used:

```
bin/akka org.akka.essentials.server.ServerSystem
```

You can use the *Ctrl + C* command to interrupt and exit the microkernel application.

Summary

In this chapter, we saw the various gating criteria that need to be adhered to before the application becomes deployable. We also understood how to write unit test cases, how to move the environment-specific configuration out of the application, and finally, how to use the built-in microkernel to deploy and run Akka applications.

In the next chapter, we will cover the different techniques available for scaling out your application using the concept of remote actors. We will cover topics such as remote actor setup, lookup, and deployment; routing and data serialization for over-the-wire transmission; and the various events generated by remote actors and how we can tap into them.

9
Remote Actors

In this chapter we will cover the different techniques available for scaling out your application using the concept of remote actors. We will see how to create remote actors and how to invoke distributed or remote actors. We will cover the following concepts:

- Remote actor setup
- Remote actor lookup
- Remote actor deployment
- Routing and data serialization for over-the-wire transmission
- Remote events generated by remote clients and servers, and how we can tap into them

Distributed computing

We have seen how the Akka actors allow the application to scale up and use the processing power of the underlying hardware, and make use of all the cores available to the application. Once the application has reached the machine limit (in terms of hardware capacity), you may want to scale out or distribute the application, so that the application can run on multiple machines. When the application runs on multiple machines, the risk of the application going down because one machine failed is also mitigated.

So, what does Akka provide that can be used to distribute the application? The answer is remote actors. Before we jump into remote actors, let's take a step back and understand some basics with respect to distributed computing.

Distributed computing refers to the concept where individual compute nodes run as autonomous entities, with each having their own local memory. The compute nodes talk to each other via **Remote Procedure Calls (RPC)**, which is like message passing. Distributed computing systems require the ability to locate the nodes where the individual compute nodes are running, in order to distribute the work.

In order to locate the nodes, we need to know the address of the nodes, the paths required to reach the node, and the mode of transport needed to reach the node.

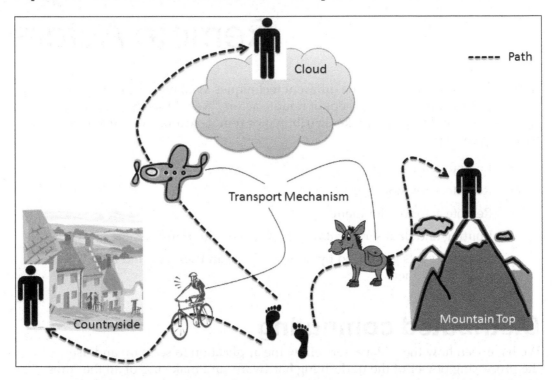

For example, in the preceding diagram, if my friends are at different places (mountain top, countryside, or cloud), then I need to know the address where they are located (mountain top name, countryside name, or which cloud), the path I need to traverse to reach the address (mountain trails, street maps, or an airplane route), and the mode of transportation required to reach the address (mule, bicycle, or airplane). In the distributed world, if I need to locate the objects, I need to know the address as well as the path of the object, along with the means of transport required to reach the object.

Let's understand distributed computing using the Java EE EJB model of distributed computing.

If you have worked with the EJBs earlier, you will know that an EJB will have two references, namely a local reference and a remote reference. The objects within the same JVM use the local reference so as to not incur the overhead of data serialization. The Java objects that are accessing the EJB from outside the container or JVM use the remote reference:

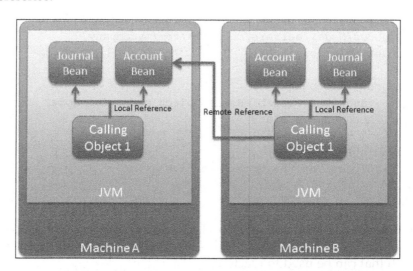

The bean lookup involves knowing where the bean is installed, either in local or remote, and then invoking a reference to the same:

```
java.lang.Object ejbHome = initialContext.lookup(
       "java:comp/env/com/mycompany/accounting/AccountEJB");
```

The application invoking the bean needs to specify whether the bean is locally deployed or remotely deployed via the lookup URLs:

```
// Look up the home interface using the JNDI name.
try {
  java.lang.Object ejbHome = initialContext.lookup(
"java:comp/env/com/mycompany/accounting/AccountEJB");

accountHome = (AccountHome)
        javax.rmi.PortableRemoteObject.narrow(ejbHome,
        AccountHome.class);
}
catch (NamingException e) {
    // Error getting the home interface
    ...
}
```

The preceding code snippet shows how the lookup is being done and that `AccountEJB` is locally deployed. For the same case, if the EJB was to be invoked on another machine instance, the lookup would use the node address as follows:

```
// Look up the home interface using the JNDI name.
try {
  java.lang.Object ejbHome = initialContext.lookup(
  "cell/nodes/Node1/servers/machineA/com/mycompany/
    accounting/AccountEJB");

accountHome = (AccountHome)
        javax.rmi.PortableRemoteObject.narrow(ejbHome,
        AccountHome.class);
}
catch (NamingException e) {
    // Error getting the home interface

}
```

Based on the location where the EJB is deployed, the calling code needs to pass the right name or path to invoke the same. This means that every bean needs to have a name or path that can be used to reach it.

In order to reach the bean that is deployed both locally and remotely, the bean will have two sets of unique addresses. Once we look up the bean, we get a reference to the bean object, namely `LocalReference` or `RemoteReference`, based on the location of the object.

Another key requirement of distributed computing is that whenever the objects are passing the JVM boundaries, they need to be serializable. Since the object reference from one JVM does not exist in the other, the objects being passed need to be serialized before they are passed to the calling node. Without messages being serialized, the data on the other side cannot be interpreted and utilized.

For any application to provide distributed computing capabilities, there are some key elements that need to be used as follows:

- Each bean object should have a unique path that allows the calling client to reach the bean object

- The lookup of the bean should provide a transparent bean reference (local or remote) depending upon the unique path of the deployed bean

- When objects are crossing JVM boundaries, the objects being passed need to be serializable

Now let's see how the same concepts of distributed computing are implemented in Akka. In Akka, everything is passed via messages and the actors communicate asynchronously via immutable messages. It means that the sender does not wait for the message to be received and can go back to its execution immediately, unlike blocking calls in the standard Java world.

For passing the message, all you need is an access to `ActorRef`. The main purpose of `ActorRef` is to allow messages to be passed to the actors it is referencing. `ActorRef` is analogous to the bean reference in the EJB world.

Now Akka uses the concept of location transparency, which means that, for the client sending the message, the location of the actor is transparent. Akka achieves this location transparency using the concept of actor paths. The actor path concept is analogous to the unique bean path. We will examine the actor path in the next section.

For object serialization, Akka provides multiple implementations that can be used for message serialization as well.

Actor path

A path is defined as the concrete series of steps that will lead us to a destination. Now the path to an actor is analogous to a filesystem or URL, where the file or HTML content is located under a series of folders. Akka uses the same philosophy as followed when identifying and locating resources on the Web. We make use of the **uniform resource locator (URL)** to identify and locate resources on the Web. The URL consists of the following:

```
scheme://domain:port/path
```

Here `scheme` defines the protocol (HTTP or FTP), `domain` defines the server name or the IP address, `port` defines which process is listening and where, and `path` specifies the resource to be fetched.

In the case of an Akka application, the default values are `akka://hostname/` or `akka://hostname:2552/` depending on whether the application uses remote actors to identify the application. To identify the resource within the application, the actor hierarchy is used to identify the location of the actor.

Let's take an example to understand the different elements of the actor path:

```
"akka://ServerSys/user/SomeActor"
```

Every Akka application that uses local actors runs at a default address of `akka://hostname/`, and the actor system provides a default guardian actor — `user` to manage the actors created underneath. The actor hierarchy allows a unique path to be created to reach any actor within the actor system. This unique path coupled with the address creates a unique address that identifies and locates an actor.

Every actor within the actor system can be identified and accessed using the actor path. The actor path first identifies the actor system — `/ServerSys` followed by the path — `/user` to the designated actor, which in this case is `/SomeActor`.

This path is used to identify the `ActorRef` that is local to the `ActorSystem`. In the case of the remote actor lookups, the actor path includes the IP address and port number of the machine where the actor, along with its actor system, is deployed:

```
akka://ServerSys@10.102.141.77:2552/user/SomeActor"
```

Looking up `SomeActor` from a distributed client means the `ActorRef` needs to pass the server name or the IP address and port number, `10.102.141.77:2552` where the `ServerSys` application is running.

At this point, let's just keep in mind that every actor has a path anchor that can be used to identify and get a reference to the Akka Actor object. The path itself signifies whether the reference is local or remote. The IP address, `10.102.141.77` is random. You may want to use the IP address of the location where the remote actors are running.

As the remote actors are accessed over the network, by default Akka uses the TCP-based remote transport mechanism based on Netty. This is pluggable. TCP using Netty is just the default.

Netty is a **New I/O (NIO)** client-server framework that enables the quick and easy development of network applications, such as protocol servers and clients. It greatly simplifies and streamlines network programming, such as the TCP and UDP socket server; `https://netty.io/`. NIO was introduced as part of the Java 1.4 to handle intensive I/O operations.

For the serialization of data when it is being sent across the JVMs, Akka provides two serialization mechanisms out of the box. One technique makes use of standard Java serialization and the second uses Google's protocol buffer library.

Protocol buffers is a data interchange format from Google. It specifies the way to encode/serialize structured data in a language-neutral, platform-neutral way. Protocol buffers is binary backward compatible. More about protocol buffers can be found at `https://developers.google.com/protocol-buffers/`.

Akka provides a pluggable model where the third-party serialization module can be plugged in. In fact, later in the chapter we will write our own object serialization mechanism and see how it can be plugged in.

Remote actors

Running Akka applications with hundreds and thousands on one system is a scale-up model, where we optimize the usage of the hardware resource available to the application, but within the boundaries of one instance. Soon, the question about how we can scale out our application arises. It explains how we can run our Akka actors on different instances and how they can be managed and controlled as a single entity:

Consider a large grid where various nodes are processing the data and all the worker actors in each of the nodes are managed centrally. Alternatively, think of a map reduce algorithm running where the data is mapped across nodes, which is passed to other nodes for reduction and aggregation:

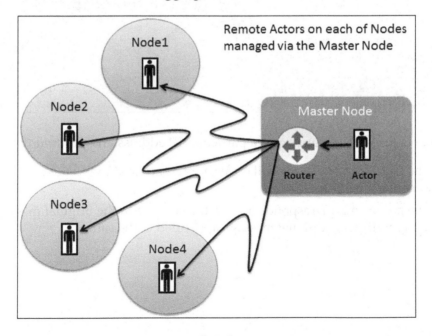

In the previous diagram, we can see each of the nodes (node1 to node4) running actors that are managed by the actor from the master node. In this case, we are have a router actor whose routees are the remote actors on each of the nodes.

So in order to make use of actors that are not part of your own actor system, we need to make use of the remote actors API. Now the remote actors may already be running on remote nodes, in which case we need to get their remote actor reference. In other cases, we can even instantiate new remote actors on the remote nodes.

Let's go ahead and start creating remote actors. We will take a simple example of a two-node application that demonstrates how the RemoteActor API is used. The RemoteActor system receives a message from the LocalActor system that is appended and returned back to the local application. The local application then prints out the message. The idea behind this application is to show how two actor systems running as two different application instances communicate with each other:

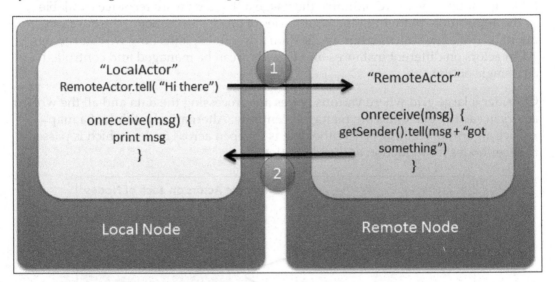

The server actor will be running on a particular IP address and port number:

1. The LocalActor system will create a reference to the RemoteActor and pass a message to RemoteActor.

2. The RemoteActor responds back to the client with the original message, along with an additional message appended to the same.

Creating the remote node application

Our remote node application basically consists of a RemoteActor and a
RemoteActorSystem that implements Bootable, so that we can deploy the
application as a microkernel application. We will start a new Java/Scala project
that will hold the remote node application and its components. First, we will see
the remote node code where we will create the actors that can be invoked remotely.

Let's go ahead and create a RemoteActor.

Java:

```java
public class RemoteActor extends UntypedActor {
  @Override
  public void onReceive(Object message) throws Exception {
    if(message instanceof String){
    //Get reference to the message sender and reply back
      getSender().tell(message + " got something");
    }
  }
}
```

Scala:

```scala
class RemoteActor extends Actor {
  def receive: Receive = {
    case message: String =>
      // Get reference to the message sender and reply back
      sender.tell(message + " got something")
  }
}
```

We created a simple RemoteActor class, which extends the UntypedActor and
implements the method onReceive(). In this method we get the message and
check for the instanceof string. Once the message type is confirmed as the string,
we append our message (" got something") to the original message and send the
message to the sender via the getSender().

Next we will create the RemoteNodeApplication class, where we read the
application.conf configuration file and load the application configuration settings.

Java:

```java
public class RemoteNodeApplication implements Bootable {
  final ActorSystem system = ActorSystem.create("RemoteSys",
          ConfigFactory.load().getConfig("RemoteSys"));
  public void shutdown() {
    system.shutdown();
  }
```

```java
    public void startup() {
      system.actorOf(new Props(RemoteActor.class), "remoteActor");
    }
  }
```

Scala:

```scala
  class RemoteNodeApplication extends Bootable {
    val system = ActorSystem("RemoteNodeApp", ConfigFactory
      .load().getConfig("RemoteSys"))

    def startup = {
      system.actorOf(Props[RemoteActor], name = "remoteActor")
    }

    def shutdown = {
      system.shutdown()
    }
  }
```

That's all. We have created `Bootable`, `RemoteNodeApplication`, where we are using the tag `RemoteSys` to read the block within the `application.conf`. In the startup method, we create a reference of the `RemoteActor`.

Until now, what we have seen has not been different from what we have been doing. So the question where we are specifying that these actors can be accessed over the network is: what is the IP address and port numbers to be used?

Two key configurations that enable the actors to be accessed remotely are as follows:

- **Provider**: For enabling remote access to the actor, we need to specify the provider class, in this case **for** `akka.remote.RemoteActorRefProvider`:

  ```
  akka {
      actor {
        provider = "akka.remote.RemoteActorRefProvider"
  }
  ```

  By default, the provider is `akka.actor.LocalActorRefProvider`, which needs to be changed to the `RemoteActorRefProvider`.

- **Remote Transport**: The second key configuration is providing the remote transport mechanism along with the hostname and port number where the actor system will be running:

  ```
  remote {
   transport = "akka.remote.netty.NettyRemoteTransport"
   netty {
     hostname = "10.102.141.14"
     port = 2552
   }
   }
  ```

All this magic is defined in the `application.conf` file given as follows:

```
RemoteSys {
  akka {
     actor {
        provider = "akka.remote.RemoteActorRefProvider"
     }
     remote {
      transport = "akka.remote.netty.NettyRemoteTransport"
      netty {
        hostname = "10.102.141.14"
        port = 2552
      }
     }
  }
}
```

The `application.conf` is defined under the `resources` folder in your project. These are the bare minimum configurations required to enable remoting for actors. This completes the minimum setup required to host the remote node application. We will package this compiled remote node application as a microkernel application, and deploy it on the `10.102.141.14` node where it will wait for remote invocations:

We create the JAR file of the **RemoteNodeApplication** project and add the JAR to the **deploy** folder under your Akka deployment folder. Next, we run the Akka script to execute the remote node application.

Creating the local node application

Once the server is up and running along with the actors enabled for remoting, the next step is to be able to look up the remote actors and invoke messages on the same.

Let's go ahead and create the `LocalActor` class and see its constituents.

Java:

```java
public class LocalActor extends UntypedActor {
  LoggingAdapter log = Logging.getLogger(getContext()
                          .system(), this);
  Timeout timeout = new Timeout(Duration.parse("5 seconds"));

  ActorRef remoteActor;

  @Override
  public void preStart() {
    //Get a reference to the remote actor
    remoteActor = getContext().actorFor(
    "akka://RemoteNodeApp@10.102.141.14:2552/user/remoteActor");
  }

  @Override
  public void onReceive(Object message) throws Exception {
    Future<Object> future = Patterns.ask(remoteActor,
                    message.toString(),timeout);
    String result = (String) Await.result(future,
                        timeout.duration());
    log.info("Message received from Server -> {}", result);
  }
}
```

Scala:

```scala
class LocalActor extends Actor with ActorLogging {

  //Get a reference to the remote actor
  val remoteActor = context.actorFor
      ("akka://RemoteNodeApp@10.102.141.14:2552/user/remoteActor")
  implicit val timeout = Timeout(5 seconds)

  def receive: Receive = {
    case message: String =>
      val future = (remoteActor ? message).mapTo[String]
```

```
        val result = Await.result(future, timeout.duration)
        log.info("Message received from Server -> {}", result)
    }
}
```

The key here is to get access to the actor reference of the remote actor.

Let's write some sample code and see how it is done.

Java:

```
    remoteActor = getContext().actorFor(
```

"akka://RemoteNodeApp@10.102.141.14:2552/user/remoteActor");

Scala:

```
    val remoteActor = context.actorFor(
        " akka://RemoteNodeApp@10.102.141.14:2552/user/remoteActor")
```

Now to create a reference to the remote actor, we need to provide the actor path to the `context.actorFor()` call. We saw, in the previous sections, how every actor has an actor path attached:

```
    akka://<ActorSystem-name>@<hostname>:<port>/<actor path>
```

The path contains the name of the `ActorSystem` with the IP address and port number specified, with the path of the `Actor` object within the context of the `ActorSystem`.

Once the `RemoteActor` reference has been created, the message can be passed to the remote actor. In the following example, we are passing the message in the request-reply mode, where we expect a response from the server.

Java:

```
    Future<Object> future = Patterns.ask(remoteActor,
                    message.toString(),timeout);

    String result = (String) Await.result(future,timeout.duration());

    log.info("Message received from Server -> {}", result);
```

Scala:

```
    val future = (remoteActor ? message).mapTo[String]

    . . .

    val result = Await.result(future, timeout.duration)

    log.info("Message received from Server -> {}", result)
```

Even in the client application, the remote provider needs to be set up in order for the client to be able to access the remote actor. We create `application.conf` under the `/resources` folder and add it to the class path:

```
LocalSys {
  akka {
      actor {
        provider = "akka.remote.RemoteActorRefProvider"
      }
  }
}
```

Next, we need to initialize the `LocalActor` and pass the message so that it can communicate with the remote actor.

Java:

```java
public class LocalNodeApplication {
  public static void main(String[] args) throws Exception {
    ActorSystem _system = ActorSystem.create("LocalNodeApp",
                ConfigFactory.load().getConfig("LocalSys"));

    ActorRef LocalActor = _system.actorOf(
                    new Props(LocalActor.class));

    LocalActor.tell("Hello");

    Thread.sleep(5000);

    _system.shutdown();
  }
}
```

Scala:

```scala
object LocalNodeApplication {

  def main(args: Array[String]): Unit = {
    val config = ConfigFactory.load().getConfig("LocalSys")
    val system = ActorSystem("LocalNodeApp", config)

    val clientActor = system.actorOf(Props[LocalActor])

    clientActor ! "Hello"

    Thread.sleep(4000)
    system.shutdown()
  }
}
```

Now when we run the local node application, we pass a message to the `LocalActor`, which in turn passes the same to the remote actor and waits for the reply. Once the reply is received, it is printed to the console.

With this we saw our first demonstration of remote actors, and how they can be deployed on one node and accessed from another. Let's see how the whole thing worked:

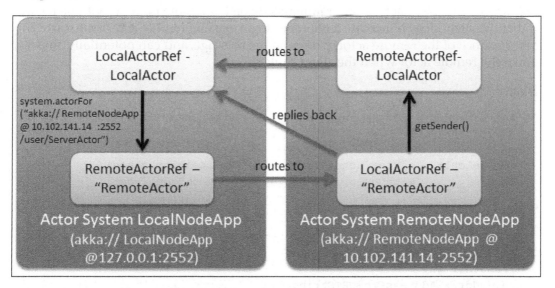

There are two actor systems, namely **LocalNodeApp** and **RemoteNodeApp**. The **RemoteNodeApp** has the **RemoteActor**, and **LocalNodeApp** hosts the **LocalActor**:

- The **LocalActor** needs to invoke the **RemoteActor** to pass the message

- The **RemoteActor** is created in the **RemoteNodeApp** by using the `system.actorOf()` command

- In the **LocalNodeApp**, we need to create a remote reference to the **RemoteActor**, which is created using the `system.actorFor()` command and passing the **RemoteActor** path (`"akka://RemoteNodeApp@10.102.141.14:2552/user/ServerActor"`)

- Once the **RemoteActor** reference is available, the **LocalActor** invokes methods on the **RemoteActor** reference object

>
> `actorOf()`: It creates new actors and is created as a direct child within the context where the method is invoked.
>
> `actorFor()`: It only creates a reference to an existing actor. It does not create a new one.

In the previous example, we saw the **LocalActor** getting the reference to the **RemoteActor** by passing the remote actor path. So what happens if the remote actor is not running, and we need to initialize and start the remote actor instance from the local actor? In that case, we can create remote actors programmatically.

Creating remote actors programmatically

We can create remote actors programmatically on the remote node. What this means is that the client does not create a reference to an existing remote actor, but starts a new instance of the remote actor, passes on the message, and can potentially shut down the remote actor when the client shuts down.

Java:

```
Address addr = new Address("akka", "RemoteNodeApp", "10.102.141.14",
2552);

remoteActor = system.actorOf(new Props(RemoteActor.class)
            .withDeploy(new Deploy(new RemoteScope(addr))));
```

Scala:

```
val addr = Address("akka", "RemoteNodeApp", "10.102.141.14", 2552)

//another way
val addr = AddressFromURIString
        ("akka://RemoteNodeApp@10.102.141.14:2552/user/RemoteActor")

val remoteActor = system.actorOf(Props[RemoteActor]
                    .withDeploy(Deploy(scope = RemoteScope(addr))))
```

What we are doing here is creating an address that takes in the parameters — protocol, ActorSystem name, IP address, and port number. Using this address object, we can create an instance of the remote actor on the remote machine.

We need to pass on the fully qualified name of the remote actor. This method requires access to the class files of the Actor object with the client. The Actor class files also need to be bundled on the client-side deployment.

In case you do not want to hardcode the physical path of the actor in the code, there is another one to specify the remote deployment location of the actor using the `application.conf` file. So for the client-actor system, we define the actor deployment location as follows:

```
akka {
  actor {
      deployment {
         /remoteActorAddr {
             remote = "akka://RemoteNodeApp@10.102.141.14:2552"
         }
      }
  }
}
```

In the following code, we can create the actor using the `system.actorOf()` command.

Java:

```
remoteActor = system.actorOf(new Props(RemoteActor.class),
        "remoteActorAddr");
```

Scala:

```
val remoteActor = system.actorOf(
    Props[RemoteActor], name = "remoteActorAddr");
```

We need to pass on the fully qualified name of the server actor class name along with the `Actor` identifier. In this case, `remoteActorAddr` is the key that is mapped to the deployment name defined in the `application.conf` file.

This allows you to write code that does not worry about the location of the actor, and at runtime, the location of the actor can be plugged in. This is a better way to access remote actors, as the actor deployment becomes transparent to the application. This method allows us to change the deployment location of the actor seamlessly, without impacting on the actual code. As long as the actor reference name has been defined in the code, the same can be used to map the actor to the remote deployment location.

 In this method of remote actor creation, just by analyzing the code, you may not be able to comprehend where the actor gets deployed; so extra precaution needs to be taken when debugging such deployments.

With this, we saw how one Akka application can access actors that are running on a different node or in another instance. Here, the applications running on each of the nodes are independent of each other and are instantiated separately.

Message serialization

Another key aspect of distributed computing is the serialization of the message data that passes the JVM boundaries. Message serialization allows us to save the state of an object into a sequence of bytes, in order to allow us to rebuild the object with the state using the byte sequence.

In the case of Akka as well, whenever the message passes the JVM boundary, the principles of object serialization get applied. In Java, the serialization of a class is enabled when the class implements the `java.io.Serializable` interface. The serialization interface does not impose that any methods be implemented, but only serves to identify the semantics of being serializable. The serializable interface only saves the object state and not the object definition.

Akka has an inbuilt extension for serialization. Akka allows us to use the built-in serializers, or be able to define our own serializable extensions.

By default, Akka uses the built-in serialization technique to serialize messages when they are crossing the JVM boundaries. Akka provides two serialization techniques. One is the default Java serialization (`java.io.Serializable`) and another is Google's `Protobuf` serialization (`com.google.protobuf.GeneratedMessage`) technique.

In Akka, you can specify which class needs to use which serialization technique. Let's see how we can define the protocols available and map them to the classes.

So in the `application.conf` file, we can define the list of available serializers as follows:

```
akka {
   actor {
     serializers {
       java = "akka.serialization.JavaSerializer"
       proto = "akka.serialization.ProtobufSerializer"
     }
   }
}
```

In case we are using any custom, third-party serializers, they can also be defined in the `application.conf` file.

Once the serializers have been defined, we need to define the classes and bind those serializers to the classes we want, as given in the following code:

```
akka {
   actor {
     serialization-bindings {
       "java.lang.Integer" = java
```

```
            "java.lang.Boolean" = java
            "com.google.protobuf.Message" = proto
          }
        }
      }
```

We define the class with their fully qualified names and map them to the serializer names, as defined in the serializer's section.

The complete `application.conf` looks as shown in the following code:

```
akka {
    actor {

      serializers {
          java = "akka.serialization.JavaSerializer"
          proto = "akka.serialization.ProtobufSerializer"
      }

      serialization-bindings {
          "java.lang.Integer" = java
          "java.lang.Boolean" = java
          "com.google.protobuf.Message" = proto
        }

    }
  }
```

So what we see is that we need to define the available serializers in akka | actor | serializers (as defined in the `application.conf`) section, with a name that is used to define and subsequently bind the serializers to the class files. By default, Akka provides the serializers for Java and Protobuf, so you need not add them to the configuration file.

Next, we define the serialization bindings in the akka | actor | serialization-bindings section. Here the classes are identified by their fully qualified names and then mapped to the serializers that need to be used for that class.

Creating your own serialization technique

In the previous section, we saw how the various serializations that are available can be defined and mapped to the class files. Now let's try to create our own serialization technique and see how it can be used to serialize and de-serialize the object state.

For writing your own serializer in Java, Akka provides the class `JSerializer` that needs to be extended.

Java:

```java
public class MySerializer extends JSerializer {

  public int identifier() {
    return 12062010;
  }

  public boolean includeManifest() {
    return false;
  }

  public byte[] toBinary(Object arg0) {

    ...

  }
  @Override
  public Object fromBinaryJava(byte[] arg0, Class<?> arg1) {

    ...

  }
}
```

You need to implement four methods in order to write your serializable. Let's go through each of the methods and see what we need to implement there:

- `identifier()`: In this we need to specify a unique identifier. It can be any number. The numbers from 0 to 16 are reserved by Akka, so you can use that range.

- `includeManifest()`: This method indicates whether we need a class definition when de-serializing the byte array.

- `toBinary(Object arg0)`: This method is where we write our logic of serializing the object into the byte array.

- `fromBinaryJava(byte[] arg0,Class<?> arg1)`: This method is where we write our logic of converting the byte array into the object itself.

Let's implement a serializable technique. We will make use of the Gson libraries from Google here (http://code.google.com/p/google-gson/), for serializing and de-serializing the object state.

 Gson is a Java library that allows you to convert Java objects into their JSON representation. The library can also convert a JSON string to an equivalent Java object.

Java:

```java
public class MySerializer extends JSerializer {
  // create the Gson object
  private Gson gson = new GsonBuilder().serializeNulls().create();
  public int identifier() {
    return 12062010;
  }
  public boolean includeManifest() {
    return true;
  }
    // "toBinary" serializes the given object to an Array of Bytes
    public byte[] toBinary(Object arg0) {
    return gson.toJson(arg0).getBytes();
  }

    // "fromBinary" deserializes the given array,
    // using the type hint (if any, see "includeManifest" above)
    // into the optionally provided classLoader.
  @Override
  public Object fromBinaryJava(byte[] arg0, Class<?> arg1) {
    return gson.fromJson(new String(arg0), arg1);
  }
}
```

Scala:

```scala
class MySerializer extends Serializer {
  def identifier = 12062010
  def includeManifest: Boolean = true
  val gson = new GsonBuilder().serializeNulls().create()

  // "toBinary" serializes the given object to an Array of Bytes
  def toBinary(obj: AnyRef): Array[Byte] = {
  gson.toJson(obj).getBytes()
  }
  // "fromBinary" deserializes the given array,
  // using the type hint (if any, see "includeManifest" above)
  // into the optionally provided classLoader.
  def fromBinary(bytes: Array[Byte],
    clazz: Option[Class[_]]): AnyRef = {
    gson.fromJson(new String(bytes), clazz.toList.first)
  }
}
```

By using the Gson library, we convert the object state into the JSON array, which is then converted into a byte array.

Java:

```
public byte[] toBinary(Object arg0) {
    return gson.toJson(arg0).getBytes();
}
```

Scala:

```
def toBinary(obj: AnyRef): Array[Byte] = {
gson.toJson(obj).getBytes()
}
```

When it comes to de-serialization, we convert the byte array into a string and pass it to the method call `fromJson()`.

Java:

```
public Object fromBinaryJava(byte[] arg0, Class<?> arg1) {
    return gson.fromJson(new String(arg0), arg1);
}
```

Scala:

```
def fromBinary(bytes: Array[Byte],
  clazz: Option[Class[_]]): AnyRef = {
  gson.fromJson(new String(bytes), clazz.toList.first)
}
```

Let's see how we can use this serializable in our code. The `application.conf` needs to define the serializers and bindings to the respective class. We'll use the following configuration as an example:

```
akka {
    actor {
      serialize-messages = on
      serializers {
         my-serialization  =  "org.akka.essentials.serializer.
MySerializer"
      }
      serialization-bindings {

         "org.akka.essentials.serializer.MyMessage" = my-serialization

      }
    }
  }
```

Let's define a message class with which we will bind the custom serializer.

Java:

```java
public class MyMessage {

  private String name;
  private Integer age;
  private String address;
  public MyMessage(String _name, Integer _age, String _address) {
  name = _name;
  age = _age;
    address = _address;
  }
  public String getName() {
    return name;
  }
  public void setName(String name) {
    this.name = name;
  }
  public Integer getAge() {
    return age;
  }
  public void setAge(Integer age) {
    this.age = age;
  }
  public String getAddress() {
    return address;
  }
  public void setAddress(String address) {
    this.address = address;
  }
  public String toString() {
    return new StringBuffer().append(name).append(",").append(age)
      .append(",").append(address).toString();
  }
}
```

Scala:

```scala
case class MyMessage( name: String, age: Int, city: String)
```

The message class is simple; it has three attributes, which are name, age, and address. We have overridden the toString() method in the case of Java, so that we can log the state of the object.

Now, let's go ahead and define an `ActorSystem` and see how we can use the custom serializer with the `MyMessage` object that we have defined.

Java:

```
ActorSystem system = ActorSystem.create("MySerializableSys",
    ConfigFactory.load().getConfig("MySerializableSys"));

Serialization serialization = SerializationExtension.get(system);

MyMessage originalMessage = new MyMessage("Munish", 36, "Bangalore");

System.out.println("The original message is as " + originalMessage);

// Get the Binded Serializer for it
Serializer serializer = serialization.findSerializerFor
(originalMessage);

// Turn the object into bytes
byte[] bytes = serializer.toBinary(originalMessage);

// Turn the byte[] back into an object,
MyMessage deSerializedMessage = (MyMessage) serializer.fromBinary(
        bytes, MyMessage.class);

System.out.println("The de-serialized message is as " +
deSerializedMessage);

system.shutdown();
```

Scala:

```
val system = ActorSystem("MySerializableSys", ConfigFactory.load()
    .getConfig("MySerializableSys"));
val log = system.log

// Get the Serialization Extension
val serialization = SerializationExtension(system)

val originalMessage = new MyMessage("Munish", 36, "Bangalore")

log.info("The original message is as {}", originalMessage)

// Get the Binded Serializer for it
val serializer = serialization.findSerializerFor(originalMessage);
```

```
// Turn the object into bytes
val bytes = serializer.toBinary(originalMessage);

// Turn the byte[] back into an object,
val deSerializedMessage = serializer.fromBinary(
    bytes, classOf[MyMessage])

log.info("The de-serialized message is as {}",deSerializedMessage)

system.shutdown
```

Let's go through the code and understand what is happening. Now, we load the `config` data for the actor system defined in the `application.conf`.

Next we get the `SerializationExtension` defined in the `application.conf`.

Java:

```
Serialization serialization = SerializationExtension.get(system);
```

Scala:

```
val serialization = SerializationExtension(system)
```

This loads the three extensions we had defined, namely `java`, `proto`, and `my-serialization`.

We create the `Message` object with the attributes.

Java:

```
MyMessage originalMessage =
    new MyMessage("Munish", 36, "Bangalore");
```

Scala:

```
val originalMessage = new MyMessage("Munish", 36, "Bangalore")
```

With the object, we again look into the `config` to get the binary serialization attached to the object. This refers to the following code:

```
Akka{
    actor {
       serialization-bindings {
         "org.akka.essentials.serializer.MyMessage" = my-serialization
      }
   }
}
```

We had defined in the `application.conf`, using the serializer for the `MyMessage` class, how we can serialize the object state into a `byte` array.

Java:

```
byte[] bytes = serializer.toBinary(originalMessage);
```

Scala:

```
val bytes = serializer.toBinary(originalMessage)
```

Next, we pass back the byte array to the `serializer` method to get the object state back.

Java:

```
MyMessage deSerializedMessage =
    (MyMessage)serializer.fromBinary(bytes, MyMessage.class);
```

Scala:

```
val deSerializedMessage =
    serializer.fromBinary(bytes, classOf[MyMessage])
```

Then we can dump the object state to verify whether the object got created properly or not.

We saw the usage of the message serialization technique that allows us to pass the messages in a format that is understood on both sides of the wire. The default serializers, namely `java.io.Serializer` or `protobuf`, would suffice your needs for most cases. If you are dealing with a proprietary message serialization technique, you will need to override and write your serialization extension.

This completes the example that demonstrated how to write your own object serialization technique and map the objects that are passed as messages between the actors.

Remote events

To monitor the remote actors, Akka provides the functionality to listen to these events. We can write an `Actor` class and register it as `Listener` to listen to these events. The events are published to the event stream, and our actor subscribes to the event stream for actor-specific, event notifications.

The following remote events are provided, which our `Listener` can subscribe to:

Event name	Description
RemoteClientConnected	Whenever an outbound connection is made. The event has information about the transport used and the outbound address that was connected to it.
RemoteClientDisconnected	Whenever an outbound connection is disconnected. The event has information about the transport used and the outbound address that the client was disconnected from.
RemoteClientStarted	Whenever an outbound client is started. The event has information about the transport used and the outbound address that the client was connected to.
RemoteClientShutdown	Whenever an outbound client is shut down. The event has information about the transport used and the outbound address that the client was connected to.
RemoteClientWriteFailed	Whenever the outbound message was not delivered. The event holds the information for the payload that was not delivered, the cause of failure (throwable), the transport used, and the outbound address that the client was connected to.
RemoteClientError	All other errors that are not classified in any other category are caught via this event. The event holds the information for the cause of failure (throwable), the transport used, and the outbound address that the client was connected to.
RemoteServerStarted	This event is generated when the inbound server is started. The event has information for the remote transport used.
RemoteServerShutdown	This event is generated when the inbound server is shutdown. The event has information for the remote transport used.
RemoteServerClient Connected	Whenever an inbound client connection is established. The event contains information about the transport used and the outbound address that the client was connected to (optional).
RemoteServerClient Disconnected	Whenever an inbound client connection is disconnected. The event contains information about the transport used and the outbound address that the client was connected to (optional).
RemoteServerClient Closed	Whenever an inbound client connection is closed. The event contains information about the transport used and the outbound address that the client was connected to (optional).

Let's see how we can write a small `Listener` for subscribing to remote events, and how we register the `Listener`.

Java:

```java
public class RemoteClientEventListener extends UntypedActor {
  @Override
  public void onReceive(Object message) throws Exception {
    if (message instanceof RemoteClientError) {
      //do something
    } else if (message instanceof RemoteClientConnected) {
      //do something
    } else if (message instanceof RemoteClientDisconnected) {
      //do something
    } else if (message instanceof RemoteClientStarted) {
    //do something
    } else if (message instanceof RemoteClientShutdown) {
      //do something
    } else if (message instanceof RemoteClientWriteFailed) {
      //do something
    }
  }
}
```

Scala:

```scala
class RemoteClientEventListener(val jobScheduler: ActorRef) extends
Actor with ActorLogging {

  def receive: Receive = {
    case event: RemoteClientError => //do something
    case event: RemoteClientConnected => //do something
    case event: RemoteClientDisconnected => //do something
    case event: RemoteClientStarted => //do something
    case event: RemoteClientShutdown => //do something
    case event: RemoteClientWriteFailed => //do something
  }
}
```

The `Listener` is a simple actor that listens to the various events. Based on the events, the `Listener` can either forward a message for corrective action or take the corrective action itself. For example, if the remote client has shut down, then one corrective mode might restart the remote client actor.

Once `Listener` is created, we need to register the `Listener` on `eventStream` for particular events.

So to register `Listener` in the actor system, we instantiate the `Listener` actor and then register it on the `eventStream` for particular messages.

Java:

```
//Actor creation
ActorRef remoteActorListener = system.actorOf(
        new Props(RemoteActorListener.class)),
        "RemoteClientEventListener");


//registration of listener on the stream
system.eventStream().subscribe(remoteActorListener,
        RemoteLifeCycleEvent.class);
```

Scala:

```
val remoteActorListener = system.actorOf(Props(
    new RemoteClientEventListener(jobControllerActor)),
    name = "RemoteClientEventListener")


system.eventStream.subscribe(remoteActorListener,
classOf[RemoteLifeCycleEvent])
```

The `subscribe` method takes two arguments, — one is `actorref` for the `Listener` class and the second is the type of lifecycle events you want to subscribe to. There are three main lifecycle events given, as follows:

- `RemoteClientLifeCycleEvent`: This is used when you want to listen primarily to outbound events originating from the remote clients

- `RemoteServerLifeCycleEvent`: This is used when you want to listen primarily to inbound events originating from the remote server

- `RemoteLifeCycleEvent`: This is used when you want to listen to all remote events

Using the remote events, you can write programs to handle remote event notifications that can then be potentially used by the supervisor strategy to handle failures.

Summary

In this chapter, we saw what the requirements of any distributed computing environment are and how Akka implements them. We saw various methods of creating actors using the remote deployment mode, and how to create remote references to remote objects.

Next we saw how object serialization happens on Akka, the various serializers provided by Akka, and how we can write our own serializers.

In the next chapter, we will the see the techniques available to monitor and manage your large, distributed application. We will cover the Akka monitoring tools and the various statistics provided by these tools.

10
Management

The availability of a large, distributed application is dependent on the quality of application monitoring. If the application is not properly monitored, outages can go undetected, leading to application unavailability. The ability to monitor the entire application stack and take corrective actions is very important.

In this chapter we will cover the following advanced topics as follows:

- Typesafe console — an Akka monitoring tool
- Graphical dashboards
- Real-time statistics
- JMX and REST interfaces

Application monitoring

Knowing application failure alerts in real time helps you to respond to alerts and take corrective actions, which in turn determines the agility of the overall application. If you are not able to gauge the health of the application in real time, you may not be able to respond to any signs of failure quickly. This leads to a situation where you come to know of failure only when a major portion of the application or service has gone down.

In a large, distributed application, monitoring and alerting capabilities are all the more important due to the sheer number of pieces that need to work together to make sure that the application performs at its optimum. In addition, it is an expected behavior to have the monitoring turned on in production systems, because, at times, system behavior at runtime is unpredictable and very difficult to reproduce under normal circumstances. This means that a monitoring system should ideally have the following characteristics:

- **Low overhead**: The monitoring system in itself should have a very low footprint and a very negligible impact on the running applications.
- **Transparent**: The application should not be aware of the monitoring solution. The application need not take anything into account, and programmers need not perform anything with respect to the monitoring solution.
- **Real time**: The monitoring system should provide runtime statistics on a real-time basis.

Akka, via its commercial arm Typesafe, provides the application monitoring capability. The Typesafe console provides a dashboard for monitoring the application built using Akka. The Typesafe console is available only for Typesafe subscription customers.

Typesafe console

The Typesafe console is a custom-built, tracing and monitoring solution for Akka's actor-based applications. The Typesafe console captures the events emitting from an actor system that are linked together via a trace ID, which is spanned across the complete message flow (including remote nodes). These events are then aggregated, consolidated, and made available to the administrators and developers via a web-based interface.

The Typesafe console provides an insight into usage trends and performance characteristics of the running system. Using the console, the operations staff can detect potential bottlenecks, understand the underlying reasons, and take corrective actions before they explode into a full-blown problem.

The Typesafe console monitoring solution is very lightweight and designed to be used in a high-volume production environment. For a very high transaction rate system, the Typesafe console uses sampling to reduce the overhead and the amount of data to be collected.

The Typesafe console provides a rich web interface to monitor the application. In addition, it also exposes the aggregated metrics and monitoring data via RESTful API and JMX. This allows the enterprise to take advantage of existing tools and integrate the Typesafe console. The Typesafe console provides both historical and current monitoring information, allowing comparison across time and trend analysis.

The Typesafe console has been implemented as a series of modules that combine together to provide complete functionality. Let's go through the console modules to understand their role, and how they integrate together to provide functionality.

Typesafe console modules

The Typesafe console is composed of the following modules:

- **Trace**: It is responsible for collecting the trace events being emitted by the actor system and storing those trace events in storage.

- **Analyze**: It is responsible for taking raw trace events from storage and producing aggregated results. These results are then stored in a separate storage.

- **Query**: It is responsible for exposing the statistical data via REST and JMX.

- **Typesafe console**: It is the web interface that uses the REST API interface to connect to the query module and provide the rich interface.

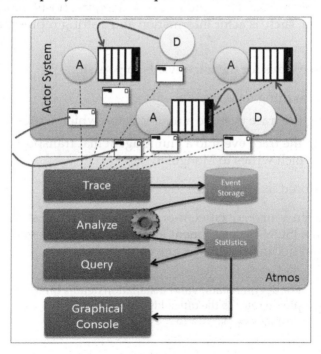

The trace, analyze, and query modules together are referred to as *Atmos*, while the frontend module is called either the Typesafe console or just console.

Atmos is able to track messages as they flow through the distributed systems (across the actor system and across networks). This means that it is possible to follow message chains in the distributed system. Atmos is able to follow distributed control paths by relying entirely on the instrumentation of a few common libraries.

Trace events are captured in a very efficient way using a combination of threads, local state, and local buffering, before they are emitted to storage for an offline analysis.

In the Akka application, we need to configure the three atmos modules, to be able to make use of the monitoring capabilities of the Typesafe console.

Let's go through the atmos modules and see their usage and configuration.

Trace

Trace events are collected in the application using the instrumented versions of a common library (`akka-actor`, `akka-remote`, `akka-kernel`, and `akka-slf4j`) of JAR files. The trace events are buffered and then asynchronously written to storage.

Each trace event holds a UUID of the trace it belongs to, and also of the trace event (the work unit) that happened in the trace before. Each trace event also carries timestamps (`currentTimeMillis` and `nanoTime`), nodes, hosts, sampling factors, and additional data, such as actor information and a string representation of the sent message.

A trace allows three ways for the trace events to persist:

- By directly writing to MongoDB
- By sending the trace event to a remote actor, which writes to MongoDB
- By sending the trace event to a Flume agent that transports to a Flume collector, which writes to MongoDB

Trace events are stored in MongoDB.

MongoDB is an open source, document-oriented NoSQL data store. It stores structured data in a JSON-like document format and provides very good support for indexing and ad hoc queries on document-style data.

 For documentation and installation details on MongoDB, please refer to the official MongoDB site: http://www.mongodb.org/

Flume is an Apache project that focuses on collecting, aggregating, and moving large amounts of data. Flume was initially written to move data into the Hadoop HDFS file system.

 For more details about Apache Flume, refer to the following URL: https://cwiki.apache.org/FLUME/

Trace configuration

In the application to be monitored, add the following minimum configuration corresponding to the `application.conf` file:

```
akka {
  loglevel = INFO
  event-handlers = ["akka.atmos.trace.Slf4jTraceContextEventHandler"]

  atmos {
    mode = mongo

    trace {
      # Enable or disable all tracing
      enabled = true
      node = node1
      mongo {
        # Name of the Mongo database
        db-name = "atmos-monitoring"

         # Connection URI to MongoDB
        db-connection-uri = "mongodb://localhost"
      }
    }


  }
}
```

To get the tracing running, we need to define the following minimum properties:

* Tracing is disabled by default, so we need to enable it for the specific actor systems that need to be monitored
* Define the node property for each node (`ActorSystem`) in the system, as this is used to identify and tag the multiple actor systems that are running

- Define the MongoDB name and URL, specifying the location of MongoDB

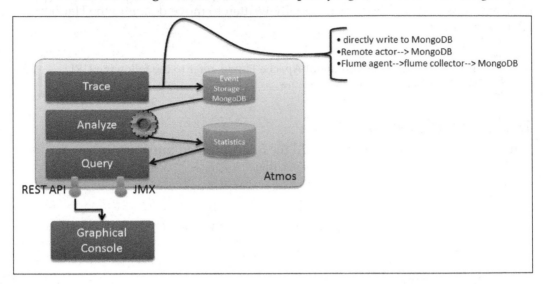

Analyze

The analyze module creates spans and then aggregates the statistics from the trace events for that particular span. The trace events are extracted from the event storage, and the statistics are then computed and stored in advance for various groupings in time and scope.

A span is the path between two trace events, and the duration between these events is the data that captures the essence of the availability and scalability of the application.

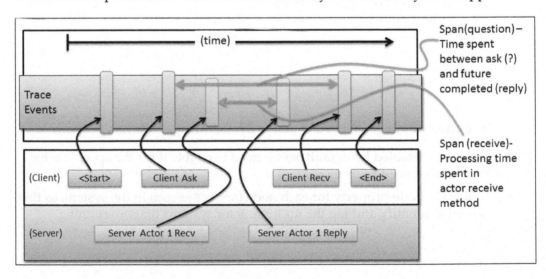

The previous diagram shows a sample span that contains information between client and server. For each activity happening on the client and server side, events are generated that are annotated and tagged to the span ID. These events are then correlated and aggregated by the analyze module.

Atmos supports the following span types:

- **Message**: A span for a message, from when it is sent until the processing of the message is completed
- **Mailbox**: A span for the waiting time of the message in the actor mailbox
- **Receive**: A span for the processing time in the actor receive method
- **Question**: A span between ask (?) and future completed (reply)
- **Remote**: A span for remote latency
- **Any user-defined marker span**: A user-defined span may start and end at any location in the message trace; that is, it may span over several actors

The trace events and span-aggregated statistics are grouped into two dimensions, namely scope and time. The scope dimension group's actors are based on the following properties:

- `actorPath`: The unique name of the actor
- `tag`: One or more tags can be assigned to an actor with configuration
- `dispatcher`: The name of the message dispatcher of the actor
- `node`: The logical name of the node, which corresponds to an actor system, and typically also a JVM, even though it is possible to run several nodes (actor systems) in the same JVM

Running analyze module

The analyze module is started with `bin/atmos -analyze -name analyze` (or `bin\bat\startAnalyze.bat` on Windows) in the distribution.

It uses `config/atmos/atmos.conf` as an analyze configuration:

```
akka {
  loglevel = INFO
  event-handlers = ["akka.atmos.trace.Slf4jTraceContextEventHandler"]


  atmos {
    mode = mongo
```

```
    analytics {
      mongo {
        # Name of the Mongo database
        db-name = ${akka.atmos.trace.mongo.db-name}

        # Connection URI to MongoDB
        db-connection-uri = ${akka.atmos.trace.mongo.db-connection-
  uri}
      }
    }
  }
```

In this configuration, it is very important to define the `mongo.db-name` and `uri`, as the aggregated statistics are stored in the database.

Query

The query module exposes the aggregated statistics and underlying trace events and spans via the REST API and JMX. Availability of the REST API and JMX allows the integration of atmos with other enterprise products, for monitoring operations.

The JMX beans expose the information using the root name `akka.atmos`. JMX information can be accessed with an ordinary JMX console, such as JConsole or JVisualVM, connected to the query node.

The Typesafe console uses the query module's REST API to display statistics in a rich web GUI.

Running query module

The query module is started with `bin/atmos -query -jmx -name query` (or `bin\bat\startQuery.bat and bin\bat\startJmx.bat` on Windows) in the distribution. It uses the `config/atmos/atmos.conf` as the query configuration.

As the query module accesses the same MongoDB instance in which the analyze module stores the aggregated statistical data, the configuration read and used is the same:

```
akka {
  loglevel = INFO
  event-handlers = ["akka.atmos.trace.Slf4jTraceContextEventHandler"]

  atmos {
    mode = mongo
```

```
    analytics {
      mongo {
        # Name of the Mongo database
        db-name = ${akka.atmos.trace.mongo.db-name}

        # Connection URI to MongoDB
        db-connection-uri = ${akka.atmos.trace.mongo.db-connection-
  uri}
      }

      jmx {
        # URL for the host and port of the REST API.
        base-url = "http://127.0.0.1:9898"

        # Time filter of the queries, such as rolling=2hours
        # "" means all time
        time-filter = ""
      }
    }

    collect {
      remote {
        hostname = "127.0.0.1"
        port = 2553
      }
    }
  }
}
```

Additional information is defined for the JMX and time-filter criteria.

Typesafe console

The Typesafe console retrieves the information from the query module and visualizes the collected information in nice-looking graphs.

The Typesafe console has been built using the Play framework.

Running Typesafe console

The console module is started with `bin/console` (or `bin\bat\startConsole.bat` on Windows) in the distribution. It uses the `config/console/console.conf` as the console configuration:

```
# Get configuration from this file (not database)
app.config=true

# The name of the application
app.name=Demo
# The URL of the endpoint, i.e. where the Atmos Query API is found
app.url="http://localhost:9898/monitoring/"

# User to login with
user.email="demo@typesafe.com"
user.password="demo"

# Secret key
application.secret=<application secret key>
```

The setting `app.config=true` means that the settings in this configuration file will be used to define the application's attributes. Any changes made in the console will be temporary and will not persist.

Define the name of the application with the `app.name` parameter. This name is the one that will be shown in the console.

The console uses the query module to retrieve information, so we need to configure `app.url` to where the query module is running.

`user.email` and `user.password` are used when there are multiple users and applications involved. `application.secret` is used by the Play framework to secure cryptographic functions.

This completes the overview, setup configuration, and the procedure on how to run the Typesafe console modules. Next, we will see what information is exposed via the Typesafe console and how we can comprehend the same.

Graphical dashboard

Let's hit the Typesafe console URL at `http://localhost:9898/monitoring/` and check out the graphical dashboard provided to monitor your Akka application.

The first screen to come up is the sign-in screen, as shown in the following screenshot. By default, the user/password applicable is what we provided in the previous section, *Running Typesafe console*.

```
user.email="demo@typesafe.com"
user.password="demo"
```

We provide the user's **Email** and **Password** and click on **SIGN IN**. Once we are successfully signed in, we are presented with the screen shown in the following screenshot:

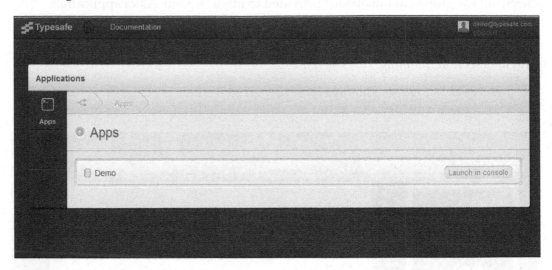

The following screenshot lists the applications that are currently being monitored. In the preceding screenshot, it shows the **Demo** application.

We click on the **Launch in console** link mentioned against the **Demo** option, shown in the preceding screenshot.

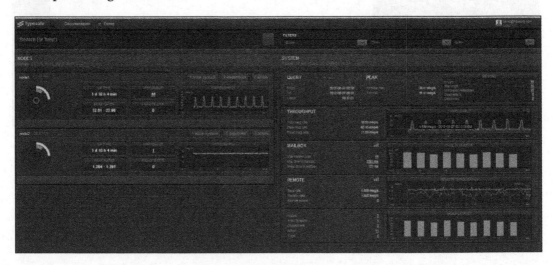

The preceding screenshot shows the overview of the whole **SYSTEM** to the right-hand side and all **NODES** to the left-hand side.

System overview

Let's look at the **SYSTEM** overview (present on the right-hand side) to see all the details that are provided:

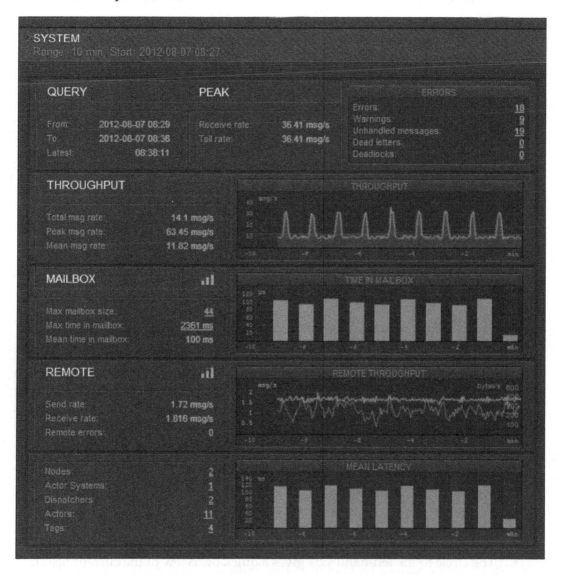

The **SYSTEM** overview displays information about the whole system. The aggregated statistics are displayed across all the actors in the whole system and all the nodes are combined.

The individual graph sections illustrate the following information:

- **QUERY (query time period)**: The data query range.

- **PEAK (peak messages rate)**: The peak number of messages received per second.

- **ERRORS**: The total number of errors and warnings recorded in the application.

- **THROUGHPUT**: The total message rate at the number of messages per second.

- **TIME IN MAILBOX**: The histogram shows the average time that the messages spend waiting in the actor mailbox queue. Each bar corresponds to 1 minute. The bar to the left-hand side is the average for the latest minute, and the bar to the right-hand side is the average for 15 minutes ago.

- **REMOTE THROUGHPUT**: The message rate and serialized message size in bytes per second.

- **MEAN LATENCY**: The histogram shows the average duration for the messages. The duration is measured from when the message was sent until the message processing has completed in the receiving actor.

Node

For each node (on the left-hand side), some key metrics are displayed. The statistics are aggregated for all the actors living in this node, as shown in the following screenshot:

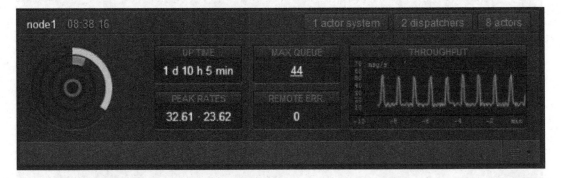

- The circle to the left-hand side gives a quick overview of the current health of the node. Corresponding time series graphs are shown in the expanded view in the previous screenshot. The inner circle becomes red if there are any errors within the selected time period.

- The next circle from the middle shows the current GC Activity, which is the time spent in garbage collection, in percentage.

- The next circle shows the current CPU usage (user plus system mode) in percentage.

- The outermost circle shows the current Java heap usage in percentage.

By clicking on the down arrow in the lower right-hand side corner, the view is expanded with more graphs and values, which are displayed as shown in the following screenshot:

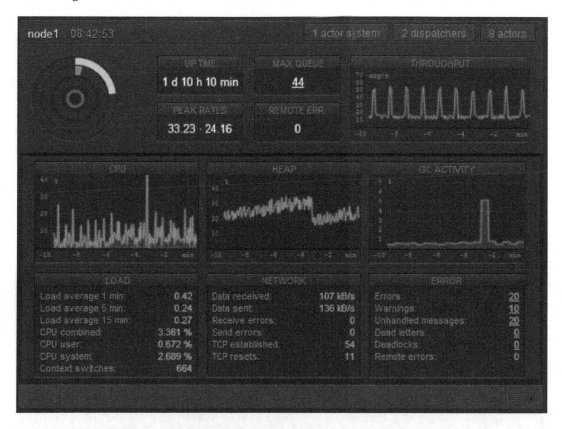

The individual graph sections illustrate the following information:

- **THROUGHPUT**: The total message rate, displayed in number of messages per second

- **CPU (CPU user)**: The CPU usage in the user mode in percentage

- **HEAP**: The current maximum usage of the Java heap in percentage

- **GC ACTIVITY**: The time spent in garbage collection, as a percentage of the wall-clock time

- **LOAD**: It displays the load in the node where the actor system is running

- **NETWORK**: The amount of data received/sent, number of socket connections, and send/receive errors
- **ERROR**: It displays the number of error/warnings recorded in the actor hierarchy, the dead letters count, and any deadlocks encountered

Next, we check out the data available for other components available in the node menu:

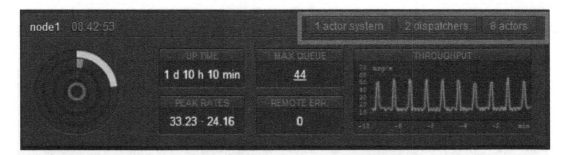

Dispatchers

For accessing the dispatchers data, click on the dispatcher link menu on the top right-hand side of the node screen.

On the right-hand side, we see all the **DISPATCHERS** associated with the application showing up. For each dispatcher, some key metrics are displayed. Note that a dispatcher belongs to a specific node, so two dispatchers with the same name may exist on different nodes. The statistics are aggregated for all the actors associated with the dispatcher.

Clicking on the down arrow in the lower right-hand side corner, the view is expanded with more graphs and values, as displayed in the following screenshot.

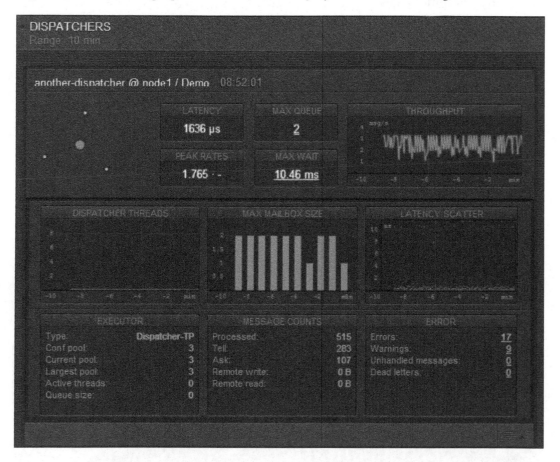

The *spider* illustrates the thread pool of the dispatcher, with one leg for each thread in the pool. The legs are highlighted to indicate an active worker thread, but that is an approximation as the dispatcher metrics are gathered periodically with a rather low frequency.

The individual graph sections illustrate the following information:

- **THROUGHPUT**: The total message rate (messages per second) of sent and received messages

- **DISPATCHER THREADS**: The number of dispatcher threads

- **MAX MAILBOX SIZE**: The maximum number of messages reached in the mailbox queue

- **LATENCY SCATTER**: It indicates the time taken to dispatch each message plus the time taken by the actor to process the message

- **EXECUTOR**: It indicates the type of dispatcher policy being used, along with the thread pool size

- **MESSAGE COUNTS**: It indicates the number of messages that have been processed until now

- **ERROR**: The number of error/warnings recorded in the actors associated with this dispatcher, the dead letters count, and the number of unhandled messages that were encountered

Actors

For accessing the **ACTORS** data, click on the menu in the top-right corner of the node screen:

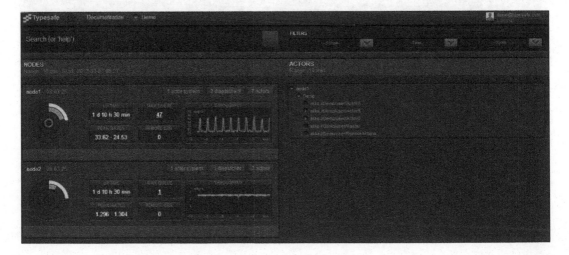

Select one of the **ACTORS** on the right-hand side. For each actor, some key metrics are displayed as follows:.

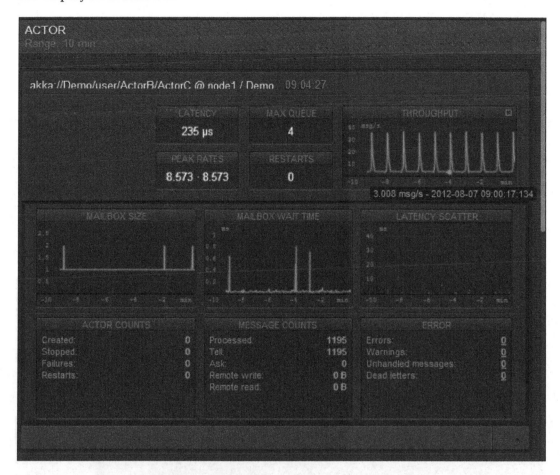

The individual graph sections illustrate the following information:

- **THROUGHPUT**: The total message rate displayed in number of messages per second

- **MAILBOX SIZE**: The number of messages waiting in the actor mailbox queue

- **MAILBOX WAIT TIME**: The time that the messages spend waiting in the actor mailbox queue

- **LATENCY SCATTER**: It indicates the time taken by the actor to process the message

- **ACTOR COUNTS**: The number of times that the actors have been stopped/started/failed
- **MESSAGE COUNTS**: It indicates the number of messages processed by this actor until now
- **ERROR**: The number of errors/warnings that were recorded in the actors, the dead letters count, and the number of unhandled messages that were encountered

Tags

Tags is the way that is provided to aggregate information across the applications running on different nodes. It is similar to the way that Twitter makes use of hashtags to aggregate data across a common thread. Multiple tags can be associated with different elements of the application.

For accessing the tag data, click on the **FILTERS** menu on the top right-hand side of the screen, as shown in the following screenshot:

In the drop-down menu, select the **Tags** option.

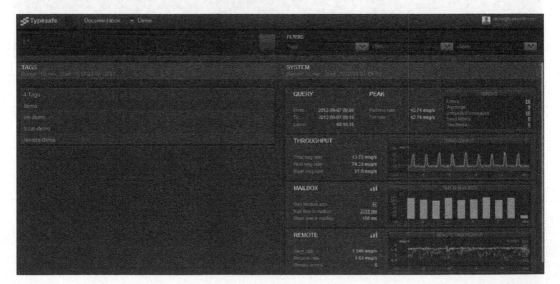

Select one of the **TAGS** displayed on the left-hand side in the previous screenshot. One or more tags can be assigned to an actor with configuration. This is a nice way of grouping the actors into logical units. For each tag, some key metrics are displayed. The statistics are aggregated for all the actors associated with the tag:

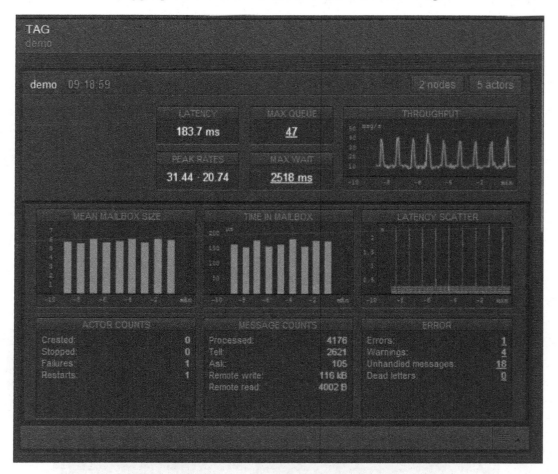

Errors

Error counts are displayed at several places, such as in the inner-red circle of the node. You can click on those values to show more detailed information about the errors, including the full tree of trace events:

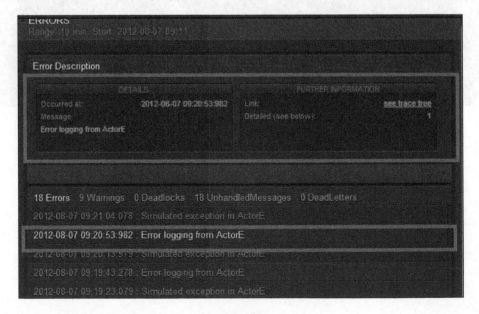

After selecting one error message from the list of errors, additional details about the error, such as when the error occurred, on which actor it occurred, and the link to the stack trace are shown, as displayed in the following screenshot:

Chapter 10

On clicking the **see trace tree** link, the detailed information about the error and the trace tree is only visible as raw JSON:

```
{
  "event" : {
    "id" : "/monitoring/trace/event/f1c42960-848f-11e1-a97f-
12313d2d1dd7",
      "trace" : "/monitoring/trace/tree/f1c20681-848f-11e1-a97f-
12313d2d1dd7",
      "parent" : "/monitoring/trace/event/f1c40250-848f-11e1-a97f-
12313d2d1dd7",
        "sampled" : 1,
        "node" : "node1",
        "host" : "ip-10-62-10-37.ec2.internal",
        "timestamp" : "2012-04-12T11:09:16:918",
        "nanoTime" : 172252222312236,
        "annotation" : {
          "type" : "ActorFailed",
          "reason" : "java.lang.RuntimeException: Simulated exception
in ActorE\n\tat akka.atmos.demo.ActorE$$anonfun$receive$2.
apply(ErrorDemo.scala:89)\n\tat akka.atmos.demo.
ActorE$$anonfun$receive$2.apply(ErrorDemo.scala:84)\n\tat akka.
actor.Actor$class.apply(Actor.scala:290)\n\tat akka.atmos.demo.
ActorE.apply(ErrorDemo.scala:83)\n\tat akka.actor.ActorCell.
invoke_aroundBody2(ActorCell.scala:617)\n\tat akka.actor.ActorCell.
invoke_aroundBody3$advice(ActorCell.scala:531)\n\tat akka.
actor.ActorCell.invoke(ActorCell.scala:1)\n\tat akka.dispatch.
Mailbox.processMailbox(Mailbox.scala:179)\n\tat akka.dispatch.
Mailbox.run(Mailbox.scala:161)\n\tat java.util.concurrent.
ThreadPoolExecutor$Worker.runTask(ThreadPoolExecutor.java:886)\n\tat
java.util.concurrent.ThreadPoolExecutor$Worker.run(ThreadPoolExecutor.
java:908)\n\tat java.lang.Thread.run(Thread.java:662)\n",
          "supervisor" : {
            "actorPath" : "akka://Demo/user/ActorD",
            "dispatcher" : "another-dispatcher",
            "remote" : false,
            "tags" : [ "err-demo", "demo" ]
          },
          "actorInfo" : {
            "actorPath" : "akka://Demo/user/ActorD/ActorE",
            "dispatcher" : "another-dispatcher",
            "remote" : false,
            "tags" : [ ]
          }
        }
      }
    }
```

This completes the Typesafe console's overview. The monitoring solution allows detecting and handling situations, as follows:

- The incoming message rate is higher than the speed at which the actors are able to process the message, leading to backlogs
- The node level statistic provides the view of the overall application usage of the resources, plenty versus starved
- Errors allow us to dig deeper and find out the cause of failure, allowing us to take proactive actions before the situation becomes alarming
- Dispatcher utilization indicates whether the `ForkJoin` or `ThreadPool` execution schemes are used, and how the underlying threads are performing

Limitations

The Typesafe console only shows a subset (via a predefined set of time periods) of all the information available in atmos. The rest of the information is queryable using the REST API. The default Typesafe console has certain limitations. The one that matters when monitoring the application in real time is that all the actors with the same actor path across all the nodes are aggregated and displayed in the current mode. When you visualize the mailbox activity of the actors, the actor with the maximum value is selected and displayed.

The Typesafe console is undergoing frequent releases, and additional features are being added to make the console more robust and provide all kinds of information about your Akka application. Some of its limitations might be getting fixed in or already be fixed in the latest release of the Typesafe console.

JMX and REST interfaces

The Typesafe console's query module exposes the monitoring statistics via two interfaces, given as follows:

- RESTful API
- JMX

RESTful API

The REST API provides an easy way to integrate atmos with other products for monitoring and surveillance. Most of the REST API calls support the search in two dimensions, namely scope and time.

The scope dimension filters the actors according to the following information:

- **Node**: The logical name of the node, which corresponds to an actor system
- **Dispatcher**: The name of the message dispatcher of the actor
- **Actor**: The unique name of the actor by using the actor path
- **Tag**: One or more tags can be assigned to an actor with configuration

The time dimension can filter queries with a rolling window or an explicit time period. The aggregated statistics are grouped by whole time period units, for example, whole hours.

For span-related queries, the name of the span type is part of the URI. For example, consider the following `/monitoring/span/summary/{spanType}` URI, which provides the statistics of the overview character for the durations of the spans.

Following are some of the important parameters provided by the different REST API calls:

Name	Description
Metadata	This parameter provides metadata about the system (span types, actor addresses, and so on).
Metadata nodes	This parameter contains details of the nodes in the system. The logical name of the (JVM) node.
Metadata dispatchers	This parameter provides names of the message dispatchers in the system.
Metadata tags	This provides the list of actor tags in the system. One or more tags can be assigned to an actor with configuration.
Metadata span types	This provides the predefined and user-defined span types in the system.
Summary span statistics	This parameter provides the statistics of the overview character for the durations of the spans.
Span time series	This parameter provides the time series for the durations of the spans. This information is typically used for producing the time series scatter plot of latencies.
Actor statistics	This parameter provides the actor lifecycle events and message processing statistics.
Mailbox time series	This parameter provides the time series for the mailbox size and message waiting time in the mailbox.
System metrics time series	This parameter provides the JVM and OS health metrics. It's possible to retrieve time series for system metrics.

Name	Description
System metrics point	This parameter provides a specific point in a time series of system metrics points.
Error statistics	This parameter provides details on the number of errors, warnings, dead letters, unhandled messages, and deadlocks in the whole system or for a specific node.
Remote status	This parameter provides details on the remote status events and counts of the lifecycle events from RemoteSupport.
Trace events	This parameter provides information about the trace events in the system.

For the complete list of parameters, please refer to the official documentation here:

http://resources.typesafe.com/docs/console/manual/rest-api.html

JMX

JMX MBeans expose the information using the root name akka.atmos. JMX information can be accessed using the JMX console provided along with JDK, such as JConsole or JVisualVM, connected to the query node.

The JMX MBeans provide a consolidated view of the monitoring statistics across all servers, which means that you do not connect to individual machines during production.

Let's take a quick look at the JMX view. Start the demo application in the distribution with bin/atmos-demo (or bin\bat\startDemo.bat on Windows).

Open **JConsole**, which is part of the JDK, and connect to the **Local Process** `akka.atmos.demo.MixedDemo.local.jmx`, as shown in following screenshot:

Go to the **MBeans** tab and expand the **akka.atmos** element by clicking on it, as shown in the following screenshot:

Note that you can double-click on a value to see a graph of that value, as shown in the following screenshot:

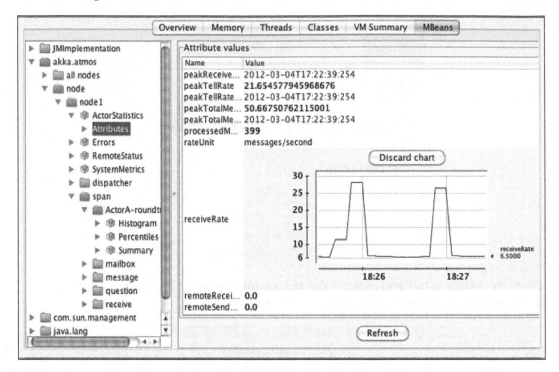

Summary

This completes the management chapter, where we saw the capabilities provided by the Typesafe console to monitor the Akka application. We explored the Typesafe console's various modules, namely trace, analyze, query, and graphical console. We saw the base configuration setting and usage for each of the modules.

We also looked at the Typesafe console, and the various dials and knobs provided to understand the runtime health of your Akka application. We also saw how monitoring data is exposed via the REST API and JMX.

In the next chapter we will cover some advanced topics, such as durable mailboxes, accessing actors over HTTP, and ZeroMQ integration.

11
Advanced Topics

In this chapter, we will cover topics that will allow your Akka application to be more resistant to failures (via durable mailboxes), interact over HTTP with other applications, and talk to other enterprise applications (using messaging). The following topics will be covered:

- Durable mailboxes
- Actors and web applications
- Integrating actors with ZeroMQ

Durable mailboxes

Imagine a large distributed application with the actor(s) running, with hundreds of messages queued in the mailbox. Suddenly, the application node where the actor(s) and its attached mailbox is hosted goes down. When the application node comes back, the actor(s) will be (re)initialized but the mailbox will lose all the messages.

This kind of scenario is not acceptable in a production environment, where the application is crunching critical data and any missing data can lead to serious inconsistencies in the application.

So, what is the option? In the messaging world, this problem has been solved using what is called persistent messages. It means that the messages coming in persist in some storage. After the message has been successfully processed, the message is removed from the queue.

Like any messaging system, Akka also supports the concept and notion of persistent or durable mailboxes. The message being received by the actor can persist via a variety of storage options. So in the case of an actor failure, when the actor node is restarted, it will start processing the messages as though nothing has happened, and the pending messages will be processed from the mailbox:

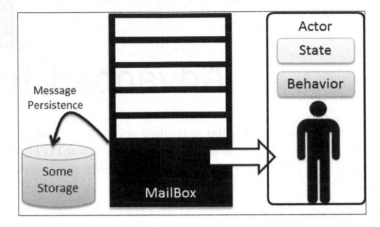

Until version 2.0.1, Akka supported durable mailboxes using the following multiple options:

- **File**: Using a transaction log on a local filesystem
- **Redis**: Using the open source, key-value store (`http://www.redis.io/`)
- **Zookeeper**: A centralized service for maintaining configuration information, and naming, providing distributed synchronization, and group services (`http://zookeeper.apache.org/`)
- **Beanstalkd**: Using the work queue feature coupled with `memcache` (`http://kr.github.com/beanstalkd/`)
- **MongoDB**: Using the open source NoSQL database storage (`http://www.mongodb.org/`)

 Except the file-based option, all the other options use additional software to provide durable mailboxes. Using a third-party persistent allows for a centralized storage in a multinode environment. But these third-party software can themselves become the single point of failure if not set up and configured properly.

From Akka 2.0.2, all the options except file-based durable mailboxes have been deprecated, and the plan is to remove their support completely from version 2.1. The idea behind deprecating the support of durable mailboxes using third-party software was to cut down on the dependency on the core Akka libraries. All the third-party durable options are now available to be taken over by the community.

We will examine the file-based option and see how our application can make use of these.

Akka support

Akka supports the file-based, durable mailbox option, `FileDurableMailboxStorage`.

Akka supports durable mailboxes via dispatchers. Dispatchers are the entities that are responsible for receiving and transmitting pure and reliable messages. Dispatchers keep track of the messages and actors, allowing them to configure the application for optimal throughput, scalability, and performance. Refer to *Chapter 5, Dispatchers and Routers*, for more details on dispatchers.

The use of dispatchers allows the application to create partitions, where you can group a set of actors to share the same dispatcher and underlying storage. The actor is not aware of whether the mailbox is durable.

Dispatcher usage

The following code snippet shows how to configure the appropriate durable mailbox scheme in the `application.conf`:

```
MyDurableMailBox {

  My-Dispatcher {
    type = PinnedDispatcher
    executor = "thread-pool-executor"
    thread-pool-executor {
      core-pool-size-min = 2
      core-pool-size-factor = 2.0
      core-pool-size-max = 10
    }
    throughput = 10
    mailbox-type = akka.actor.mailbox.FileBasedMailboxType
  }

akka {
  actor{ 0
```

```
        mailbox {
          file-based {
            directory-path = "./_mb"
            max-items = 2147483647
            max-size = 2147483647 bytes
            max-items = 2147483647
            max-item-size = 2147483647 bytes
            max-age = 0s
            max-journal-size = 16 MiB
            max-memory-size = 128 MiB
            max-journal-overflow = 10
            max-journal-size-absolute = 9223372036854775807 bytes
            discard-old-when-full = on
            keep-journal = on
            sync-journal = off
          }
        }
      }
    }
  }
```

Java:

```
system = ActorSystem.create("DurableMailBoxApp",
        ConfigFactory.load().getConfig("MyDurableMailBox"));
actor = system.actorOf(new Props(WorkerActor.class).
        withDispatcher("My-Dispatcher"), "myActor");
actor.tell("Hello");
```

Scala:

```
val config = ConfigFactory.load()
val system = ActorSystem("DurableMailBoxApp" ,
            config.getConfig("MyDurableMailBox"))
val actor = system.actorOf(Props[WorkerActor].
        withDispatcher("My-Dispatcher"), name = "myActor")
actor ! "Hello"
```

We create `DurableEventBasedDispatcher` with a defined namespace, and a durable mailbox scheme is to be used.

In this case, the `FileDurableMailboxStorage` scheme is being used to persist the messages. To use the appropriate durable scheme, we need to specify the correct storage option when defining the dispatcher.

To use the durable mailboxes, your Maven projects need to define additional dependencies in the pom.xml file:

```
<dependency>
    <groupId>se.scalablesolutions.akka</groupId>
    <artifactId>akka-mailboxes-common</artifactId>
    <version>2.0</version>
</dependency>

<dependency>
    <groupId>se.scalablesolutions.akka</groupId>
    <artifactId>akka-file-mailbox</artifactId>
    <version>2.0</version>
</dependency>
```

For the file-based, durable-persistent scheme, there are additional configurations that need to be made.

FileDurableMailboxStorage

The simplest and easiest way to administer it is the file-based durable mailbox. There is no extra piece of hardware or software that is required. In most cases this option will suffice for your application needs. The file-based durable mailbox can be fine-tuned to use additional settings in the section based on akka.actor.mailbox.file of the akka.conf configuration file:

```
akka {
  actor {
    mailbox {
      file-based {
        directory-path = "./_mb"
        max-items = 2147483647
        max-size = 2147483647
        max-item-size = 2147483647
        max-age = 0
        max-journal-size = 16777216 # 16 * 1024 * 1024
        max-memory-size = 134217728 # 128 * 1024 * 1024
        max-journal-overflow = 10
        max-journal-size-absolute = 9223372036854775807
        discard-old-when-full = on
        keep-journal = on
        sync-journal = off
      }
    }
  }
}
```

The parameters that can be fine-tuned are as follows:

Parameter name	Description
directory-path	The directory location where the durable queue will reside.
max-items	Defines the maximum number of messages that can be held in the queue. Any attempts to add a message after this will fail.
max-size	Defines the maximum size of the queue in bytes.
max-item-size	Sets the maximum size of a message in the queue (in bytes).
max-age	Defines the maximum expiration of a message in the queue.
max-journal-size	Defines the maximum journal size before the journal is rotated. Similar to log rotation, when the logfile reaches the predefined size.
max-memory-size	Defines the maximum size of the queue before it drops into the read-behind mode, which means that the messages are coming in faster than they are getting processed.
max-journal-overflow	Defines the maximum overflow of the journal file before it is recreated.
max-journal-size-absolute	Defines the maximum size of the journal file until it is rebuilt.
discard-old-when-full	Drops the old messages when the queue is full.
keep-journal	Determines whether the journal file should be kept.
sync-journal	Determines whether to keep the journal in sync for every transaction.

To use the file-based durable mailboxes, your Maven projects need to define additional dependencies in pom.xml:

```xml
<dependency>
  <groupId>se.scalablesolutions.akka</groupId>
  <artifactId>akka-file-mailbox</artifactId>
  <version>2.0</version>
</dependency>
```

The file-based durable mailbox is provided as a blueprint for implementations around other storage mechanisms. The deprecated mailboxes are not part of Akka but will be available as community-supported projects.

Actors and web applications

If you are building a web-based application or distributed application, it becomes very important that you can make use of the HTTP protocols for the received messages to be processed by the actors.

To expose actors over the HTTP protocol, the recommended framework is the Play framework (http://www.playframework.org/).

The Play framework is an open source, web application-development framework based on the **Model-View-Controller** (**MVC**) paradigm. The framework is written in Scala. The Play 2.0 is part of the Typesafe Stack 2.0. We will not cover the Play framework in its entirety as a part of this section, but we will see how we can expose the actors over REST using the framework.

For the purpose of exposing the actors via HTTP, we will cover the basic minimum requirements. For additional details on the Play framework, please refer to the official documentation of the Play framework at http://www.playframework.org/

The Play framework allows both Scala and Java to be used as the underlying programming model for creating web applications. We will cover only the Java part of exposing the actors.

Let's go ahead and create the project template for exposing our actor over HTTP. Let's call our application HttpActors. Our application should be able to receive the message over HTTP and pass the message to the actor, which will process the message and return the message back to the client as a response:

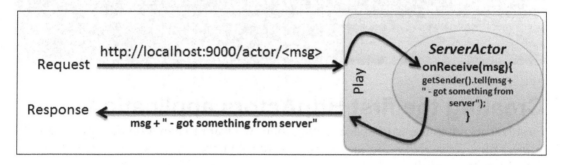

We shall go through the basic setup requirements to get the Play framework up, and to run and create the default project template.

Installing play

To run play, we need to have at least JDK 1.6 installed. Download the play package from the site and extract the archive file to a suitable location.

After that, add the location of the folder where play is extracted to the system PATH directive:

```
export PATH=$PATH:/<folder location>/play-2.0
```

In Windows, we set it in the global environment variables minus the export directive.

Next go to the shell prompt and launch the play help command as follows:

```
$ play help
```

If everything is properly installed, we should see the basic help screen as it is shown in the following screenshot:

Creating the first HttpActors application

First let's move to the workspace folder where we want to generate the application project files. Once there, the easiest way to create a new application is to use the play new command as follows:

```
$ play new HttpActors
```

This will ask for some information, as follows:

- **The application name**: It is used just for displaying purposes and will be used later in several messages.

- **The template to be used for this application**: You can choose either a default Scala application, a default Java application, or an empty application. In our case, we choose a Java application as shown in the following screenshot:

```
D:\workspace\Akka-Essentials>play new HttpActors

         _            _
  _ __  | | __ _ _  _| |
 | '_ \ | |/ _` | || |_|
 | .__/ |_|\__,_|\_, (_)
 |_|            |__/

play! 2.0, http://www.playframework.org

The new application will be created in D:\workspace\Akka-Essentials\HttpActors

What is the application name?
> HttpActors

Which template do you want to use for this new application?

  1 - Create a simple Scala application
  2 - Create a simple Java application
  3 - Create an empty project

> 2

OK, application HttpActors is created.

Have fun!
```

This completes the default project application template that needs to be generated.

Launching the console

To launch the console, enter any existing play application directory and run the `play` script as follows:

```
$ play
```

```
D:\workspace\Akka-Essentials>cd HttpActors

D:\workspace\Akka-Essentials\HttpActors>play
[info] Loading project definition from D:\workspace\Akka-Essentials\HttpActors\project
[info] Set current project to HttpActors (in build file:/D:/workspace/Akka-Essentials/HttpActors/)

         _            _
  _ __  | | __ _ _  _| |
 | '_ \ | |/ _` | || |_|
 | .__/ |_|\__,_|\_, (_)
 |_|            |__/

play! 2.0, http://www.playframework.org

> Type "help play" or "license" for more information.
> Type "exit" or use Ctrl+D to leave this console.

[HttpActors] $ run
```

Next, we use the `run` command to run the current application in development mode:

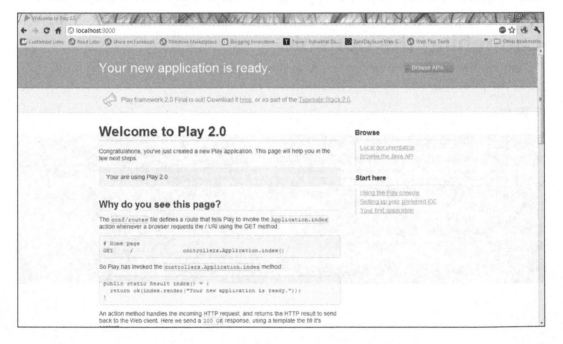

In this mode the server will be launched with the auto-reload feature enabled, which means that for each request, play will check your project and recompile the required sources. If needed the application will restart automatically.

Next, we open the browser at `localhost:9000` and see the default application running, as shown in the following screenshot:

We can see the complete structure of the project template in the preceding screenshot.

```
$ cd HttpActors
$ ls
```

```
D:\workspace\Akka-Essentials\HttpActors>dir
 Volume in drive D is Local Disk
 Volume Serial Number is 221D-00DE

 Directory of D:\workspace\Akka-Essentials\HttpActors

04/09/2012  11:40 AM    <DIR>          .
04/09/2012  11:40 AM    <DIR>          ..
03/13/2012  04:22 AM                60 .gitignore
04/09/2012  11:29 AM    <DIR>          app
04/09/2012  11:29 AM    <DIR>          conf
04/09/2012  11:40 AM    <DIR>          logs
04/09/2012  11:39 AM    <DIR>          project
04/09/2012  11:29 AM    <DIR>          public
03/13/2012  04:22 AM               151 README
04/09/2012  11:40 AM    <DIR>          target
               2 File(s)            211 bytes
               8 Dir(s)  56,222,236,672 bytes free

D:\workspace\Akka-Essentials\HttpActors>
```

The layout of the play application is standardized to keep things as simple as possible.

We will be interested in the **app** directory, which contains all executable artifacts, such as Java and Scala source code, templates, and compiled assets' sources.

There are three standard packages in the **app** directory, one for each corresponding component of the MVC architectural pattern, as follows:

- app/controllers
- app/models
- app/views

The **conf** directory contains the application's configuration files. There are two main configuration files, as follows:

- application.conf: It is the main configuration file for the application, which contains standard configuration parameters
- routes: It is the routes definition file

In the **conf** directory we will add the following code snippet for the purpose of our demo, and we will expose the /actor URI for which we will define the route in the routes file:

```
GET      /actor/:msg                      controllers.ServerActorApp.
process(msg: String)
```

Here we have defined the /actor URI with the dynamic part — msg. The URI is then mapped to the controller class static method — process() with the parameter type (in this case String).

In the /app/controllers folder, we will define the ServerActorApp controller class, which will handle the HTTP request.

Java:

```java
package controllers;

import play.*;
import play.mvc.*;

import views.html.*;

import static akka.pattern.Patterns.ask;
import play.libs.Akka;
import akka.actor.*;
import play.libs.F.Function;
import org.akka.essentials.remoteActor.sample.ServerActor;

public class ServerActorApp extends Controller {

  private static ActorRef myServerActor = Akka.system()
               .actorOf(new Props(ServerActor.class));

  public static Result process(String msg){

    return async(
    Akka.asPromise(ask(myServerActor,msg, 1000)).map(
      new Function<Object,Result>() {
        public Result apply(Object response) {
          return ok(response.toString());
        }
      }
    )
  );
  }
}
```

ServerActorApp extends the controller and implements the process (String) as a static method. We define our ServerActor instance as follows:

Java:

```
private static ActorRef myServerActor = Akka.system()
                .actorOf(new Props(ServerActor.class));
```

In the process() method, we invoke ServerActor. As we are making a send and receive request, our actor will return the Future object. We need to convert the Future object to the play Promise using the conversion method provided in play. libs.Akka.asPromise().

Java:

```
public static Result process(String msg){

    return async(
    Akka.asPromise(ask(myServerActor,msg, 1000)).map(
      new Function<Object,Result>() {
        public Result apply(Object response) {
          return ok(response.toString());
        }
      }
    )
  );
```

Our ServerActor class is defined as follows.

Java:

```
package org.akka.essentials.remoteActor.sample;

import akka.actor.UntypedActor;

public class ServerActor extends UntypedActor {

  @Override
  public void onReceive(Object arg0) throws Exception {

    if(arg0 instanceof String){
      getSender().tell(arg0 + " - got something from server");
    }
  }
}
```

That's it! We have exposed our actor on the HTTP protocol.

Let's hit the URL `http://localhost:9000/actor/Hi`, where we are invoking the `/actor` URI with the **Hi** message, as shown in the following screenshot:

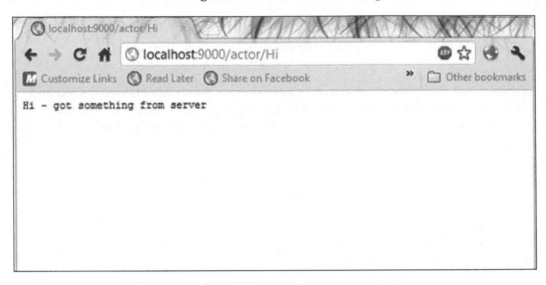

We can see our `ServerActor` responding back with the message, as shown in the previous screenshot.

This completes a very simple demonstration on how to expose actors over HTTP. For additional information on the play framework, refer to the play framework documentation at `http://www.playframework.org/`.

If you do not want to develop the complete HTTP application but just want to expose the actors as REST API, we can make use of the play-mini `https://github.com/typesafehub/play2-mini/`. The play-mini provides REST API on top of the play framework.

In addition, Akka integrates very well with the following frameworks, which allow exposing actors over HTTP/REST API. All the frameworks are geared towards the Scala developers:

- **Spray (built using Akka)**: `https://github.com/spray/spray`
- **Socko web (built using Akka)**: `http://sockoweb.org/`
- **Unfiltered**: `http://unfiltered.databinder.net/Unfiltered.html`
- **Scalatra**: `http://www.scalatra.org/`

Integrating actors with ZeroMQ

ZeroMQ is a high-performance, asynchronous messaging library used for highly scalable, distributed, or concurrent applications. ZeroMQ is an embeddable networking library. ZeroMQ sockets provide a layer of abstraction on top of the traditional socket AP, and carry whole messages across various transports, such as in-process, inter-process, TCP, and multicast. Applications using sockets for communication and data exchange, make use of patterns such as fanout, PubSub, task distribution, and request-reply. ZeroMQ provides an asynchronous I/O model, which allows you to write scalable multicore applications, built using asynchronous, message-processing tasks. For more information on ZeroMQ, refer to www.zeromq.org.

Akka provides an integrated ZeroMQ module that allows Akka actors to act as listeners to the ZeroMQ connections. The message to be passed can be in the proprietary format or can make use of Akka's supported ProtoBuf binary protocol. The socket actor(s) is fault-tolerant by default, and when you use the newSocket method to create new sockets, it will properly reinitialize the socket.

As ZeroMQ communication is done in an asynchronous fashion (by default), the application using the ZeroMQ module needs to explicitly declare the number of background I/O threads. The ZeroMQ library itself handles all the thread logic. As a result, in Akka, akka.zeromq.socket-dispatcher always needs to be configured to a PinnedDispatcher, because the thread that created it can only access the actual ZeroMQ socket.

Akka provides native support to the ZeroMQ C++ library using **Java Native Access (JNA)** support, with the ZeroMQ binding in Scala. As a result, to use and run ZeroMQ with Akka, all you need is for the compiled ZeroMQ library to be in the class path. This means that for accessing the ZeroMQ library, you do not need the JNI-binding API library.

Akka supports the following connectivity patterns using ZeroMQ:

- Publisher-subscriber connection
- Request-reply connection
- Router-dealer connection
- Push-pull connection

For each of the supported connectivity patterns, we will explore the usage.

Publisher-subscriber connection

Publish-subscribe is a data distribution messaging pattern, where the senders of messages, called publishers, do not program the messages to be sent directly to specific receivers, called subscribers. The publisher publishes the message for a set of topics, and subscribers can subscribe to one or more topics to receive those messages. The publisher has no knowledge of the subscribers, and there is no direct interaction between the publisher and subscriber.

In the context of the Akka environment, pub-sub connections are used when an actor sends messages to one or more actors that do not interact with the actor that sent the message.

The ZeroMQ pub/sub model requires multicast messaging to work properly, as the filtering of events for the topics happens on the client side. This allows for all the events to always be broadcasted to every subscriber:

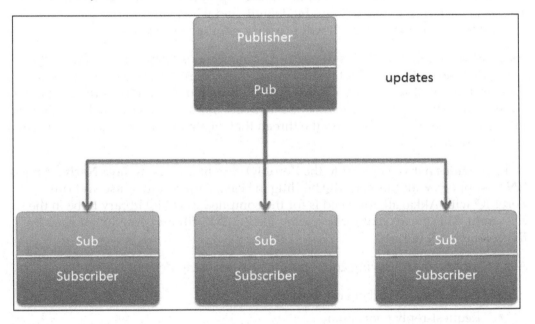

Usage

ZeroMQ uses sockets for connecting or accepting connections. Akka supports socket creation using `akka.zeromq.ZeroMQExtension`.

Let's go ahead and create `PublisherActor` that encompasses the publisher socket.

Java:

```java
public class PublisherActor extends UntypedActor {
  public static final Object TICK = "TICK";
  int count = 0;
  Cancellable cancellable;
  ActorRef pubSocket = ZeroMQExtension.get(getContext().system())
      .newPubSocket(new Bind("tcp://127.0.0.1:1237"));

  @Override
  public void preStart() {
    cancellable = getContext()
        .system()
        .scheduler()
        .schedule(Duration.parse("1 second"),
            Duration.parse("1 second"), getSelf(), TICK);
  }

  @Override
  public void onReceive(Object message) throws Exception {
    if (message.equals(TICK)) {
      pubSocket.tell(new ZMQMessage(
                new Frame("someTopic"), new Frame(
          "This is the workload " + ++count)));

      if(count==10)
        cancellable.cancel();
    }
  }
}
```

Scala:

```scala
case class Tick
class PublisherActor extends Actor with ActorLogging {
  val pubSocket = ZeroMQExtension(context.system)
      .newSocket(SocketType.Pub, Bind("tcp://127.0.0.1:1234"))
  var count = 0
  var cancellable:Cancellable = null
  override def preStart() {
    cancellable = context.system
          .scheduler.schedule(1 second, 1 second, self, Tick)
  }
  def receive: Receive = {
    case Tick =>
      count += 1
```

```
        var payload = "This is the workload " + count;
        pubSocket ! ZMQMessage(Seq(Frame("someTopic"),
                                   Frame(payload)))

        if(count == 10){
          cancellable.cancel()
        }
    }
}
```

So we have created `PubSocket` using `ZeroMQExtension`, which is bounded on the `127.0.0.1` IP address with port `1237`, using the TCP protocol.

Java:

```
ActorRef pubSocket = ZeroMQExtension.get(getContext().system())
  .newPubSocket(new Bind("tcp://127.0.0.1:1237"));
```

Scala:

```
val pubSocket = ZeroMQExtension(context.system)
  .newSocket(SocketType.Pub, Bind("tcp://127.0.0.1:1234"))
```

The published socket can now publish the message on a given topic.

Java:

```
pubSocket.tell(new ZMQMessage(new Frame("someTopic"),
                  new Frame("This is the workload)));
```

Scala:

```
var payload = "This is the workload " + count;
pubSocket ! ZMQMessage(Seq(Frame("someTopic"),
                           Frame(payload)))
```

In this code, we are publishing a message using `ZMQMessage`, which takes in two frames. The first frame signifies the topic name against which the message is to be published. The second frame contains the message payload itself:

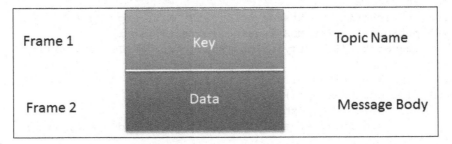

Next, we will create the Subscriber actor that will implement the subscriber socket, which will subscribe to the topic and receive the messages.

Java:

```java
public class WorkerTaskA extends UntypedActor {
  ActorRef subSocket = ZeroMQExtension.get(getContext().system())
    .newSubSocket(new Connect("tcp://127.0.0.1:1237"),
    new Listener(getSelf()), new Subscribe("someTopic"));

  LoggingAdapter log = Logging.getLogger(
              getContext().system(), this);

  @Override
  public void onReceive(Object message) throws Exception {
    if (message instanceof ZMQMessage) {
      ZMQMessage m = (ZMQMessage) message;
      String mesg = new String(m.payload(1));
      log.info("Received Message @ A -> {}",mesg);
    }
  }
}
```

Scala:

```scala
class WorkerTaskA extends Actor with ActorLogging {
  val subSocket = ZeroMQExtension(context.system)
          .newSocket(SocketType.Sub,
            Connect("tcp://127.0.0.1:1234"),
            Listener(self), Subscribe("someTopic"))

  def receive = {
    case m: ZMQMessage =>
      var mesg = new String(m.payload(1))
    log.info("Received Message @ A -> {}", mesg)
  }
}
```

We create SubSocket using ZeroMQExtension. The socket connects to the IP address and port. In addition, we define the actor self() to be Listener for the messages and, lastly, we indicate the topic for which we want to subscribe the messages.

Whenever a message is published, our Subscriber actor will receive the message that can be read and acted upon by the actor.

We can bind all the publishers and subscribers together to get the communication going.

Java:

```
ActorSystem system = ActorSystem.create("zeromqTest");
system.actorOf(new Props(WorkerTaskA.class), "workerA");
system.actorOf(new Props(WorkerTaskB.class), "workerB");
system.actorOf(new Props(PublisherActor.class), "publisher");
```

Scala:

```
val system = ActorSystem("zeromqTest")
system.actorOf(Props[PublisherActor], name = "publisher")
system.actorOf(Props[WorkerTaskA], name = "workerA")
system.actorOf(Props[WorkerTaskB], name = "workerB")
```

You see two workers, A and B, defined and created above. The `WorkerTaskB` actor is similar to `WorkerTaskA` and needs to be defined separately.

Request-reply connection

Request-reply is a simple, message exchange pattern, where the requester sends a message to the replier system, which receives the message, processes the message, and sends back a reply to the requester system. This pattern is implemented in a synchronous way when implementing web service calls, where the requester waits until the response is returned back. This pattern is typical of the client-server implementation, as shown in following diagram:

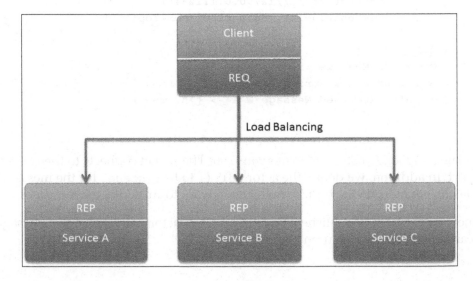

Usage

Let's go ahead and create an actor that encompasses the replier socket.

Java:

```java
public class ServerActor extends UntypedActor {
  ActorRef repSocket = ZeroMQExtension.get(getContext().system())
    .newRepSocket(new SocketOption[] {
        new Bind("tcp://127.0.0.1:1237"),
        new Listener(getSelf()) });

  @Override
  public void onReceive(Object message) throws Exception {
    if (message instanceof ZMQMessage) {
      ZMQMessage m = (ZMQMessage) message;
      String mesg = new String(m.payload(0));
      repSocket.tell((new ZMQMessage(
          new Frame(mesg + " Good to see you!"))));
    }
  }
}
```

Scala:

```scala
class ServerActor extends Actor with ActorLogging {
  val repSocket = ZeroMQExtension(context.system)
    .newSocket(SocketType.Rep, Bind("tcp://127.0.0.1:1234"),
    Listener(self))

  def receive: Receive = {
    case m: ZMQMessage =>
      var mesg = new String(m.payload(0));
      repSocket ! ZMQMessage(Seq(Frame(mesg +
              " Good to see you!")))
  }
}
```

So we have created `RepSocket` using `ZeroMQExtension`, which is bounded on the `127.0.0.1` IP address with port `1237`, using the TCP protocol. In addition, we define the actor `self()` to be `Listener` for the messages.

Now whenever a request comes, our replier socket can receive the message, process the message, and send back the reply.

Next, we will create the requester actor that will implement the requester socket, which will send a message to the replier system and get the response back.

Java:

```java
public class ClientActor extends UntypedActor {
  public static final Object TICK = "TICK";
  int count = 0;
  Cancellable cancellable;
  ActorRef reqSocket = ZeroMQExtension.get(getContext().system())
      .newReqSocket(new SocketOption[] {
          new Connect("tcp://127.0.0.1:1237"),
      new Listener(getSelf()) });
  LoggingAdapter log = Logging.getLogger(
                  getContext().system(), this);

  @Override
  public void preStart() {
    cancellable = getContext()
        .system()
        .scheduler()
        .schedule(Duration.parse("1 second"),
            Duration.parse("1 second"), getSelf(), TICK);
  }

  @Override
  public void onReceive(Object message) throws Exception {
    if (message.equals(TICK)) {
      // send a message to the replier system
      reqSocket.tell(new ZMQMessage(new Frame("Hi there! ("
          + getContext().self().hashCode() + ")->")));
      count++;
      if (count == 10)
        cancellable.cancel();
    } else if (message instanceof ZMQMessage) {
      ZMQMessage m = (ZMQMessage) message;
      String mesg = new String(m.payload(0));
      log.info("Received msg! {}", mesg);
    }
  }
}
```

Scala:

```scala
case class Tick

class ClientActor extends Actor with ActorLogging {
  val reqSocket = ZeroMQExtension(context.system)
          .newSocket(SocketType.Req,
          Connect("tcp://127.0.0.1:1234"), Listener(self))

  var count = 0
  var cancellable: Cancellable = null
  override def preStart() {
    cancellable = context.system.scheduler
              .schedule(1 second, 1 second, self, Tick)
  }

  def receive: Receive = {
    case Tick =>
      count += 1
      var payload = "Hi there! (" +
                    context.self.hashCode() + ")->"
      reqSocket ! ZMQMessage(Seq(Frame(payload)))
      if (count == 5) {
      cancellable.cancel()
      }
    case m: ZMQMessage =>
      var mesg = new String(m.payload(0))
      log.info("recieved msg! {}", mesg)
  }
}
```

We create `SubSocket` using `ZeroMQExtension`. The socket connects to the IP address and port. In addition, we define the actor `self()` to be `Listener` for the messages.

We will send a message to the replier system, and our requester actor will receive the response message that can be read and acted upon by the actor.

We can bind all the request and reply actors together to get the communication going. First, on the reply side, we get `ActorSystem` started and the actor created and running.

Java:

```java
ActorSystem system = ActorSystem.create("zeromqServerTest");
system.actorOf(new Props(ServerActor.class), "server");
```

Scala:

```
val system = ActorSystem("zeromqServerTest")
system.actorOf(Props[ServerActor], name = "server")
```

Similarly, on the request side, we will start another `ActorSystem` that connects to the request sockets and starts the communication.

Java:

```
ActorSystem system = ActorSystem.create("zeromqClientTest");
system.actorOf(new Props(ClientActor.class)
    .withRouter(new RoundRobinRouter(3)), "client");
```

Scala:

```
val system = ActorSystem("zeromqTest")
system.actorOf(Props[ClientActor].withRouter(
    RoundRobinRouter(nrOfInstances = 3)), name = "client")
```

We use a `RoundRobinRouter` to create multiple request actors that will connect to the same reply socket.

Router-dealer connection

The router-dealer message pattern helps in dealing with the tight coupling of the request-reply connections. If I need to add additional replier systems to handle the incoming, requester system requests, how do I do that? To help this, the concept of the router-dealer connection comes into the picture. The router-dealer is a little message queuing broker that has two endpoints, one that binds to the requester and another that binds to the replier. The broker then monitors these two endpoints and shuffles the messages between its two sockets.

So, the router-dealer provides a non-blocking, request-response mechanism:

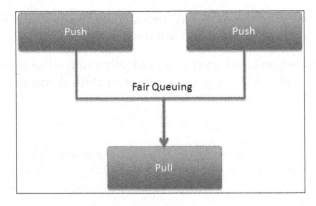

Usage

Let's go ahead and create an actor that encompasses the dealer socket.

Java:

```
public class WorkerTaskA extends UntypedActor {
    ActorRef subSocket = ZeroMQExtension.get(getContext().system())
        .newDealerSocket(new SocketOption[]
                        { new Connect("tcp://127.0.0.1:1237"),
                new Listener(getSelf()),
                new Identity("A".getBytes()) });

    @Override
    public void onReceive(Object message) throws Exception {

      if (message instanceof ZMQMessage) {
        ZMQMessage m = (ZMQMessage) message;
        String mesg = new String(m.payload(0));
        subSocket.tell((new ZMQMessage(new Frame(mesg
            + " Processed the workload for A"))));
      }
    }
}
```

Scala:

```
class WorkerTaskA extends Actor with ActorLogging {
  val subSocket = ZeroMQExtension(context.system)
                  .newSocket(SocketType.Dealer,
                    Connect("tcp://127.0.0.1:1234"),
                            Listener(self),
                            Identity("A".getBytes()))

  def receive = {
    case m: ZMQMessage =>
      var mesg = new String(m.payload(0))
      subSocket.tell((new ZMQMessage(Frame(mesg
        + " - Workload Processed by A"))))
  }
}
```

So we have created a DealerSocket using ZeroMQExtension, which connects to the 127.0.0.1 IP address with port 1237, using the TCP protocol. In addition, we define the self() actor to be Listener for the messages. For example, for objects in Java, we use this to indicate the object's own instance, in the same way that the actor's self() refers to its own actor reference. We add another attribute called Identity, which identifies the service name so that the message is routed to the right service.

Now whenever a request is received, our replier socket can receive the message, process the message, and send back the reply.

Next, we will create the router actor that will implement the router socket, which will send a message to the replier system and get the response back.

Java:

```java
public class RouterActor extends UntypedActor {
  public static final Object TICK = "TICK";

  Random random = new Random(3);
  int count = 0;
  Cancellable cancellable;

  ActorRef routerSocket = ZeroMQExtension.get(
                            getContext().system())
      .newRouterSocket(
          new SocketOption[] {
                      new Listener(getSelf()),
              new Bind("tcp://127.0.0.1:1237"),
              new HighWatermark(50000) });

  LoggingAdapter log = Logging.getLogger(getContext().system(),
                      this);

  @Override
  public void preStart() {
    cancellable = getContext()
        .system()
        .scheduler()
        .schedule(Duration.parse("1 second"),
          Duration.parse("1 second"), getSelf(), TICK);
  }

  @Override
  public void onReceive(Object message) throws Exception {
    if (message.equals(TICK)) {
      if (random.nextBoolean() == true) {
        routerSocket.tell(new ZMQMessage(new Frame("A"),
                    new Frame("This is the workload for A")));
      } else {
        routerSocket.tell(new ZMQMessage(new Frame("B"),
                    new Frame("This is the workload for B")));
      }
      count++;
      if (count == 10)
        cancellable.cancel();
```

```java
    } else if (message instanceof ZMQMessage) {
        ZMQMessage m = (ZMQMessage) message;
        String replier = new String(m.payload(0));
        String msg = new String(m.payload(1));
        log.info("Received message from {} with mesg -> {}",
                    replier, msg);
    }
  }
}
```

Scala:

```scala
case class Tick

class RouterActor extends Actor with ActorLogging {
  val pubSocket = ZeroMQExtension(context.system)
                    .newSocket(SocketType.Router,
                      Bind("tcp://127.0.0.1:1234"),
                      Listener(self), HighWatermark(50000))

  var random = new Random(3);

  var count = 0
  var cancellable: Cancellable = null

  override def preStart() {
    cancellable = context.system.scheduler
                    .schedule(1 second, 1 second, self, Tick)
  }

  def receive: Receive = {
    case Tick =>
      count += 1
      if (random.nextBoolean() == true) {
        pubSocket ! ZMQMessage(Seq(Frame("A"),
                        Frame("This is the workload for A")))
      } else {
        pubSocket ! ZMQMessage(Seq(Frame("B"),
                        Frame("This is the workload for B")))
      }
      if (count == 10) {
      cancellable.cancel()
      }

    case m: ZMQMessage =>
      var replier = new String(m.payload(0))
      var msg = new String(m.payload(1))
      log.info("received message from {} with mesg -> {}",
                replier, msg)
  }
}
```

We create RouterSocket using ZeroMQExtension. The socket binds to the IP address and port. In addition, we define the self() actor to be Listener for the messages. We also define the HighWatermark attribute that defines the maximum queue limit.

We will send a message to the replier system, and our requester actor will receive the response message that can be read and acted upon by the actor.

We define a random Boolean variable to send messages to the dealer sockets. When the replier system responds back, we get both the requester name and message.

To get the communication started, we will use the ActorSystem and get the routers and worker actors started.

Java:

```
ActorSystem system = ActorSystem.create("zeromqTest");
system.actorOf(new Props(WorkerTaskA.class), "workerA");
system.actorOf(new Props(WorkerTaskB.class), "workerB");
system.actorOf(new Props(RouterActor.class), "router");
```

Scala:

```
val system = ActorSystem("zeromqTest")
system.actorOf(Props[RouterActor], name = "router")
system.actorOf(Props[WorkerTaskA], name = "workerA")
system.actorOf(Props[WorkerTaskB], name = "workerB")
```

You see two workers, A and B, defined and created in the preceding code. The WorkerTaskB actor is similar to WorkerTaskA and needs to be defined separately.

Push-pull connection

Another connection type is the push-pull pattern. The push socket distributes tasks to the workers. The push-pull sockets function in a one-way pattern only:

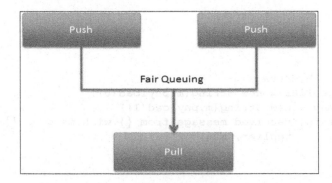

Usage

Let's go ahead and create an actor that encompasses the push socket.

Java:

```java
public class PushActor extends UntypedActor {
  public static final Object TICK = "TICK";
  int count = 0;
  Cancellable cancellable;
  ActorRef pushSocket = ZeroMQExtension.get(
                          getContext().system())
      .newPushSocket(new SocketOption[] {
                  new Bind("tcp://127.0.0.1:1237"),
              new Listener(getSelf()) });

  @Override
  public void preStart() {
    cancellable = getContext()
        .system()
        .scheduler()
        .schedule(Duration.parse("1 second"),
            Duration.parse("1 second"), getSelf(), TICK);
  }

  @Override
  public void onReceive(Object message) throws Exception {
    if (message.equals(TICK)) {
      count++;
      pushSocket.tell(new ZMQMessage(
          new Frame("Hi there (" + count + ")")));
      if (count == 5)
        cancellable.cancel();
    }
  }
}
```

Scala:

```scala
case class Tick

class PushActor extends Actor with ActorLogging {
  val pushSocket = ZeroMQExtension(context.system)
                    .newSocket(SocketType.Push,
                    Bind("tcp://127.0.0.1:1234"), Listener(self))

  var count = 0
  var cancellable: Cancellable = null
```

```
    override def preStart() {
      cancellable = context.system.scheduler
                .schedule(1 second, 1 second, self, Tick)
    }

    def receive: Receive = {
      case Tick =>
        count += 1
        var payload = "Hi there! (" + count + ")"
        pushSocket ! ZMQMessage(Seq(Frame(payload)))
        if (count == 5) {
          cancellable.cancel()
        }
    }
  }
```

So we have created `PushSocket` using `ZeroMQExtension`, which binds to the `127.0.0.1` IP address with port `1237`, using the TCP protocol. In addition, we define the `self()` actor to be `Listener` for the messages.

Now, our actor can start sending the message out to the pull-socket actors.

Next, we will create the pull actor that will implement the pull socket, which will pull the messages in load-balanced mode.

Java:

```
public class PullActor1 extends UntypedActor {
  ActorRef pullSocket = ZeroMQExtension.get(
                        getContext().system())
      .newPullSocket(new SocketOption[] {
                new Connect("tcp://127.0.0.1:1237"),
          new Listener(getSelf()) });
  LoggingAdapter log = Logging.getLogger(
                        getContext().system(), this);

  @Override
  public void onReceive(Object message) throws Exception {

    if (message instanceof ZMQMessage) {
      ZMQMessage m = (ZMQMessage) message;
      String mesg = new String(m.payload(0));
      log.info("Received Message -> {}", mesg);
    }
  }
}
```

Scala:

```
class PullActor1 extends Actor with ActorLogging {
  val pullSocket = ZeroMQExtension(context.system)
              .newSocket(SocketType.Pull,
                    Connect("tcp://127.0.0.1:1234"),
                    Listener(self))

  def receive: Receive = {
    case m: ZMQMessage =>
      var mesg = new String(m.payload(0))
      log.info("Received Message -> {}", mesg)
  }
}
```

We create `PullSocket` using `ZeroMQExtension`. The socket connects to the IP address and port. In addition, we define the `self()` actor to be `Listener` for the messages.

The pull sockets will get the messages pushed by `PushActor`, and the pull actors can then process the messages.

To get the communication started, we will use the `ActorSystem` and get the routers and worker actors started.

Java:

```
ActorSystem system = ActorSystem.create("zeromqTest");
system.actorOf(new Props(PushActor.class), "push");
system.actorOf(new Props(PullActor1.class), "pull1");
system.actorOf(new Props(PullActor2.class), "pull2");
```

Scala:

```
val system = ActorSystem("zeromqTest")
system.actorOf(Props[PushActor], name = "push")
system.actorOf(Props[PullActor1], name = "pull1")
system.actorOf(Props[PullActor2], name = "pull2")
```

You will see two pull actors, A and B, defined and created above. The `PullActor2` actor is similar to `PullActor1` and needs to be defined separately.

This completes the `ZeroMQ` section, where we explored the various socket connection types supported by `ZeroMQExtension`, and how it is very well integrated with the actors' messaging system.

Summary

In this chapter, we learned techniques that come in handy when creating enterprise-level applications.

We saw how durable mailboxes allow us to overcome the actor failure or crash and not lose out on the messages, and how the actor application can be integrated with the play framework to build an asynchronous web application; we also saw how to make use of the `ZeroMQ` library with Akka actors, and integrate an Akka application using the integration patterns within the enterprise.

Index

A

ACID (atomicity, consistency, isolation, and durability) 166
Active Object pattern
  used, for implementing typed actor 78, 79
actor behavior 14
actor classes, Java application
  AggregateActor.java 40, 41
  MapActor.java 37, 38
  MasterActor.java 41-43
  ReduceActor.java 39, 40
actor classes, Scala application
  AggregateActor.scala 51
  MapActor.scala 48, 49
  MasterActor.scala 53-55
  ReduceActor.scala 50
ACTOR COUNTS 266
actorFor() method 231
actor model
  about 10
  principles 11
actorOf() method 62, 231
actor path 221, 222
actorPath property 253
ActorRef class 19, 62, 221
actor reference
  access to 194, 195
actorRef.underlyingActor() 194
actors
  about 13, 59, 124
  actor state 14
  behavior 14
  creating 61, 62
  creating, with default constructor 62
  creating, within actor hierarchy 63, 64
  creating, with non-default
    constructor 62, 63
  defining 61
  hierarchy 125
  integrating, with ZeroMQ 289
  killing 73
  lifecycle, monitoring 73
  lifecycle, phases 60
  lifestyle 16
  mailbox 15
  recursive actor hierarchy 125
  specialized actors, managing 124
  stopping 71, 72
  supervisor actors 124
ACTORS
  individual graph section 265, 266
actor state 14
actor statistics parameter 271
actor system 13
ActorSystem class 62
ActorSystem context 82
Address objects 113
agents
  about 187
  creating 188
  stopping 190
  using, in application 188
  values, reading 189
  values, updating 188, 189
AggregateActor class 52
AggregateActor.java 40, 41
AggregateActor.scala 51
aggregate task 24
air traffic controllers. *See* **ATCs**

Akka
about 7
actor model 10, 11
actor system 13
background 7
concurrent systems 8, 9
container-based applications 10
directory structure 29
dispatchers 99, 100
fault tolerance 17
key constructs 20
location transparency 18
Maven project, creating 30-35
modules 29
transactions 19, 20
URL 12
URL, for downloading distribution 28
use cases 21
akka-actor 29
akka-agent 29
Akka application
actor behavior, testing 195, 196
actor reference, accessing 194, 195
deployment mode 213
exception scenarios, testing 196, 197
requisites 23, 24
testing 191, 192
unit test, testing with TestActorRef 192-194
akka-camel 29
akka-dataflow 29
Akka extensions
used, for managing application
   configuration 208-213
akka.first.app.mapreduce package 47
Akka framework
features 12
akka-kernel 29
Akka Maven project
creating, steps for 30-35
Akka, modules
akka-<storage-system>-mailbox 29
akka-actor 29
akka-agent 29
akka-camel 29
akka-dataflow 29
akka-kernel 29
akka-osgi 29

akka-remote 29
akka-slf4j 29
akka-testkit 29
akka-transactor 29
Akka-zeromq 29
akka-osgi 29
akka-remote 29
akka-slf4j 29
akka-<storage-system>-mailbox 29
akka-testkit 29
akka-transactor 29
Akka-zeromq 29
All-For-One strategy 131, 146-153
analytics 21
analyze module, Typesafe console
about 252
running 253
scope dimension groups actors,
   properties 253
span 252, 253
span, types 253
any user-defined marker span span 253
application.conf
router usage via 112, 113
application.conf class 93
application configuration
managing, Akka extensions used 208-213
**application development environment,
   prerequisites**
Akka 28, 29
Eclipse 27
Java 26
Maven 27
Scala 27
application.secret 256
ask() method 65, 67, 81
ATCs 96

B

balancing dispatcher
about 103
features 103
batch processing 21
Beanstalkd
URL 276
blocking queue 104

BlockingQueue method 101
Boolean variable 302
BoomActor 197
Bootable class 214
bounded mailbox 104
bounded priority mailbox 104
bounded queue 104
broadcast router 110
BroadcastRouter, router type 112
BurstyMessageRouter class 115
business intelligence 21

C

Calculator class 82, 89
CallingThreadDispatcher.global 195
CAS 168
close() method 190
Compare and Swap. *See* CAS
compile command 57
conf directory 285
config.getString() 210
context() actor 212
context.actorOf() method 54
Continuous Integration (CI) 191
coordinated.atomic() block 185
coordinated.coordinate() method 170
coordinated transactions
  about 169, 170
  money, transferring between multiple
      accounts 171-182
  multiple transactions, managing 170
CPU (CPU user) 261
createCustomRoute() method 117
Creator() method 84
CustomRoute class 118
CustomRoute() method 117

D

data mining 21
decouple 79
destinationsFor() method 118
directory-path parameter 280
discard-old-when-full parameter 280
dispatcher, configuration parameters
  executor parameter 106
  fork-join-executor parameter 106

key parameters 108
mailbox-capacity (optional) parameter 107
mailbox-type (optional) parameter 107
thread-pool-executor parameter 106-108
throughput parameter 106
type parameter 106
dispatcher property 253
dispatchers
  about 92, 95, 263
  ACTORS 264, 265
  application.conf class 93
  as pattern 97
  balancing dispatcher 103
  configuration parameters 106
  default dispatcher 101
  default dispatchers, features 101
  default mailbox implementations 100
  ERRORS 268-270
  fork join executor 105, 106
  in Akka 99, 100
  individual graph section 264
  pinned dispatcher 102
  TAGS 266, 267
  thread dispatcher 103
  thread pool executor 105
  types 100
  usage 105
  using 92
DISPATCHER THREADS 264
distributed actors
  router usage for 113
distributed computing
  about 217
  Java EE EJB model used 218-220
  key elements 220
durability 166
dynamic proxy classes
  implementing, in JDK 80

E

EchoActor testing 197, 202
Eclipse
  URL, for downloading 27
ERROR 262-266
ERRORS 260
error statistics parameter 272

evaluateExpression() method 37, 38, 48, 49
execution class, Java application
 defining 44
 MapReduceApplication.java class 44, 45
execution class, Scala application
 defining 55
 MapReduceApplication.scala class 55-57
executor
 constructor 98
 ForkJoinPool 98
 in Java 97
 ThreadPoolExecutor 98
EXECUTOR 264
executor parameter 106
extension 208
ExtensionId 208
ExtensionIdProvider interface 211

F

fault tolerance model
 about 161-163
 let it crash 125, 126
file-based, durable mailbox option
 about 277
 dispatcher usage 277-279
 FileDurableMailboxStorage 279, 280
FileDurableMailboxStorage scheme
 about 277, 278
 directory-path parameter 280
 discard-old-when-full parameter 280
 keep-journal parameter 280
 max-age parameter 280
 max-item-size parameter 280
 max-items parameter 280
 max-journal-overflow parameter 280
 max-journal-size-absolute parameter 280
 max-journal-size parameter 280
 max-memory-size parameter 280
 max-size parameter 280
 sync-journal parameter 280
finalReducedMap variable 41, 52
Finish button 33
fire and forget messages 65, 66
fire and forget mode, typed actors 84, 85
Flume
 about 251

URL 251
foldLeft() method 49
fork join executor 105, 106
fork-join-executor parameter 106
ForkJoinPool 98
ForwardingActor testing 197, 203
fromBinaryJava(byte[] arg0,Class<?> arg1)
 method 236
future construct 67
Future object 287
Future return type 81

G

GC ACTIVITY 261
getContext().actorOf() method 42
getContext().become() method 74
getContext().unbecome() method 74
getSender() construct 38
graphical dashboard
 about 257, 258
 dispatchers 262, 263
 limitations 270
 SYSTEM overview 259

H

HEAP 261
High Availability (HA) 21
HighWatermark attribute 302
HotSwap 74, 75
HttpActors application
 creating 282, 283

I

IDE 23
identifier() method 236
IllegalArgumentException
 exception 196, 205
includeManifest() method 236
individual graph section, ACTORS
 about 265
 ACTOR COUNTS 266
 ERROR 266
 LATENCY SCATTER 265
 MAILBOX SIZE 265
 MAILBOX WAIT TIME 265

MESSAGE COUNTS 266
THROUGHPUT 265
individual graph section, dispatchers
DISPATCHER THREADS 264
ERROR 264
EXECUTOR 264
LATENCY SCATTER 264
MAX MAILBOX SIZE 264
MESSAGE COUNTS 264
THROUGHPUT 264
individual graph section, node
CPU (CPU user) 261
ERROR 262
GC ACTIVITY 261
HEAP 261
LOAD 261
NETWORK 262
THROUGHPUT 261
**individual graph section, SYSTEM over-
    view**
ERRORS 260
MEAN LATENCY 260
PEAK (peak messages rate) 260
QUERY (query time period) 260
REMOTE THROUGHPUT 260
THROUGHPUT 260
TIME IN MAILBOX 260
instanceof string 225
Integrated Development Environment.
    See **IDE**
integration testing 192
int state variable 135
isolation 165
Iterable<Destination> object 118

J

Java application
about 30
actor classes, defining 37, 38
Akka Maven project, creating 30-35
message classes, defining 35
URL, for installing 26
java.lang.reflect.Method object 80
Java Native Access (JNA) 289
Java Platform, Enterprise Edition (JEE) 10

java.util.concurrent.TimeoutException
    exception 81
JMX MBeans 272, 273
JUnit 4.1 library
URL 192

K

keep-journal parameter 280
kill() message 73

L

LATENCY SCATTER 264, 265
Launch in console link 258
let it crash paradigm 123, 124
lifecycle monitoring
actor, monitoring for termination 155-160
guidelines 154
LOAD 261
LocalActor class 228
LocalActorRef 195
LocalActor system 224
local node application
creating 228-231
lookup() method 211

M

mailbox-capacity (optional) parameter 107
mailboxes
about 15, 104
bounded mailbox 104
bounded priority mailbox 104
bounded queue 104
durability 275
types 104
unbounded mailbox 104
unbounded priority mailbox 104
mailboxes, durability
Beanstalkd 276
file 276
MongoDB 276
options 276
Redis 276
Zookeeper 276
MAILBOX SIZE 265
mailbox span 253

mailbox time series parameter 271
mailbox-type (optional) parameter 107
MAILBOX WAIT TIME 265
MapActor class 37, 38, 48, 49
MapActor.java 37, 38
MapActor.scala 48, 49
MapData.java 35
MapData message 35, 38
MapData object 37, 42
MapReduceApplication.java class 44, 45
MapReduceApplication.scala class 55-57
MapReduce method 23
map task 24
master actor 25
MasterActor class 54
MasterActor.java 41, 42, 43
MasterActor object 38
MasterActor.scala 53, 55
Maven
  URL, for downloading 27
max-age parameter 280
max-item-size parameter 280
max-items parameter 280
max-journal-overflow parameter 280
max-journal-size-absolute parameter 280
max-journal-size parameter 280
MAX MAILBOX SIZE 264
max-memory-size parameter 280
maxNrOfRetries argument 132
max-size parameter 280
MBeans tab 273
MEAN LATENCY 260
messageBurst rate 115
message classes, Java application
  defining 35, 36
  MapData.java 35
  ReduceData.java class 36
  Result.java class 36
  WordCount.java class 35, 36
message classes, Scala application
  defining 47
MESSAGE COUNTS 264, 266
messages
  about 64
  fire and forget messages 65, 66
  forwarding 70
  receiving 67, 69

replying to 70
sending 65-69
tell() method 66
message serialization
  about 234, 235
  serializations, creating 235-242
message span 253
messages, typed actors
  receiving 88, 89
messaging model. *See* messages
metadata dispatchers parameter 271
metadata nodes parameter 271
metadata parameter 271
metadata span statistics parameter 271
metadata span types parameter 271
metadata tags parameter 271
Microkernel 214, 215
microprocessor evolution
  advancement 7
  URL 8
Model-View-Controller (MVC) 281
MongoDB
  about 250
  URL 250, 276
monitoring tool
  pre-requisites 248
  Typesafe console 248
multi-JVM sbt plugin
  URL 208
mutable 166

N

Netty 222
NETWORK 262
New I/O (NIO) client server framework 222
new() method 195
node
  about 260
  individual graph section 261
node property 253

O

One-For-One strategy 131-145
onReceive() method 37, 40, 41, 69, 135
optimism 167
Option return type 81

P

pattern
  dispatchers as 97
PCB 7
PEAK (peak messages rate) 260
persistent messages 275
PingPongActor class 75
pinned dispatcher
  about 102
  features 102
Plain Old Java Object (POJO) 78
play
  console, launching 283-288
  installing 282
play framework
  URL 281
postRestart() method 60
postStop() method 60, 72, 87
preRestart() method 60
preStart method 61
preStart() method 60, 64, 87, 141
printed circuit board. *See* PCB
process() method 287
project leads (PLs) 125
project managers (PMs) 125
Props 62
protocol buffers
  about 223
  URL 223
publish-subscriber connection
  about 290
  usage 290-294
PubSocket 292
push-pull connection
  about 302
  usage 303-305

Q

query module, Typesafe console
  about 254
  running 254, 255
QUERY (query time period) 260
question span 253

R

random router 110
RandomRouter, router type 111
receive() method 48, 53, 196
receive span 253
Redis
  URL 276
ReduceActor class 40, 50
ReduceActor.java 39, 40
ReduceActor.scala 50
ReduceData 47
ReduceData class 36
ReduceData.java class 36
ReduceData message 41
ReduceData object 42
reduce() method 40, 50
reduce task 24
RemoteActor class 225
remote actors
  about 223, 224
  creating, programmatically 232, 233
  local node application 228-232
  remote node application, creating 225-228
RemoteActor system 224
RemoteClientConnected, remote event 243
RemoteClientDisconnected, remote
      event 243
RemoteClientError, remote event 243
RemoteClientLifeCycleEvent 245
RemoteClientShutdown, remote event 243
RemoteClientStarted, remote event 243
RemoteClientWriteFailed, remote event 243
remote events
  about 242
  RemoteClientConnected 243
  RemoteClientDisconnected 243
  RemoteClientError 243
  RemoteClientShutdown 243
  RemoteClientStarted 243
  RemoteClientWriteFailed 243
  RemoteServerClientClosed 243
  RemoteServerClientConnected 243
  RemoteServerClientDisconnected 243
  RemoteServerShutdown 243
  RemoteServerStarted 243

RemoteLifeCycleEvent 245
remote node application 225-227
RemoteNodeApplication class 225
Remote Procedure Calls (RPC) 218
RemoteServerClientClosed, remote
        event 243
RemoteServerClientConnected,
        remote event 243
RemoteServerClientDisconnected,
        remote event 243
RemoteServerLifeCycleEvent 245
RemoteServerShutdown, remote event 243
RemoteServerStarted, remote event 243
remote span 253
remote status parameter 272
REMOTE THROUGHPUT 260
request-reply connection
    usage 294-297
RESTful API
    about 270
    actor statistics parameter 271
    error statistics parameter 272
    mailbox time series parameter 271
    metadata nodes parameter 271
    metadata parameter 271
    metadata span statistics parameter 271
    metadata span types parameter 271
    metadata tags parameter 271
    parameters documentation, URL 272
    remote status parameter 272
    scope dimension 271
    span-related queries 271
    span time series parameter 271
    system metrics point parameter 272
    system metrics time series parameter 271
    time dimension 271
    trace events parameter 272
Result class 36
Result.java class 36
Result message 42
round robin router 110
RoundRobinRouter 111
routees 109
RouterActorRef 110
RouterConfig interface 115
router-dealer connection
    about 298

    usage 299, 302
routers
    about 109
    broadcast router 110
    custom router 115-120
    mechanisms 110
    random router 110
    RandomRouter 111
    resizing, dynamically 114
    round robin router 110
    RoundRobinRouter 111
    scatter gather first complete router 110
    smallest mailbox router 110
    SmallestMailboxRouter 111
    usage 110
    usage, for distributed actors 113
    usage, via application.conf 112, 113
    using 93
run command 284

S

SBT 26, 28
Scala application
    about 46
    actor classes, defining 47-49
    execution class, defining 55-57
    message classes, defining 47
    URL, for downloading 27
ScalaSTM
    about 167
    example 168
    URL 169
ScalaTest
    URL 202
Scalatra
    URL 288
ScatterGatherFirstCompletedLike
        interface 115
ScatterGatherFirstCompletedRouter,
        router type 112
scatter gather first completed router 110
scope dimension groups actors
    actorPath property 253
    dispatcher property 253
    node property 253
    tag property 253

self()actor 299
send and receive message mode 65, 67
send and receive mode, typed actors 84, 85
SequencingActor testing 197, 203, 204
ServerActorApp controller class 286
ServerActor class 287
service gateways/hubs 21
service providers 21
shared state 166
Simple Build Tool. *See* SBT
smallest mailbox router 110
SmallestMailboxRouter, router type 111
Socko web
  URL 288
Software Development Lifecycle
    (SDLC) 191
Software Transactional Memory. *See* STM
span time series parameter 271
span, types
  mailbox span 253
  message span 253
  question span 253
  receive span 253
  remote span 253
split() method 49
Spray
  URL 288
STM
  about 19, 166, 167
  optimism 167
  principles 12
  ScalaSTM 167
  URL 167
STOP signal 71
String message 42
String object 48
sub-ordinates 127
Subscriber actor 293
super.testActor() 202
supervision
  about 127
  on failure of sub-ordinate actor 127
  strategies 130
supervision, strategies
  All-For-One strategy 131
  One-For-One strategy 131

Supervisor Actor (S1) 163
SupervisorActor testing 197, 205-207
sync-journal parameter 280
system.actorOf() command 231
system metrics point parameter 272
system metrics time series parameter 271
SYSTEM overview
  about 259
  node 260

T

tag property 253
tell() method 65, 66
TestActor 197
TestActorRef reference
  about 194-196
  unit testing, writing with 192-194
TestKit
  about 191, 192
  integration testing with 197-202
  using, within application 192
threaded dispatcher
  calling 103
  features 104
thread pool executor 105
ThreadPoolExecutor, router type 98
thread-pool-executor parameter 106-108
Thread.sleep() method 45, 56
THROUGHPUT 260, 264, 265
throughput parameter 106
TickTock actor
  testing 194
TIME IN MAILBOX 260
toBinary(Object arg0) method 236
toString() method 239
trace events parameter 272
trace module, Typesafe console
  about 249, 250
  configuration 251
  properties, defining 251
  trace events, persisting ways 250
transaction
  about 165
  isolation 165
transaction processing 21

transactor
  about 184
  money, transfering between multiple
    accounts 185-187
TransferActor object 171
TypedActor context 91
TypedActor implementation 91
typedActorOf() method 83
TypedActor.PostRestart interface 88
TypedActor.PostStop interface 87
TypedActor.PreStart interface 87
typed actors
  about 78
  creating 82
  defining 80-82
  fire-and-forget mode 85
  hierarchy, creating 91
  implementing, Active Object pattern
    used 78, 79
  lifecycle, callbacks 87, 88
  lifecycle, monitoring 87
  messages, receiving 88, 89
  messages, sending 84
  messaging model 84
  send and receive mode 85
  stopping 86
  supervisor, strategy 90, 91
  with default constructor 83
  with non-default constructor 83, 84
TypedProps class 83
TypedProps parameter 83
type parameter 106
Typesafe console
  about 248
  features 248
  JMX 272, 274
  modules 249
  RESTful API 270-272
  running 256
Typesafe console, modules
  about 249
  analyze module 249-253
  query module 249-255
  trade module 249, 250

U

unbecome() method 75
unbounded mailbox 104
unbounded priority mailbox 104
unhandled() method 37
Uniform Resource Locator (URL) 18, 221
unit testing
  about 192
  writing, with TestActorRef 192, 194
UntypedActor class 69
UntypedActorFactory function 63
user.email 256
user.password 256

V

void return type 81

W

web-based application
  building, on distributed application 281
withDispatcher() method 109
withinTimeRange argument 132
withRouter() method 42, 54
WordCount class 35
WordCount.java class 35, 36
WordCount object 35, 47
World Wide Web (WWW) 18

Z

ZeroMQ
  about 289
  connectivity patterns 289
Zookeeper
  URL 276

Thank you for buying
Akka Essentials

About Packt Publishing

Packt, pronounced 'packed', published its first book *"Mastering phpMyAdmin for Effective MySQL Management"* in April 2004 and subsequently continued to specialize in publishing highly focused books on specific technologies and solutions.

Our books and publications share the experiences of your fellow IT professionals in adapting and customizing today's systems, applications, and frameworks. Our solution based books give you the knowledge and power to customize the software and technologies you're using to get the job done. Packt books are more specific and less general than the IT books you have seen in the past. Our unique business model allows us to bring you more focused information, giving you more of what you need to know, and less of what you don't.

Packt is a modern, yet unique publishing company, which focuses on producing quality, cutting-edge books for communities of developers, administrators, and newbies alike. For more information, please visit our website: www.packtpub.com.

About Packt Open Source

In 2010, Packt launched two new brands, Packt Open Source and Packt Enterprise, in order to continue its focus on specialization. This book is part of the Packt Open Source brand, home to books published on software built around Open Source licences, and offering information to anybody from advanced developers to budding web designers. The Open Source brand also runs Packt's Open Source Royalty Scheme, by which Packt gives a royalty to each Open Source project about whose software a book is sold.

Writing for Packt

We welcome all inquiries from people who are interested in authoring. Book proposals should be sent to author@packtpub.com. If your book idea is still at an early stage and you would like to discuss it first before writing a formal book proposal, contact us; one of our commissioning editors will get in touch with you.

We're not just looking for published authors; if you have strong technical skills but no writing experience, our experienced editors can help you develop a writing career, or simply get some additional reward for your expertise.

Apache Maven 3 Cookbook

ISBN: 978-1-849512-44-2   Paperback: 224 pages

Over 50 recipes towards optimal Java software engineering with Maven 3

1. Grasp the fundamentals and extend Apache Maven 3 to meet your needs

2. Implement engineering practices in your application development process with Apache Maven

3. Collaboration techniques for Agile teams with Apache Maven

4. Use Apache Maven with Java, Enterprise Frameworks, and various other cutting-edge technologies

Java 7 New Features Cookbook

ISBN: 978-1-849685-62-7   Paperback: 384 pages

Over 100 comprehensive recipes to get you up-to-speed with all the exciting new features of Java 7

1. Comprehensive coverage of the new features of Java 7 organized around easy-to-follow recipes

2. Covers exciting features such as the try-with-resources block, the monitoring of directory events, asynchronous IO and new GUI enhancements, and more

3. A learn-by-example based approach that focuses on key concepts to provide the foundation to solve real world problems

Spring Security 3

ISBN: 978-1-847199-74-4   Paperback: 396 pages

Secure your web applications against malicious
intruders with this easy to follow practical guide

1. Make your web applications impenetrable.

2. Implement authentication and authorization
   of users.

3. Integrate Spring Security 3 with common
   external security providers.

4. Packed full with concrete, simple, and
   concise examples.

Jenkins Continuous Integration Cookbook

ISBN: 978-1-849517-40-9   Paperback: 344 pages

Over 80 recipes to maintain, secure, communicate,
test, build, and improve the software development
process with Jenkins

1. Explore the use of more than 40 best of
   breed plugins

2. Use code quality metrics, integration testing
   through functional and performance testing
   to measure the quality of your software

3. Get a problem-solution approach enriched
   with code examples for practical and easy
   comprehension

Please check **www.PacktPub.com** for information on our titles

Lightning Source UK Ltd.
Milton Keynes UK
UKOW05f0305260917
309858UK00003B/205/P